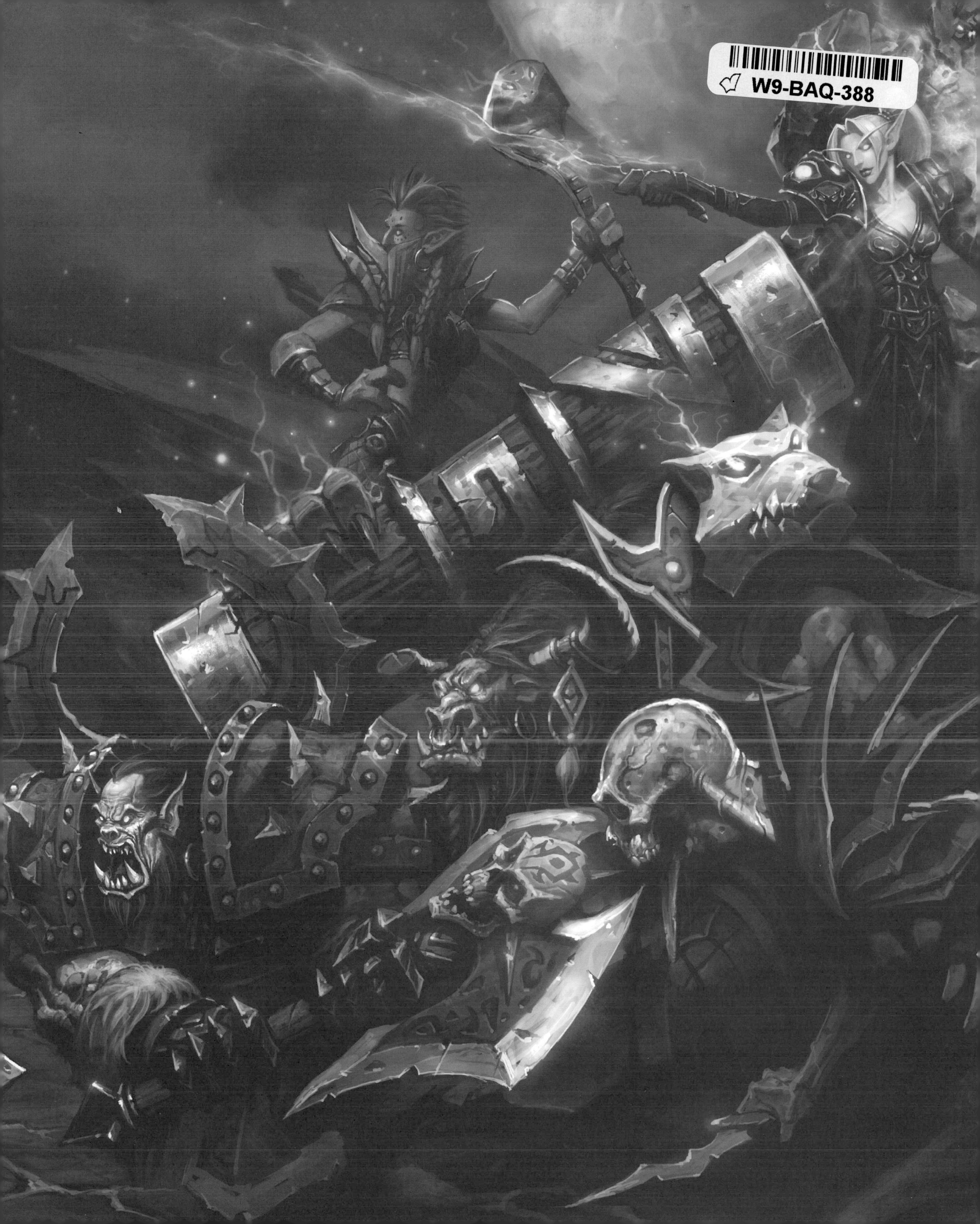

WORLD OF WARCRAFT

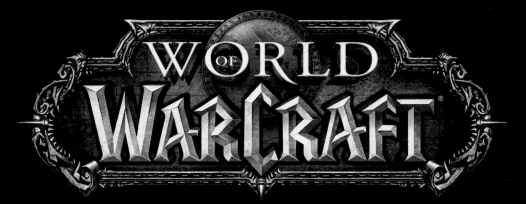

ULTIMATE VISUAL GUIDE

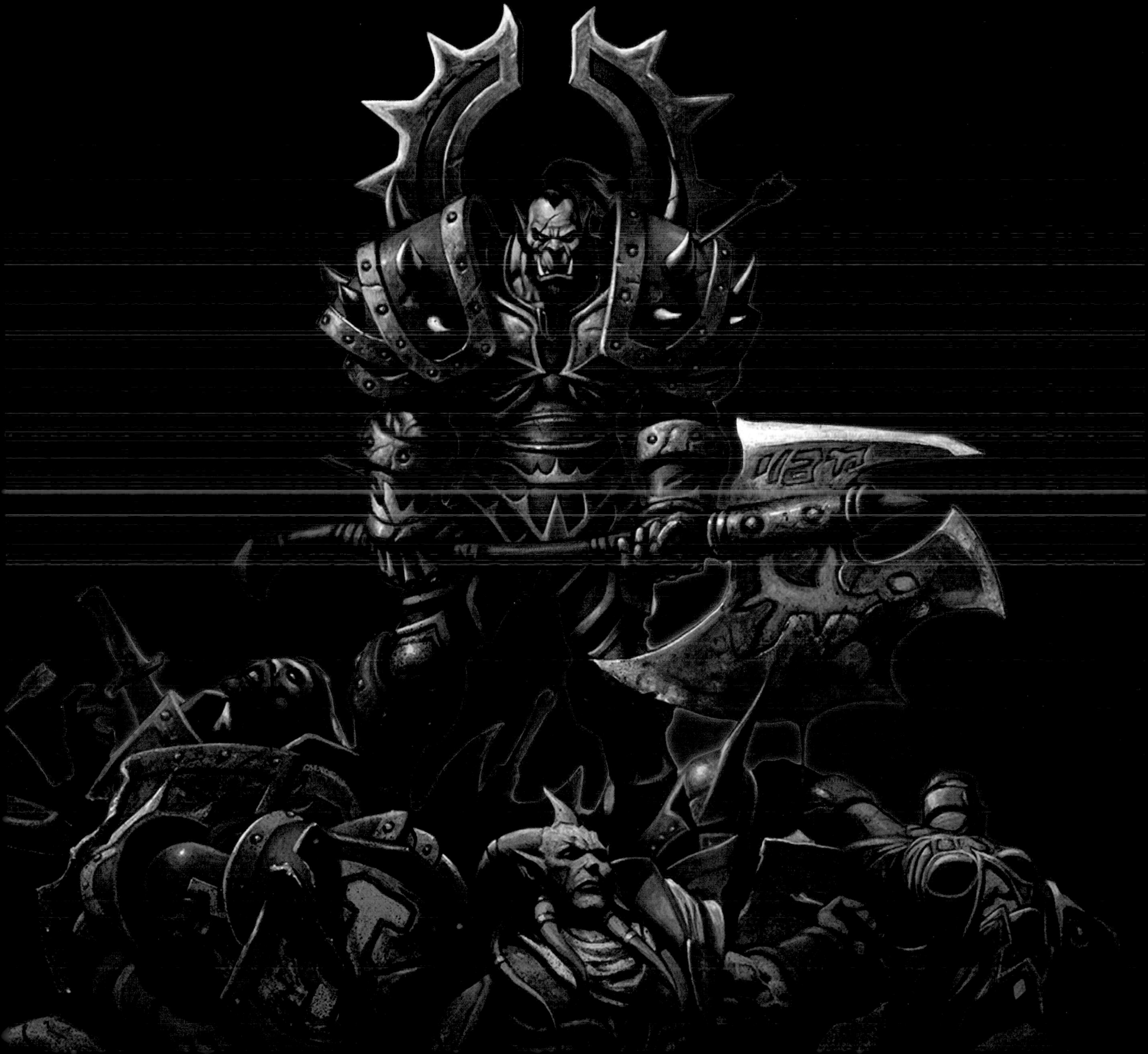

LONDON, NEW YORK, MELBOURNE, MUNICH, AND DELHI

DORLING KINDERSLEY
Senior Editor Alastair Dougall
Editor David Fentiman
Senior Designer and Brand Manager
Robert Perry
Designers Nick Avery, Richard
Horsford, Lauren Rosier, Jon Hall
Design Manager Maxine Pedliham
Managing Editor Laura Gilbert
Art Director Ron Stobbart
Publishing Manager Julie Ferris
Publishing Director Simon Beecroft
Senior Pre-Production Producer
Jennifer Murray
Senior Producer Danielle Smith

BRADYGAMES
Title Manager Tim Fitzpatrick
Senior Designer Keith Lowe
Development Editor Jennifer Sims
Senior Development Editor
Ken Schmidt
Manuscript Editor Matt Buchanan
Senior Production Designer Areva

BLIZZARD ENTERTAINMENT
Production Joshua Horst,
Skye Chandler, Leanne Huynh
Editor Micky Neilson
Lore Sean Copeland
Lore Editor Cate Gary
Licensing Matthew Beecher,
Jerry Chu, Audrey Vicenzi
Art Direction Jeremy Cranford

First published in the United States in 2013 by
DK Publishing. 345 Hudson Street, New York, New York 10014.
10 9 8 7 6 5 4 3 2 1
001-183103-October/13

WORLD OF WARCRAFT

ULTIMATE VISUAL GUIDE

Written by
Kathleen Pleet
and Anne Stickney

CONTENTS

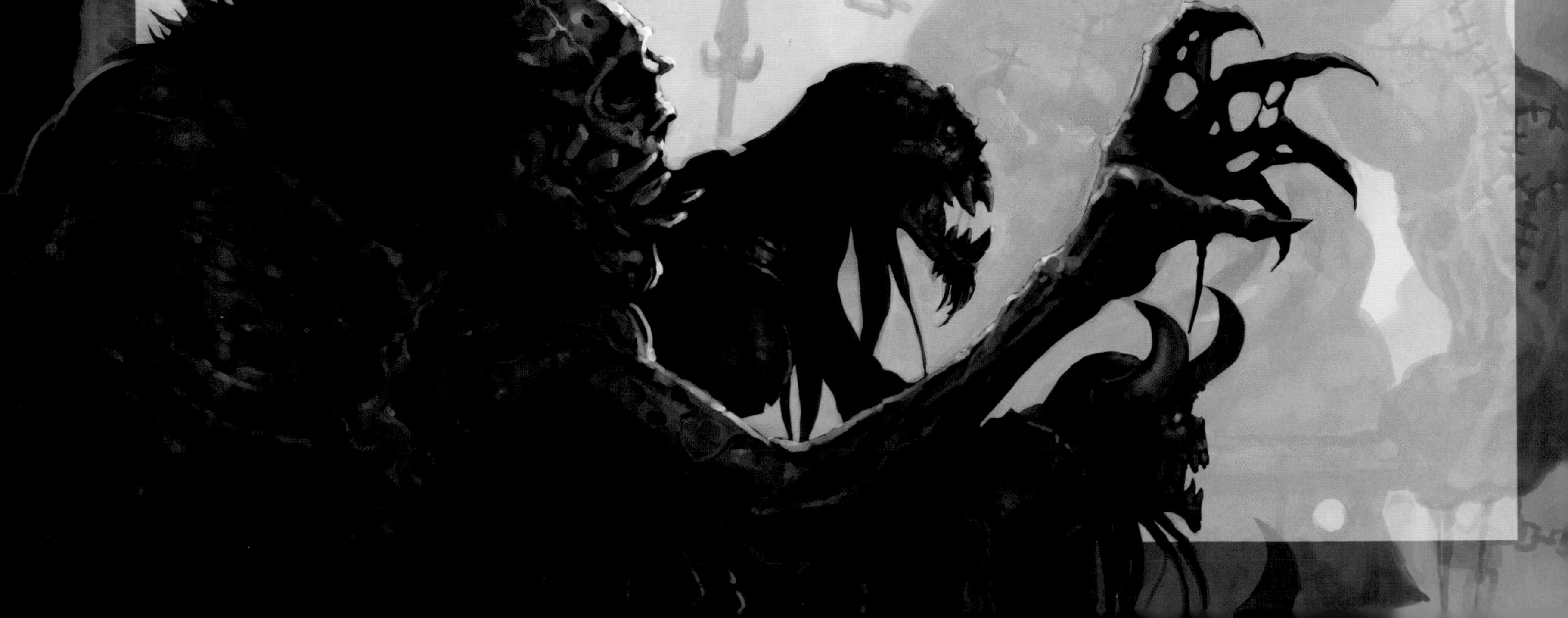

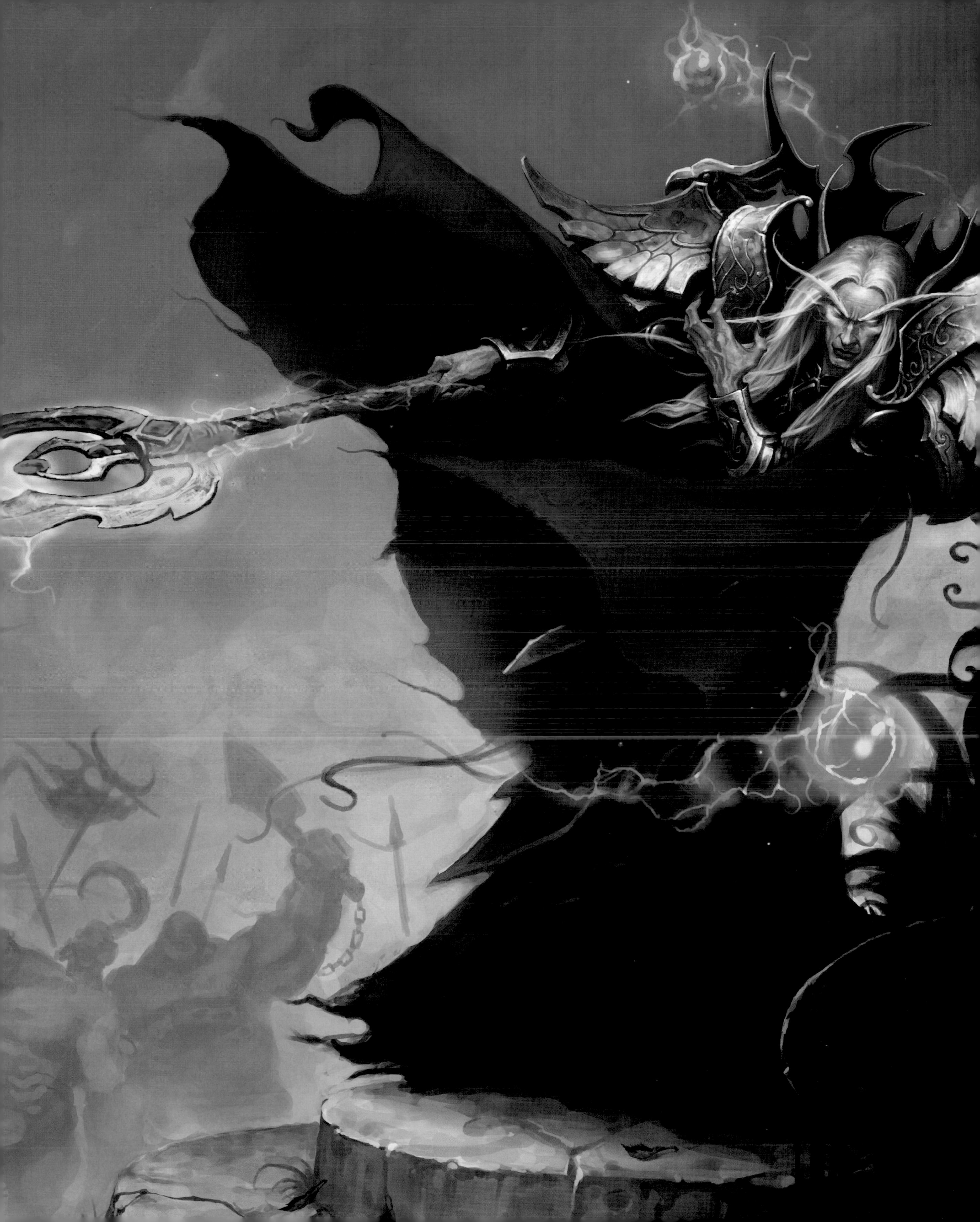

FOREWORD

World of Warcraft is a strange and powerful beast, a battle-scarred hybrid. A pop culture chimera. *WoW*'s roots can be traced back to Blizzard Entertainment's 1994 real-time strategy game *Warcraft: Orcs & Humans*. The first *Warcraft* proved to be a critical and commercial success, and was praised for its groundbreaking art and design. Perhaps most importantly, it was the first game to really embody Blizzard's "don't ship it 'til it's ready" philosophy.

Warcraft was followed by two sequels and two expansions over the next nine years. All of this world-building served to lay the foundations for a rich history that we continue to build on today—not just through our games, but through novels, comics, and other media.

When I first learned of the idea to break *Warcraft* out of the real-time strategy mold, I was skeptical—a dynamic world allowing players to embark on group quests or explore solo... a constantly evolving virtual reality with a low barrier to entry and rewarding high-end content... could such a game really have something for everyone? Time would tell.

The development process took five years. In true Blizzard style, the game wasn't shipped until we felt it was ready. On November 23, 2004, the game was finally ready... but our servers were not.

The number of *WoW* players exceeded our long-term estimated capacity within the first month. Gamers flocked to Azeroth in droves, and any reservations I (or anyone) might have had about its potential were put to rest. But what makes the game so popular?

Simply put, everyone's invited. In *WoW* you can battle giants or you can collect herbs. You can quest alone or you can team up with friends or even complete strangers. The game remains a source of liberation, escape, glory, triumph, and fulfillment. It's a place where people from all ages and walks of life can come together in pursuit of common goals, and in the years since its release, it has pervaded our pop culture consciousness.

What you hold in your hands is a visual testament to the beauty, history, complexity, and appeal of the most popular massively multiplayer online role-playing game ever created.

So sit back, relax, and enjoy the *World of Warcraft: Ultimate Visual Guide*.

See you in Azeroth.

Micky Neilson

Lead Story Developer, Blizzard Entertainment

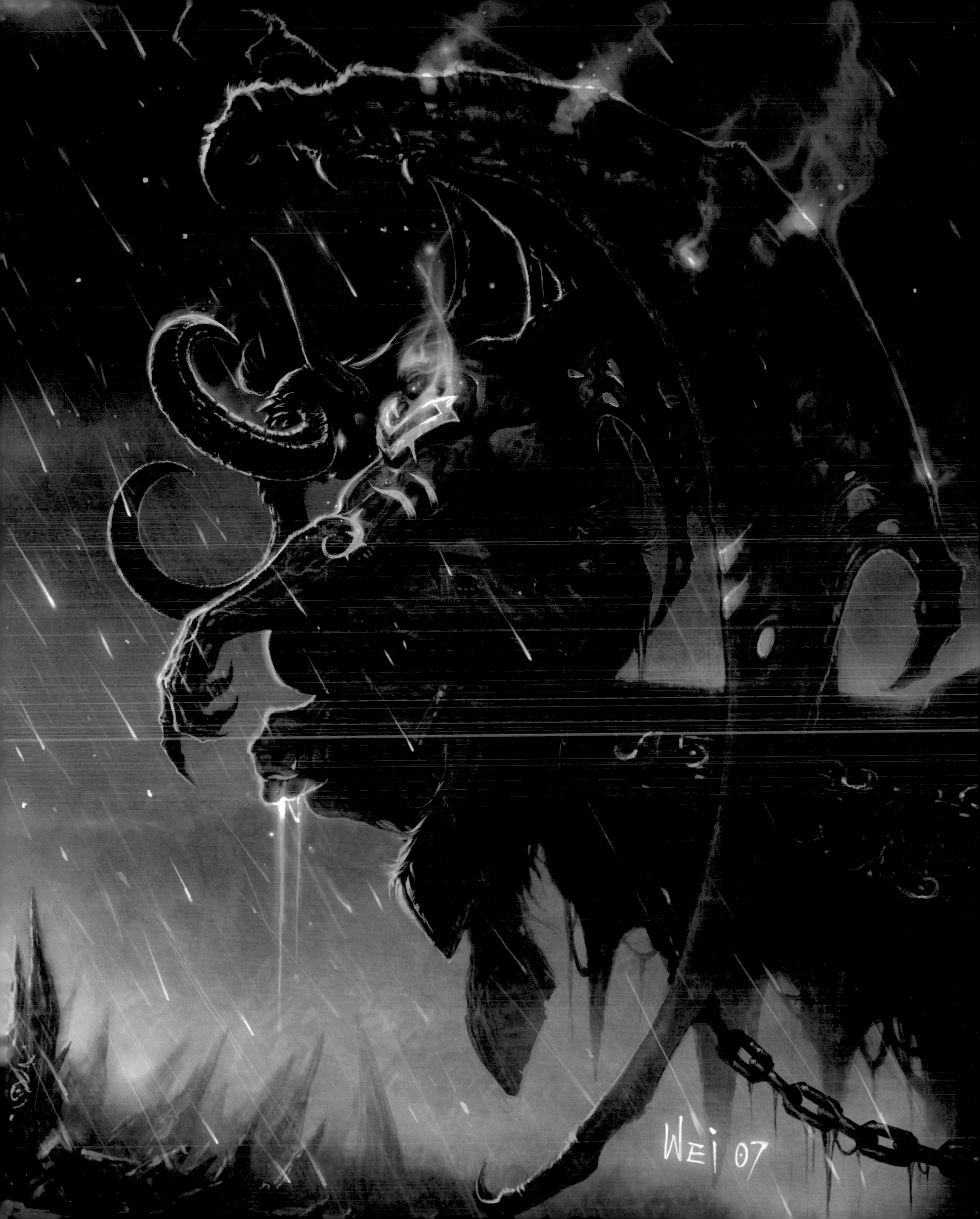

Wei 07

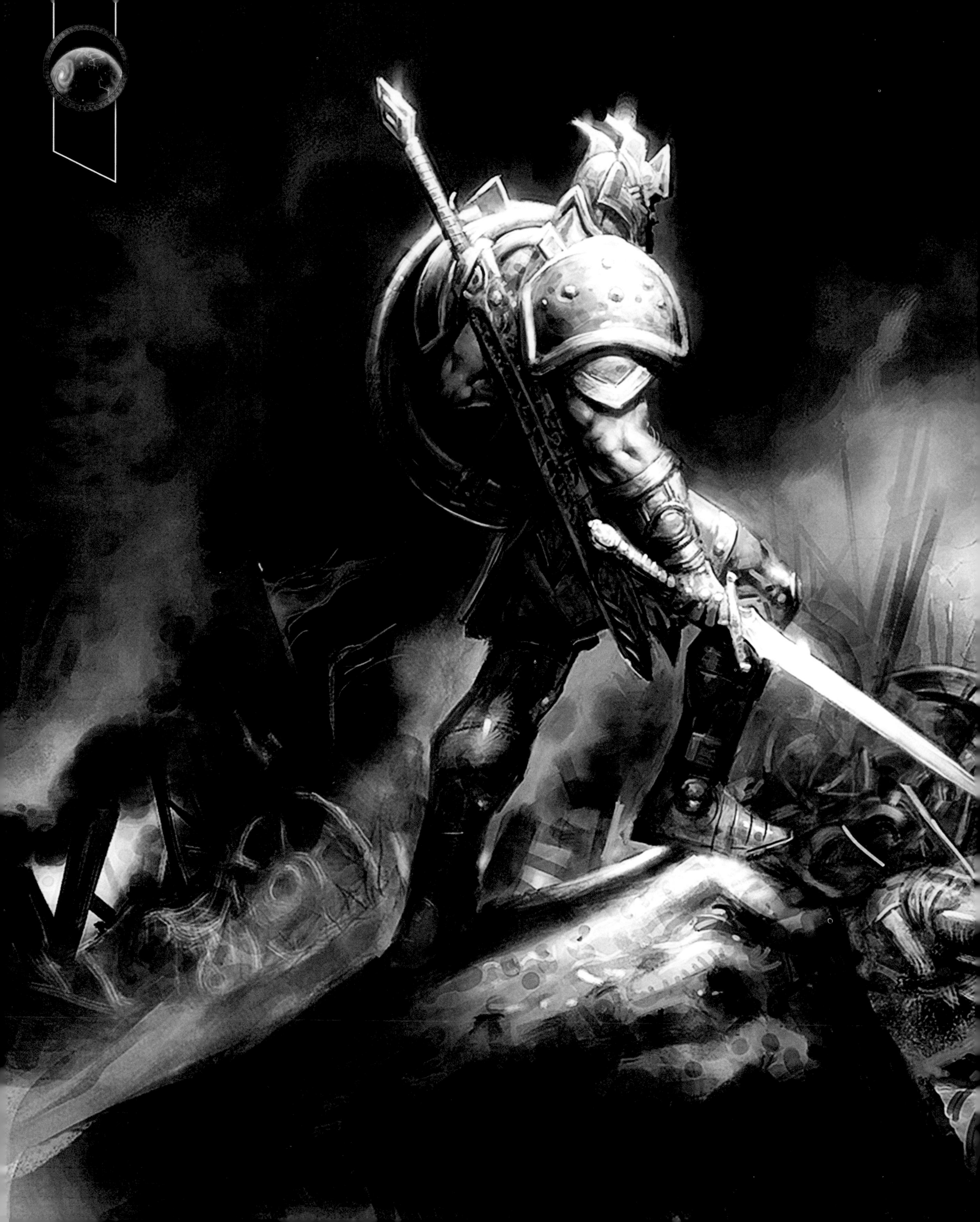

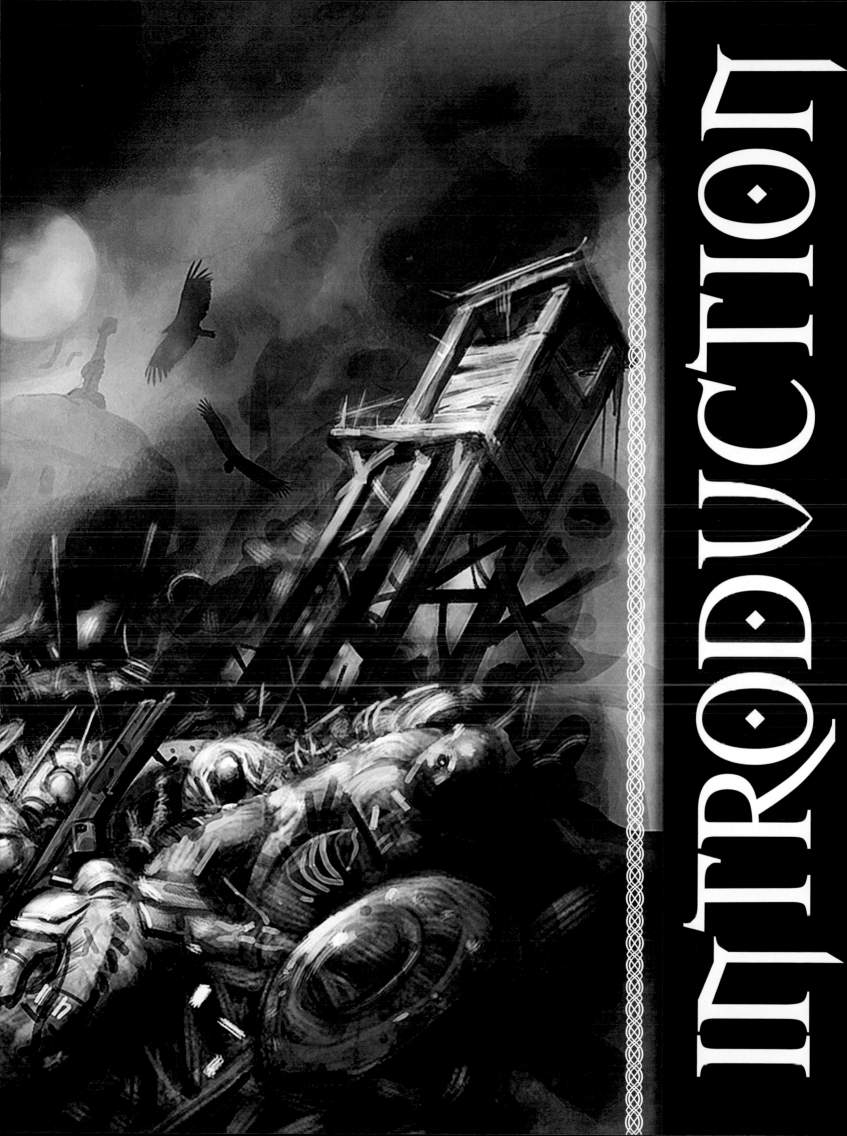

INTRODUCTION

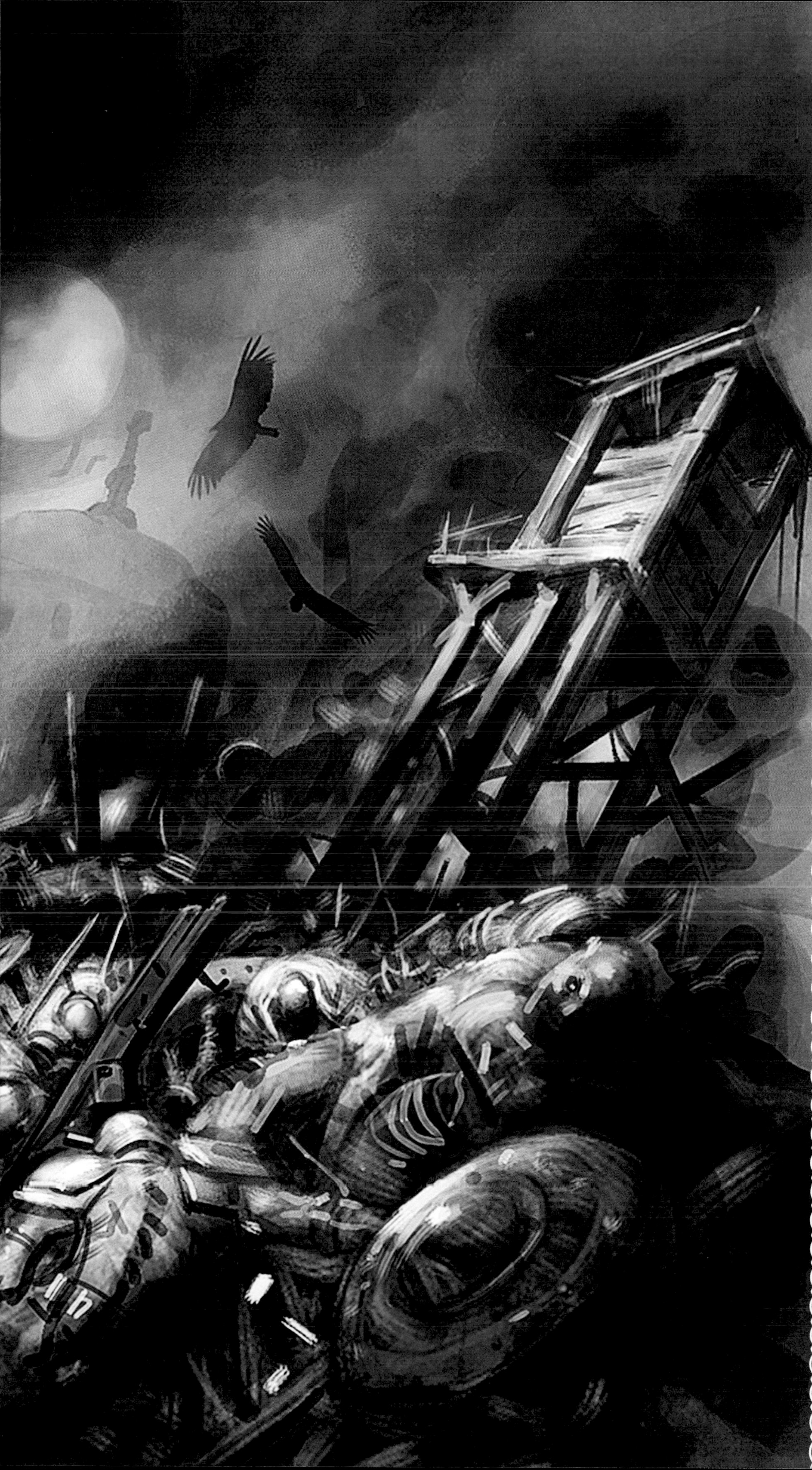

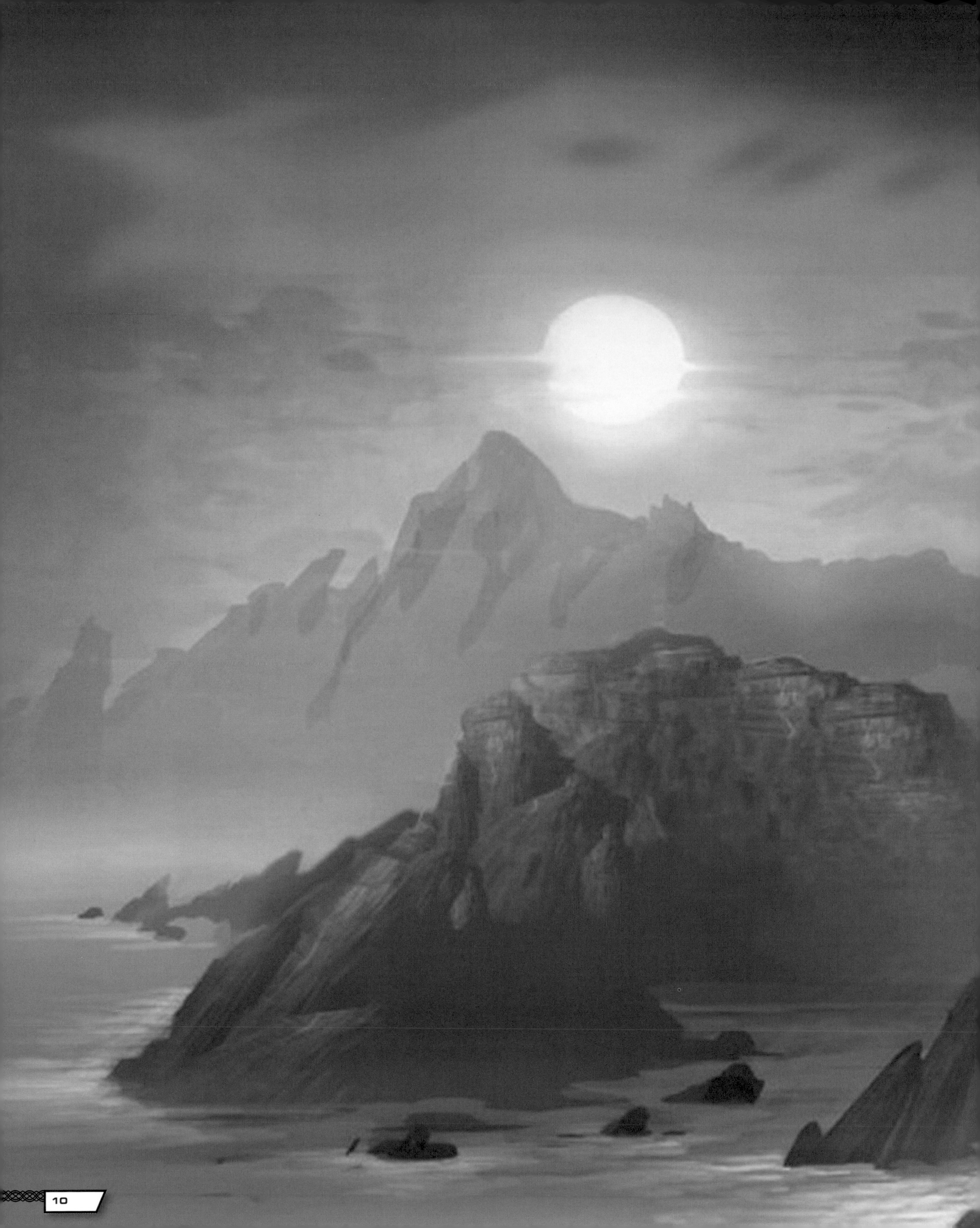

THE WORLD OF AZEROTH

Floating within the infinite reaches of the Great Dark Beyond lies the shimmering world of Azeroth. Powerful forces and titanic creations were made to shape the world, which later fell to corruption by the malefic Old Gods. The dwarf-like earthen, fashioned from magical, living stone, helped carve out the deep places of the world. Immense but gentle sea giants were created to dredge the seas and lift the land from the sea floor. For many ages, these creations moved and shaped the earth, until at last there remained one perfect continent.

Soon, Azeroth was populated by a multitude of different creatures. Some had potent connections to nature itself, such as the Ancients—powerful demigods that worked to protect the world. There were also a number of sentient races that came into prominence—trolls, elves, humans, and others. Before long, many of these races had organized into settlements and tribes, claiming territories within Azeroth.

Yet Azeroth was also the target of enemies from beyond. For millennia, from the realm of the Twisting Nether, a vast force of chaos and destruction known as the Burning Legion has made Azeroth its target. Each subsequent invasion has brought new denizens to Azeroth—many terrifying, others holding aspirations of their own for this fragile world. Only through the concerted and dedicated efforts and sacrifices of Azeroth's defenders has the Burning Legion been defeated and kept at bay. The aftermath of Legion attacks continues to affect the world, and the Burning Legion will never allow Azeroth to exist in peace. Those that dwell within the world, whether native or not, must maintain constant vigilance against the Burning Legion's eternal threat.

Those responsible for Azeroth's safety are not a united group. There are fundamental racial, cultural, and philosophical differences among them, and Azeroth's history is filled with wars and conflicts. Today, there are two major political factions, the Alliance and the Horde, which represent the unification of various racial, cultural, and philosophical groups. There are also a number of independent factions, which function as moderating or altruistic organizations, or seek to cause further dissent.

Azeroth's very existence faces formidable threats from the malevolent Old Gods, from the Burning Legion, and from internal warfare. Yet, throughout the ages, the actions of Azeroth's heroes have inspired others to become greater, to fight harder, and behave with more honor, nobility, and valor than they ever thought possible.

This is Azeroth. A dangerous, beautiful, magical, and inspiring world. A world filled with discovery, innovation, and wonder. A world worth fighting for. A world worth protecting.

REALMS OF AZEROTH

In ancient times, Azeroth was composed of one large continent, called Kalimdor. At the center of the continent was the Well of Eternity, a vast font of arcane power. At the conclusion of the War of the Ancients, the Well imploded. The waters of the oceans poured into Kalimdor's center, becoming the seething, massive whirlpool known as the Maelstrom. As the seas rushed in, nearly eighty percent of Azeroth's landmass was flooded. The existing landmasses are all that survived this sundering.

The continent of Kalimdor is home to the night elves, worgen, and draenei, along with small pockets of human settlements. The orc, tauren, troll, and goblin races are also primarily settled in Kalimdor, with various settlements in the central regions.

WILDLIFE

Azeroth and Outland are both home to a unique assortment of wildlife. While some creatures have been successfully tamed and used as beasts of burden, explorers agree that most of the world's wildlife should be approached with caution.

Zhevra

Whitetail Frenzy

Scorpid

Kodo

Jormungar

Devilsaur

THE NORTH SEA

DARNASSUS

THE EXODAR

Nordrassil

BILGEWATER HARBOR

ORGRIMMAR

THUNDER BLUFF

THE ECHO ISLES

Ruins of Theramore

THE VEILED SEA

KALIMDOR

Uldum

Tempest Keep

The Dark Portal

The Black Temple

OUTLAND

The Dark Portal is a huge, magical gateway that originally connected the worlds of Azeroth and Draenor. In time, the portal was closed, and Draenor was blasted apart. When the portal was rebuilt, explorers discovered a fragment of Draenor, renamed Outland. The Dark Portal is still used to travel between these two locations.

The icy reaches of Northrend were the site of a hard-fought campaign against the Scourge. While Northrend is still home to the now dormant Lich King, it boasts a wild array of climates, and holds many secrets of the titans.

UNDISCOVERED LANDS

Many other small islands, such as Kezan, the Lost Isles, and the Wandering Isle, dot Azeroth's oceans. However, explorers agree that much remains to be discovered in Azeroth, and new lands or events may yet reveal more about the nature of the world.

- Ulduar

- ICECROWN CITADEL

- Dalaran

NORTHREND

- The Sunwell

- SILVERMOON CITY

EASTERN KINGDOMS

UNDERCITY •
(formerly
Capital City)

THE MAELSTROM

GILNEAS CITY •

THE FORBIDDING SEA

GNOMEREGAN • • IRONFORGE

THE GREAT SEA

• Blackrock Mountain

STORMWIND CITY •

PANDARIA

• The Dark Portal

- The Shado-Pan Monastery

THE SOUTH SEAS

Temple of the Jade Serpent •

The island of Pandaria is home to several races including the pandaren. Shrouded in dense mists for ten thousand years, Pandaria's very existence was a mystery until only recently. It now represents a neutral but contested territory for both Alliance and Horde.

The northern reaches of the Eastern Kingdoms are mainly home to the blood elves and Forsaken. The human kingdom of Stormwind, along with its dwarf and gnome allies, takes up the central portion of the continent, with small settlements that stretch into the southern regions.

A WORLD DIVIDED

Azeroth has been home to many great cultures and civilizations. Currently, the world is divided between two major political factions, known as the Horde and the Alliance. Notwithstanding brief periods of peace, and even cooperation, their shared history has been defined by conflict and bloodshed.

THE HORDE AND ALLIANCE

Both the Horde and the Alliance have seen a shift in their membership over the years. The Alliance began as a union of seven human kingdoms, but later included many different races in its ranks. The Horde started as a horrifying orc invasion force, sweeping across the Eastern Kingdoms and leaving a swath of devastation in its wake. Over time, the Horde has also evolved into a collection of disparate races, but it still lives in the shadow of its dark origins. This legacy has led to tensions between Alliance and Horde that continue to this day. Yet both Alliance and Horde have treasured Azeroth, believing it should be cared for and protected, and in times of grave danger, both factions are willing to work together in the face of a common foe. Despite this common belief, alliances between the two factions have invariably dissolved into tension and conflict once the greater evil is defeated.

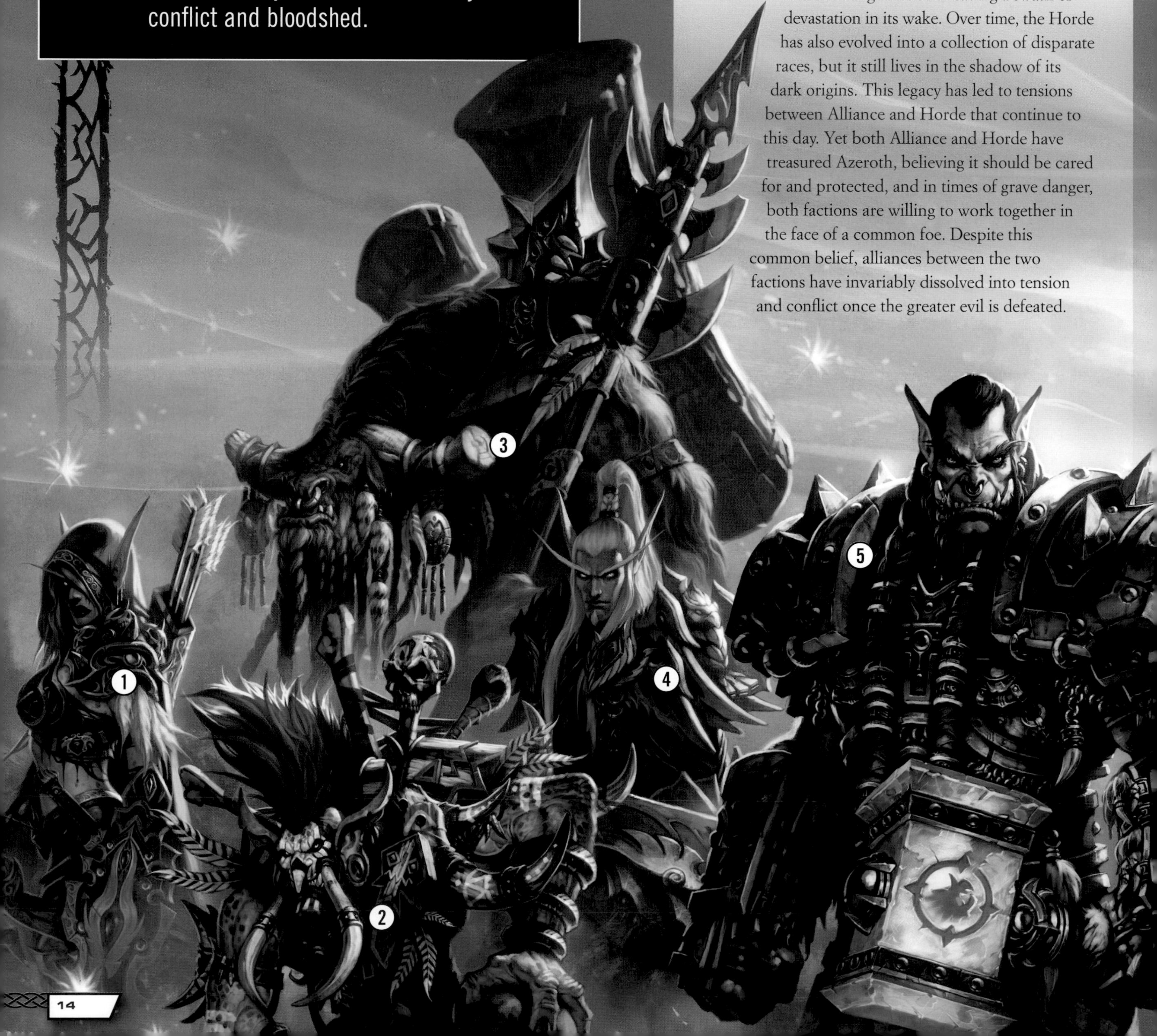
3
5
1
4
2

A HISTORY OF CONFLICT

The first contact between the Horde and the Alliance was bloody. The Horde was originally an invasion force under the control of the demonic Burning Legion, and the Alliance formed principally to protect the kingdoms of Azeroth from the Horde. The orcish invasion saw Alliance lands burned and their people slaughtered by the rampaging Horde. When the Horde was finally defeated in the Second War, most of its former combatants were placed in internment camps. The Horde eventually freed itself, first from imprisonment in the camps and then from the Burning Legion. Although the Horde has now undergone significant changes, there are those on both sides who remember the bloody battles and atrocities committed. Many in the Alliance will never trust their old enemies and will always view them as savages. Within the Horde, past grievances must be answered, and the cultural emphasis of proving oneself through glorious combat doesn't help matters. For both sides, vengeance for past wrongs is a difficult temptation to ignore. Peace must be hard fought for, and trust comes slowly, to people who have lived surrounded by war.

THE LEADERS OF THE HORDE

1. Sylvanas Windrunner

2. Vol'jin

3. Baine Bloodhoof

4. Lor'themar Theron

5. Thrall

THE LEADERS OF THE ALLIANCE

6. Varian Wrynn

7. Velen

8. Magni Bronzebeard

9. Gelbin Mekkatorque

10. Tyrande Whisperwind

THE RACES OF AZEROTH

The world of Azeroth is home to many different races. Some of them are native to the world, while others have come from worlds beyond. Nonetheless, they have all carved out territory for themselves, and their explorers, adventurers, and defenders continue to expand their spheres of influence.

DWARVES

The Ironforge dwarves hold the majority of the mountainous Khaz Modan region, in the Eastern Kingdoms. Settled areas include Dun Morogh, Loch Modan, and the Wetlands. Another dwarven stronghold, held by the Wildhammer clan, is Aerie Peak, in the Hinterlands.

HUMANS

The human kingdom of Stormwind controls territory in the Eastern Kingdoms, from Elwynn Forest and Westfall to Duskwood and the Redridge Mountains. In addition, human strongholds can be found throughout Azeroth and even beyond, in Outland.

WORGEN

The kingdom of Gilneas was once home to the worgen, but damage sustained during the Cataclysm and the Forsaken occupation left the kingdom deserted. The worgen now reside in the Howling Oak, located in the night elf capital of Darnassus.

BLOOD ELVES

The ancient nation of Quel'Thalas, including the region known as the Ghostlands and the isle of Quel'Danas, is home to the blood elves. Although long settled in the forests of the region, the blood elves still occasionally fight over territory with the Amani trolls.

GNOMES

Recent efforts by the gnomes have resulted in a partial reclamation of their ancestral home, Gnomeregan, and the establishment of a base of operations the gnomes have dubbed New Tinkertown. Although many gnomes have relocated, some still reside in the dwarven capital of Ironforge.

ORCS

Orcs make their primary home in the harsh lands of Durotar, and the Northern and Southern Barrens, in Kalimdor. While most orcs now call Azeroth home, small pockets of orc settlement can also be found on their former home world, the shattered planet of Draenor, now called Outland.

TAUREN

Most of the formerly nomadic tauren tribes now call the lands of Mulgore home, although tauren settlements can also be found elsewhere in Kalimdor.

NIGHT ELVES

The night elves live primarily in the World Tree Teldrassil, although settlements extend all over Kalimdor. Night elf homes can be found as far south as Feralas, although the majority of settlements can be found in the forests of Ashenvale, Darkshore, and Felwood.

GOBLINS

The goblins hail from the island of Kezan, but many were forced to flee the island after it faced volcanic destruction. They have since taken up residence in Azshara in Kalimdor, terraforming the land to suit their own needs.

TROLLS

Troll tribes can be found throughout Azeroth, including in the Hinterlands, Stranglethorn, and Tanaris. The Darkspear tribe, members of the Horde, have claimed the Echo Isles located just off the coast of Durotar as their home.

DRAENEI

The draenei, refugees from the distant world of Argus, once settled on the planet Draenor. However, events led to their flight from Draenor and crash-landing on Azeroth. Most draenei reside on the Azuremyst and Bloodmyst isles off the coast of Kalimdor, although some still remain on Draenor, now called Outland.

FORSAKEN

The undead Forsaken control the ruined human kingdom of Lordaeron. This includes Tirisfal Glades, Silverpine Forest, and Hillsbrad Foothills. However, Forsaken schemes are far ranging, and they also have a significant presence in the Plaguelands.

PANDAREN

Most pandaren live on the island of Pandaria, however some were born and raised on the Wandering Isle, a giant turtle that moves through the oceans of Azeroth. Many former residents of the Wandering Isle now have homes with the Alliance and Horde.

BASTIONS OF POWER

Azeroth is a world of vast magic and power. These energies are most apparent beneath the earth as well as in special locations—centers of elemental forces, otherworldly powers, and mystical energies. Warlocks, druids, shaman, and magi study to master these bastions of power.

THE MAELSTROM

During the Great Sundering, the first Well of Eternity was destroyed, collapsing into itself. Its waters became the center of the Great Sea, and an immense, violent whirlpool formed where the Well had once been. Called the Maelstrom to this day, the water churns constantly in a dizzying storm of tidal and arcane energy that seems to have no end.

DALARAN

Formerly ruled by the magocracy of the Kirin Tor, Dalaran was one of the city-states that made up the Arathorian Empire, the first great human civilization. Once situated in the Eastern Kingdoms' Alterac Mountains, Dalaran was devastated during the Third War. Rebuilt by magic and raised into the sky, the floating city was moved to Northrend, where it became a neutral base for Horde and Alliance. Dalaran has since joined the Alliance, reaffirming past connections.

THE WELL OF ETERNITY

Created when the world was young, the first Well of Eternity was destroyed during the War of the Ancients. Illidan Stormrage saved vials of water from the Well, later using some of them to transform a lake on Mount Hyjal into a new Well of Eternity. To safeguard the world from those that would abuse the Well's power, the dragonflights planted the World Tree Nordrassil in its waters, using a single seed from the Mother Tree G'Hanir.

KARAZHAN

No one knows who created the tower of Karazhan, located in the depths of Deadwind Pass. The former home of the legendary Guardian Medivh, Karazhan is a source of immense and ancient magical power. Able to seemingly grant visions and bend time itself, Karazhan later attracted the attentions of the Burning Legion. Today, few creatures walk its dusty halls apart from demonic entities, and the haunted spirits of the restless dead.

THE WORLD TREES

World Trees are ancient, massive trees, typically the home of night elves. The first of these was Nordrassil (far left), created by the dragonflights after the War of the Ancients. It was almost destroyed during the Battle of Mount Hyjal, but began recovering immediately afterward. The second World Tree, Teldrassil (left), stands as the current home of the night elves off the coast of Kalimdor. A third World Tree, Vordrassil, was created in the Grizzly Hills region of Northrend. It was corrupted by the Old Gods and, as a result, later destroyed by the druids.

THE NEXUS

The Nexus sits in the region of Coldarra, just off the coast of the Borean Tundra in Northrend. Home to the blue dragonflight, the Nexus was once occupied by the Dragon Aspect Malygos. Now nearly deserted, the Nexus serves as a storage facility for dangerous magical artifacts to be cataloged and studied.

THE EMERALD DREAM

The Emerald Dream is a mysterious, ethereal realm linked to Azeroth. In essence, it is what Azeroth would be without the presence or influence of sentient beings. It is a place of greenery, growth, and the wild aspect of nature, a conduit between nature and the physical world. Those in touch with the Emerald Dream sleep in Azeroth as their consciousness roams through the realm of nature. Ysera, Aspect of the green dragonflight, was given guardianship of the Emerald Dream by the titans, and it is now maintained and protected by her druid allies.

THE DARK PORTAL

This dimensional gateway was constructed to connect Azeroth and the world of Draenor. It was created by the joint efforts of the orc Gul'dan, his Shadow Council, and the Guardian Medivh, who was possessed by Sargeras, leader of the Burning Legion. The Dark Portal was the gateway through which the orcs invaded Azeroth. The Azeroth side was destroyed after the Horde was driven back at the end of the Second War. The Draenor side was destroyed by Alliance forces to prevent the magical backlash of that world's end from also destroying Azeroth. Dormant for years, the Dark Portal was rebuilt and reopened by the demon Lord Kazzak. Now, both Alliance and Horde forces regularly use the Dark Portal to travel between Azeroth and what remains of Draenor.

REALMS OF MAGIC

Few forces are as potent as magic. It can even bring about the destruction of entire worlds. The forms of magic found in Azeroth derive from different, ever-present energies. In Azeroth, volatile arcane magic was once concentrated in the Well of Eternity. Its destruction spread arcane power throughout the world. The nature and uses of magic are vigorously debated, but the magnitude of what it can accomplish cannot be doubted.

A HISTORY OF MAGIC

Thousands of years ago, the night elves were the masters of arcane magic. The most gifted among them, the Highborne, harnessed the powers of the Well of Eternity with such skill that they attracted the attentions of the Burning Legion. The War of the Ancients resulted, and the Well was destroyed. The surviving Highborne were forbidden to practice arcane magic. When they continued to do so, they were banished to the Eastern Kingdoms. Becoming high elves, they founded the nation of Quel'Thalas and created the Sunwell, a new magical fount, using water from the original Well. In later years, the high elves of Quel'Thalas began to teach humans the arcane arts. Those humans founded the city-state of Dalaran and formed the organization of the Kirin Tor magi as its ruling council.

The Guardian of Tirisfal was a solitary sorcerer champion gifted with immense power by the Council of Tirisfal. The Guardian's purpose was to protect Azeroth and fight against the Burning Legion.

The magocratic city-state of Dalaran was governed by the Kirin Tor. Nearly destroyed in the Third War, the city was rebuilt and is now a bastion of magical study and knowledge.

DRUIDISM

The druids' magic derives from nature, enabling them to channel natural energies and transform into animals. The first druid was Malfurion Stormrage, who was taught the art by Cenarius, demigod of nature. Druids maintain a deep connection to nature through the Emerald Dream, a primordial realm that encompasses all aspects of nature.

WARLOCKS

Warlocks are magical practitioners that seek to understand darker, fel-based magics, including destructive spells. While many warlocks willingly follow the Burning Legion, there are those who work against it, using their magic to fight against evil. Warlocks have proven themselves to be powerful allies—as well as powerful foes.

FEL MAGIC

Fel magic is a destructive form of magic often used by members of the Burning Legion. Its use frequently results in corruption that manifests in a physical transformation, such as a change to an individual's eyes or skin color. All of the Burning Legion carry the taint of fel magic within their very blood, allowing them to spread greater evil.

NECROMANCY

Few things are as abhorrent and horrifying as necromancy, the study and use of magic to raise and control the dead. Necromancers are the enemies of life itself, and all hands are raised against them. Some of the worst evils in Azeroth's history have been perpetrated by necromancers, and they deserve their malevolent reputation.

SHAMANISM

Shamanism is a deeply spiritual form of elemental magic that involves a connection with both the natural and the spirit worlds. Shaman do not normally enslave elementals, but honor them, asking the elements to heed their call. Shaman are not inherently imbued with magic—they harness the powers of the elements through ceremonial totems.

MAGIC WEAPONS

Gifted crafters can focus magical energies into potent weapons. These weapons often enhance the abilities of the wielder, whether by honing their spellcraft, or enhancing their martial abilities. Wielded by heroes and villains alike, many of these weapons have stories as varied, complex, and fascinating as those that claim their power.

THE LIGHT

The Light is a mysterious and benevolent force in the universe. Those connected to the Light can harness it to heal, cleanse, and protect. Most practitioners of the Light are either priests or paladins, devoted to cleansing the universe of darkness. The naaru, enigmatic beings composed of pure energy, taught the use of the Light to the draenei race, but other races have come into the study and practice of Light-based magic of their own accord.

TECHNOLOGY

Azeroth was crafted by technology. The titans, immense, metallic-skinned beings of unimaginable power, shaped Azeroth, leaving evidence of their technological prowess all over the world. Titan ruins often hide gigantic engines of creation, and sometimes, weapons capable of massive destruction. Although the titans are mysteriously absent, their creations, and their descendants, show a keen interest in technological advancement to this day.

The malefic Old Gods created the Curse of Flesh to corrupt the titans' creations, slowly transforming the early races of Azeroth from metal and stone into skin, blood, and bone. Unable to cure the curse, the titans created machines to produce new protobeings, thus leading to the creation of the dwarves and gnomes.

ALLIANCE TECHNOLOGY

Many Alliance races have embraced technology. The two most fervent in their pursuit have origins that lead back to the titans themselves. The gnomes, who are descended from robotic creatures called mechagnomes, display remarkable intelligence, strong engineering skills, and a zest for using those skills to improve the quality of life wherever they see fit. The dwarves, descendants of an early stone-built race known as earthen, tend to focus their technological prowess on the manufacturing of weapons and armor. Perhaps the most technologically advanced of the Alliance are the draenei, who use highly advanced, naaru-based technology, enhanced by magic, to cross dimensions. Although not all of the Alliance races are obsessed with technology, all reap its benefits in one way or another.

HORDE TECHNOLOGY

The many races of the Horde are far more primitive than those of the Alliance, and thus are not nearly as technologically advanced. Most advances have taken place in the field of war machines and weaponry, and the Horde had to employ technological "consultants"—goblins—to create the city of Orgrimmar. The introduction of the blood elves into the Horde sparked an increase in technological knowledge, although the technology of the blood elves is greatly augmented by their vast skills in the magical arts. However, the permanent inclusion of goblins, with their emphasis on engineering and mechanical development, into the Horde has opened up tremendous technological potential. Today, the Horde is slowly realizing real gains through technology, both for military and domestic purposes.

TRANSPORTATION

The Alliance and Horde are unions of races spanning vast stretches of territory, making transportation of paramount importance. While both factions rely on traditional beasts of burden, each has also developed its own methods of mass transportation. The Horde prefers to travel by air, in goblin-engineered zeppelins. The Alliance prefers to travel by sea, in great ships. The Alliance also possesses one of the greatest achievements of gnomish technology: The Deeprun Tram. This massive subterranean tram spans the Eastern Kingdoms, running between the dwarven capital of Ironforge, and the human capital of Stormwind City.

Gunships are massive, armored airships, created by gnomes for the Alliance and by goblins for the Horde. Two of the most famous are *Orgrim's Hammer* (Horde, left) and the *Skybreaker* (Alliance, right), which patrol over Icecrown Glacier in Northrend.

LEGENDARY WEAPONS

Throughout Azeroth's history, heroes and villains have wielded legendary weapons, sometimes infused and enchanted by magic. These legendary weapons have stories of their own, passed down through the ages into lore. These artifacts have been lost, cursed, blessed, corrupted, and restored, and many of them are sure to play a significant role in future events.

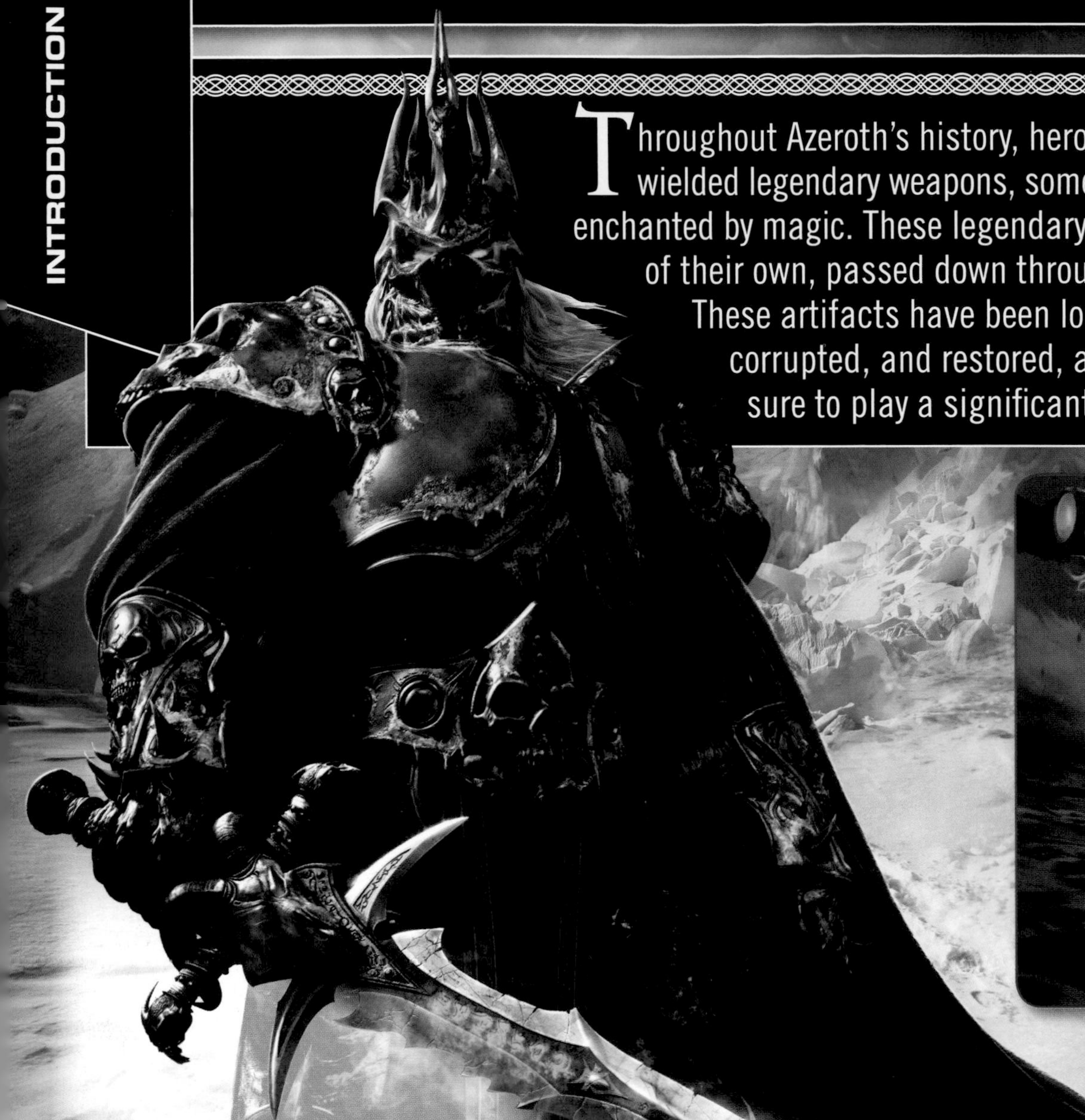

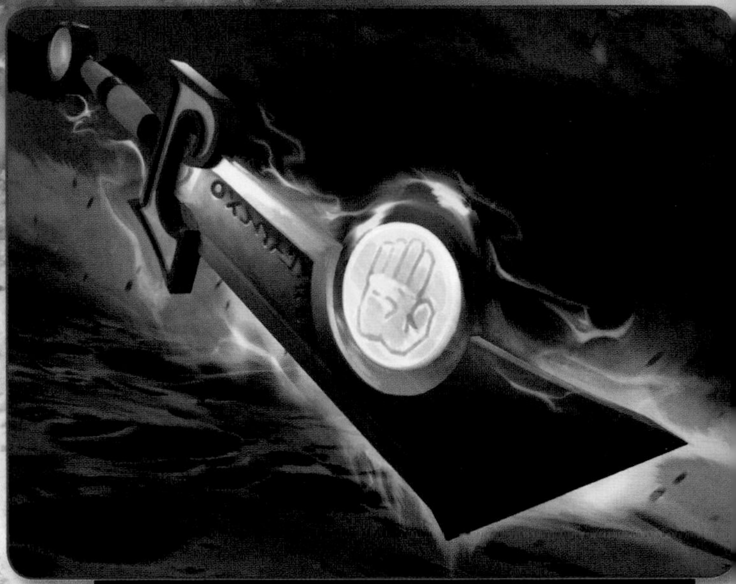

THE ASHBRINGER

King Magni Bronzebeard forged the Ashbringer for paladin Alexandros Mograine from a piece of crystal purified by wielders of the Holy Light. This gave it strange, Light-bearing powers. Named for its ability to slaughter undead, leaving nothing but ash in its wake, the Ashbringer was corrupted when it was used by Alexandros' son, Renault, to murder his father. Recovered by Alexandros' younger son, Darion, the corrupted blade was cleansed by paladin Tirion Fordring at the Battle for Light's Hope Chapel. Tirion later used the blade to shatter the Lich King's runeblade Frostmourne, and still carries the weapon.

FROSTMOURNE

Frostmourne was a cursed runeblade of unimaginable evil, capable of imprisoning the souls of those slain by its blade. It held part of the Lich King's consciousness and linked him with Frostmourne's wielder, Prince Arthas Menethil, during the Third War, which concluded with Arthas becoming the Lich King himself. As the Lich King, Arthas continued to wield the runeblade until his death in combat with Highlord Tirion Fordring, Supreme Commander of the Argent Crusade. Frostmourne was shattered by Tirion's sword, the Ashbringer, and the whereabouts of the shards and the sword's battered hilt remain a mystery to this day.

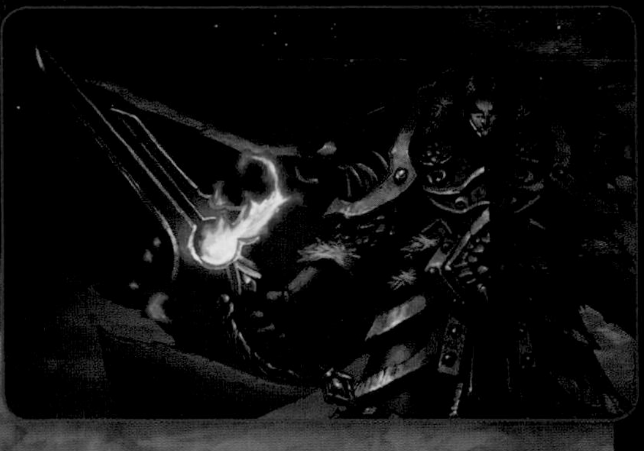

SHALAMAYNE

Varian Wrynn, King of Stormwind, wields the legendary sword Shalamayne. It was once two night elven blades, Shalla'tor and Ellemayne, gifted to the split aspects of Varian's personality by Lady Jaina Proudmoore. When the black dragon Onyxia inadvertently merged the aspects of Varian back into one individual, the swords were merged into one mighty weapon.

THE BLADES OF AZZINOTH

Azzinoth was a doomguard commander during the War of the Ancients. He was killed by Illidan Stormrage, who took his fearsome weapons as his own. These glaives, which can be joined into a single weapon or separated into two, became Illidan's weapons of choice. He used them during his ill-fated duel with Arthas Menethil, as well as in his campaign in Outland against the Burning Legion.

GOREHOWL

The axe Gorehowl was named for the unique screaming howl it made as it sliced through the air. It was the weapon of the orc Grom Hellscream, a fearsome warrior who was the first orc to drink the cursed blood of the pit lord Mannoroth and succumb to the corruption of the Burning Legion. Yet Grom's story ended with redemption. He used Gorehowl to strike the final blow against Mannoroth, bringing the pit lord's life to an untimely end and freeing the orcish race from the blood curse once and for all. The axe was later passed on to Grom's son, Garrosh, by Warchief Thrall.

DOOMHAMMER

A great warhammer originating with the Blackrock Clan on Draenor, Doomhammer was passed to Orgrim upon the death of his father, with these words: *"It is said that the last of the Doomhammer line will use it to bring first salvation and then doom to the orc people. Then it will pass into the hands of one who is not of the Blackrock clan, all will change again, and it will once again be used in the cause of justice."* The prophecy came to pass. After using Doomhammer in the First and Second Wars, Orgrim bequeathed the weapon to Thrall as he died. Thrall has wielded the weapon with pride, and justice, ever since.

MORE WEAPONS OF LEGEND

Many other weapons appear in Azeroth's history. Thori'dal, the Stars' Fury, a famous bow; Atiesh, Greatstaff of the Guardian, once wielded by the Guardian Medivh, and now held by his son Med'an; the Bladefist, wielded by Kargath Bladefist, Warchief of the Fel Horde; Shadowmourne, an axe created by Darion Mograine to combat the Lich King's runeblade Frostmourne; Sulfuras, Hand of Ragnaros, wielded by Ragnaros the Firelord; Val'anyr, Hammer of the Ancient Kings, a titan-created weapon given to Urel Stoneheart, the first earthen king; and Ashkandi, Greatsword of the Brotherhood, rumored to have belonged to Sir Anduin Lothar.

Thori'dal

Atiesh

Shadowmourne

Sulfuras

Ashkandi

Bladefist

Val'anyr

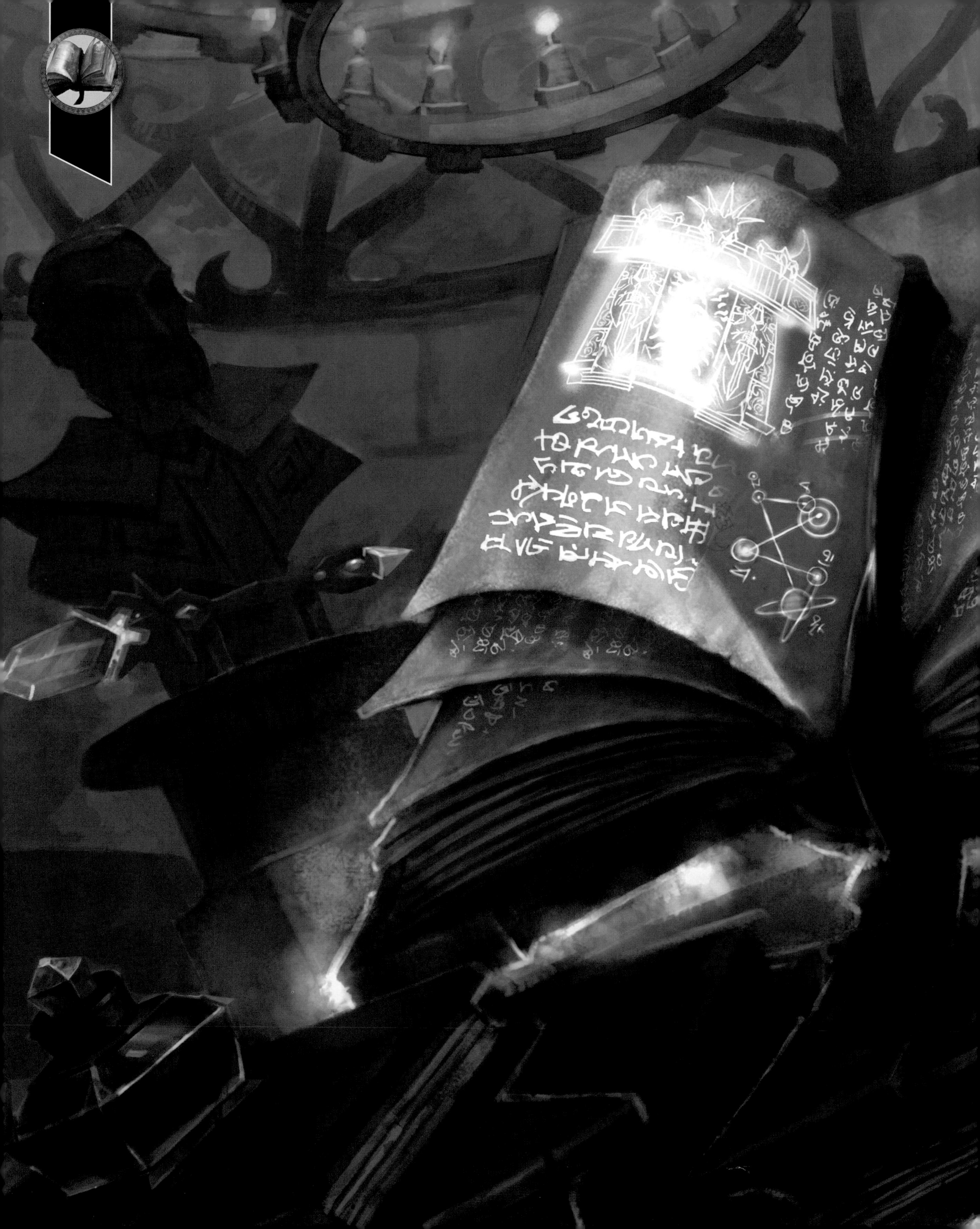

THE CHRONICLES
OF AZEROTH

YEAR 18 THE NEW HORDE

The orcs held in the Alliance's internment camps are freed by Orgrim Doomhammer, Grom Hellscream, and Thrall, an orc who was raised by humans as a slave and gladiator. Thrall is named warchief of the new Horde.

YEAR 20 THE THIRD WAR

The Burning Legion launches another assault on Azeroth using the Lich King. The Plague of Undeath spreads through the kingdom of Lordaeron, resulting in the rise of the Scourge in Lordaeron. Prince Arthas Menethil falls to corruption, taking up the cursed runeblade Frostmourne and murdering his father King Terenas II. The Sunwell is defiled, and the demon lord Archimonde is summoned into Azeroth. Many survivors flee to Kalimdor, including humans led by Lady Jaina Proudmoore, and orcs led by Thrall.

YEAR 21 THE BATTLE OF MOUNT HYJAL

On Kalimdor, the orcs establish a home in Durotar, allying with the Darkspear trolls and the tauren. The survivors in Kalimdor are brought together by the Prophet Medivh, and unite against Archimonde's onslaught. Archimonde is defeated at Mount Hyjal, but the World Tree Nordrassil is badly damaged, resulting in the night elves losing their immortality.

YEAR 22 RISE OF THE LICH KING

Arthas Menethil travels to Northrend. Former high-elf ranger-general turned banshee Sylvanas Windrunner establishes the Forsaken, taking control of the former kingdom of Lordaeron. Arthas ascends Icecrown Glacier, shattering the Frozen Throne and taking his place as the Lich King.

YEAR 25 THE GATHERING STORM

King Varian Wrynn of Stormwind is kidnapped, and his son Anduin Wrynn is temporarily crowned. The black dragon Onyxia is discovered in Stormwind City. An assault is launched on Blackwing Lair, home of the black dragon Nefarian. In the deserts of Silithus, the qiraji launch an invasion at the behest of the Old God C'thun. Kel'Thuzad launches an attack on Azeroth from the dread citadel Naxxramas in the Eastern Kingdoms.

YEAR 26 — THE BURNING CRUSADE

The blood elves of Quel'Thalas join the Horde. In Kalimdor, the draenei crash-land off the northern coast, and ally with the Alliance. The Dark Portal is rebuilt and re-opened by Lord Kazzak, and both Horde and Alliance forces travel to Outland. There the orc Garrosh Hellscream is discovered by Warchief Thrall, and taken back to Azeroth to act as an advisor. Prince Kael'thas Sunstrider of the blood elves allies with the Burning Legion, attempting to summon the demon lord Kil'jaeden to Azeroth. The Sunwell is restored with the heart of the naaru M'uru.

YEAR 27 — THE WRATH OF THE LICH KING

The Lich King launches a new assault on Azeroth, attacking Stormwind City and Orgrimmar. Alliance and Horde forces both travel to Northrend to combat the Lich King. The Argent Crusade is established. Death knight defectors from the Lich King's armies form the Knights of the Ebon Blade, allying with both Alliance and Horde. Garrosh Hellscream is sent to lead the Horde forces in Northrend. The Lich King is defeated.

YEAR 28 — THE CATACLYSM

Thrall steps down from his position as warchief and appoints Garrosh Hellscream as the new leader of the Horde. The former Dragon Aspect Deathwing bursts through into Azeroth from the Elemental Plane, shattering the surface of the world as tensions between the Alliance and Horde continue to build. The worgen of Gilneas join the Alliance, and the goblins of the Bilgewater Cartel join the Horde. The Elemental Lords Ragnaros and Al'Akir are slain, as well as Cho'gall, leader of the Twilight Cult. The Dragon Aspects expend the last of their power to kill Deathwing, and the Age of Mortals begins.

YEAR 30 — THE INVASION OF PANDARIA

All-out war erupts between Alliance and Horde when Warchief Garrosh Hellscream destroys the city of Theramore with a mana bomb. Archmage Rhonin dies, and Lady Jaina Proudmoore takes his place as leader of the Kirin Tor, a council of some of Azeroth's most powerful magi. Pandaren residents of the Wandering Isle ally with both Alliance and Horde as the continent of Pandaria is discovered. The sha are released on Pandaria, and the Thunder King Lei Shen is resurrected. Garrosh orders the assassination of the Darkspear leader, Vol'jin. Jaina forcibly removes the Horde from Dalaran, throwing the magocratic city-state's support behind the Alliance. Vol'jin begins the Darkspear Rebellion, pitting Horde against Horde. The Alliance covertly assists the Darkspear rebels, seeking to end Garrosh's reign as warchief.

TITANS AND OLD GODS

Golganneth

Eonar

Aman'Thul

Norgannon

Khaz'goroth

Aggramar

Sargeras

THE PANTHEON

The titans are ruled by an elite sect known as the Pantheon. Each member of the Pantheon possesses an important role in shaping the worlds they encounter. Aman'Thul is the Highfather, oldest and wisest, the leader of the Pantheon. Eonar serves as patron of all life and nature. Khaz'goroth is the shaper and forger of worlds. Norgannon is the lorekeeper and keeper of celestial magics, while Golganneth is known as the lord of the skies and roaring oceans. Although Sargeras once served as the champion of the Pantheon, he deserted the Pantheon after seeing his war as unwinnable; his lieutenant, Aggramar, later stepped in to fill the role.

The titans are massive, metallic-skinned gods from the far reaches of the cosmos. While their origins remain a mystery, it is known that the titans travel the cosmos bringing order to worlds, and even empowering the primitive races of those worlds to maintain their integrity. Bastions of purity and good, the titans are unable to conceive of evil or wickedness in any form, and constantly struggle to find a way to protect their creations from the chaotic forces of evil that threaten them. Although none know the current whereabouts of the titans, over a hundred million worlds have been brought to order by their hands.

Algalon the Observer is a cos entity, charged with observin Azeroth to watch for any sign corruption. In the event that Algalon deems the world corrupted, his message to the titans results in re-origination the immediate destruction an re-creation of the planet.

The desert sands of Uldum hold the re-origination device set in place by the titans. If Azeroth were deemed corrupted, the device would destroy the world.

AZEROTH AND THE OLD GODS

Long ago, the world of Azeroth became threatened by malignant beings of unfathomable evil. Known as the Old Gods, these entities of chaos and destruction wreaked havoc on the world. In ages past, the Old Gods commanded great armies led by four Elemental Lords; Ragnaros the Firelord, Al'Akir the Windlord, Therazane the Stonemother, and Neptulon the Tidehunter. The Elemental Lords and the Old Gods were defeated and imprisoned by forces of the titans, yet ages later, their influence still continues to affect the world. In the far reaches of Silithus, the Old God C'Thun influenced the insectoid silithid race to invade Kalimdor, eventually giving rise to the War of the Shifting Sands. C'Thun was sealed inside the city Ahn'Qiraj and locked behind a massive gate, but the Old God continued its dread plan, resulting in a second war years later. In Northrend, the Old God Yogg-Saron was chained beneath the mighty fortress of Ulduar, and eventually corrupted its warden to try to escape. The great Old God N'Zoth remains largely a mystery, but was responsible for the spark of the Emerald Nightmare. And in Pandaria, the dread Old God Y'Shaarj breathed one last, terrible breath from its seven heads before it perished, bringing forth the sha, terrifying entities formed of negative emotion. Although imprisoned, the Old Gods, their minions, and their mission of chaos still remain a disquieting threat.

The mighty stronghold of Ulduar in Northrend serves as prison to the Old God Yogg-Saron.

Ragnaros the Firelord was one of four Elemental Lords—raging entities once enslaved by the Old Gods, and forced to serve them.

Sargeras was once the great champion of the titans. For millennia, Sargeras traveled among countless worlds, eradicating hordes of demons from existence. Yet the horrors Sargeras witnessed wore heavy on him, and, in time, he lost hope and embraced despair. Sargeras now believed that the titans' mission of creation was hopelessly flawed. He became bonded entirely to evil, and created the Burning Legion, an army dedicated to the destruction of all creation.

SARGERAS

"Great Enemy of all life, the Destroyer of Worlds."

GOD OF FEL AND FLAME

Sargeras' constant battles in the Twisting Nether took their toll. Once loyal and true, he eventually became corrupted by the very demons he was tasked to destroy.

Sargeras was a titan, a race of beings that worked throughout the universe to shape worlds of order and justice. A paragon of virtue, Sargeras was dispatched by the Pantheon, the ruling council of titans, to fight against the evil demons that dwelled in the Twisting Nether. These demons constantly threatened the titans' creations, and for thousands of years, Sargeras performed his duties without question or fail. His might was unmatched, and his altruism did not waver. However, years of continual strife began to change him. Seeing so much evil made it hard for the titan to retain his belief that the universe could ever be made a bastion of peace. He came to believe that a flaw in the fabric of creation set up an unwinnable battle against evil. His fellow titans were unable to assuage these emotions, and Sargeras stormed from their ranks forever, seeking his own place in the universe. The titans could not have foreseen how far Sargeras was willing to go. Their former champion descended into the Twisting Nether, where he freed the demons he had once imprisoned, and began to corrupt races of all kinds. He named his new army the Burning Legion, and chose two great champions of evil—Kil'jaeden and Archimonde—to lead his forces. Sargeras instructed them to search the universe for any signs of the titans' handiwork, and to conquer and burn all they found. This task has become known as the Burning Crusade.

THE DEATH OF BROXIGAR

During the War of the Ancients, the Burning Legion's first invasion of Azeroth, Sargeras waited in the Twisting Nether to cross into the world. The great orc Broxigar, who had traveled backward in time and was fighting alongside Kalimdor's defenders, threw himself into the dimensional portal between Azeroth and the Twisting Nether. Broxigar managed to wound Sargeras, delaying him long enough for the night elves to disrupt the portal. Sadly, the heroic Broxigar died, impaled on Sargeras' broken sword.

AVATAR OF SARGERAS

Sargeras later sent an avatar of himself into the world, knowing that Aegwynn (pictured right), the powerful Guardian of Tirisfal and protector of Azeroth, would try to kill him. Aegwynn slew Sargeras' avatar with disconcerting ease, and hid the body in a tomb beneath the Great Sea. Aegwynn had fallen into Sargeras' trap; unknown to her, the spirit of Sargeras had infused her body. His essence later passed on to her son, Medivh, who would be driven to do Sargeras' will.

GUL'DAN'S FATE

Sargeras found another pawn in the orc warlock Gul'dan. Sargeras convinced Gul'dan that in exchange for manipulating the orcs of Draenor into conquering Azeroth, he would be rewarded with unimaginable power. Gul'dan sought the Tomb of Sargeras, hoping the Eye of Sargeras housed within would sate his appetite for god-like supremacy. Instead, he found only demons, madness, and death. Gul'dan's final words are inscribed in that tomb, in his own blood.

KEY DATA

NAME Sargeras

GENDER AND RACE
Male titan

AFFILIATION Burning Legion

STATUS Unknown

TITLES Lord of the Burning Legion, The Destroyer, The Destroyer of Worlds, Dark Titan, Fallen Titan

Clad in black armor, Sargeras is a massive being of near limitless power, surrounded by the fel flames that infuse the Burning Legion.

While Sargeras once hunted demons in the Twisting Nether, he now resides there, controlling his demon armies and sending them forth to conquer.

ATTACK ON AZEROTH

During the War of the Ancients, Sargeras manipulated the night elf Queen Azshara and her counselor, Lord Xavius, into helping him unleash his Burning Legion upon Azeroth. As Sargeras tried to enter the world via a portal in the depths of the Well of Eternity, it imploded, causing horrific devastation. The continent of Kalimdor fractured, and the Well site collapsed into the sea. The waters rushed in to form a vortex above the Well's remains, now known as the Maelstrom.

ARCHIMONDE

Archimonde was one of the leaders of the eredar, ruling his people alongside Kil'jaeden and Velen in peace and harmony. When Sargeras offered power in exchange for loyalty, Archimonde eagerly accepted. He loyally served Sargeras and the Burning Legion for thousands of years, before his destruction during the Third War.

THE DEFILER

Archimonde's death was the culmination of a great conflict. As he battled toward the World Tree, night elf, human, and orc forces came together to oppose him. Even the Burning Legion could not triumph against a united Azeroth.

Archimonde was one of the eredar, a race of incredibly talented magic-users from the planet Argus. He ruled his people hand in hand with Kil'jaeden and Velen. When Sargeras arrived on Argus, seeking powerful forces to bolster the Burning Legion, he made the trio an offer: whoever served him would gain vast power. Archimonde and Kil'jaeden chose Sargeras, and Velen, fearing what would befall his people, fled. Archimonde became Sargeras' military commander, triumphing on many worlds. Yet Azeroth, it seemed, would elude him—the forces of the Burning Legion were thwarted during the War of the Ancients.

Undaunted, Archimonde raged in the Twisting Nether, plotting a second invasion per the will of Sargeras. He finally got his chance when a summoner, Kel'Thuzad, brought him back into the world during the Third War. Initially, his wrath seemed unstoppable. His first act was to destroy the city of Dalaran; his second, to attack Kalimdor and try to take control of the second Well of Eternity. Yet even as he worked to rip the World Tree Nordrassil from the Well, the mortals of Azeroth struck back. Malfurion Stormrage called upon the spirits of nature, who surrounded Archimonde as he assaulted Nordrassil, which then detonated. Archimonde was destroyed, and the forces of the Burning Legion soon collapsed without their leader.

Archimonde was so brutal that he became known for killing even those who served him. Failure at any level was often punishable by death.

WAR OF THE ANCIENTS

Thousands of years ago, Sargeras, aided by Archimonde, led his first campaign against Azeroth. The resultant war would have been successful if not for the intervention of Malfurion Stormrage and Tyrande Whisperwind. Joined by a host of others, including the dragonflights, the combined forces pushed Archimonde's demons back into the portal from whence they came. The Well of Eternity imploded, cleaving the world, but the war was over.

KEY DATA

NAME Archimonde

GENDER AND RACE Male eredar

AFFILIATION Burning Legion

STATUS Deceased

TITLES The Defiler, Eredar Overlord of the Legion Forces

RELATIVES None known

"Let the echoes of doom resound across this wretched world, that all who live may hear them and despair."

KIL'JAEDEN

Kil'jaeden once ruled the utopian planet Argus, homeworld of the eredar, alongside Archimonde and Velen. The dark titan Sargeras offered almost unlimited power to the three, which Archimonde and Kil'jaeden accepted. Now a powerful leader in Sargeras' Burning Legion, Kil'jaeden serves his master with terrifying fealty, filled with a consuming desire to destroy all life.

Kil'jaeden is a horrifying adversary. Those who oppose him are faced with the prospect of torture and suffering.

THE DECEIVER

Once an eredar of Argus, Kil'jaeden has transformed into a creature of unimaginable evil. Implicitly loyal to Sargeras, the dark titan that rules the Burning Legion, Kil'jaeden has used his intelligence and strategic savvy to further his master's goals. Instead of wading through enemy lines like Archimonde, he sought out the darkest races in the universe and recruited them into Sargeras' ranks—it was through Kil'jaeden's influence that the Old Horde was formed.

Kil'jaeden was partially successful in entering Azeroth at the Sunwell Plateau. His plans were thwarted in part by the efforts of the Shattered Sun Offensive, an army of blood elf and draenei heroes brought together by the naaru.

Infuriated by the failure of the orc shaman Ner'zhul to fully give the orcs over to the Burning Legion, Kil'jaeden later shaped Ner'zhul into the Lich King and sent forth the undead armies of the Scourge. Still, Ner'zhul betrayed him yet again, and the Scourge were lost to Kil'jaeden. Undaunted, Kil'jaeden sought a stronger instrument to destroy the Lich King, eventually tempting the night elf demon hunter Illidan Stormrage to accept his command. In the end, Illidan also proved a failure, and Kil'jaeden's goal of destroying the Lich King remained unfulfilled. Prince Kael'thas Sunstrider, Illidan's retainer, proved more malleable than his master. He was manipulated into summoning Kil'jaeden himself into the world through the Sunwell, a fount of mystical power. Through the Shattered Sun Offensive, Kael'thas and Kil'jaeden's plans were thwarted, and Kil'jaeden was once again sent back to the Twisting Nether. While his current whereabouts are unknown, it can be assumed that Kil'jaeden still waits and schemes, searching for a way to further his master Sargeras' endeavors.

KEY DATA

NAME Kil'jaeden

GENDER AND RACE Male eredar

AFFILIATION Burning Legion

STATUS Living

TITLES Great One, Lord of Flame, The Deceiver, The Beautiful One

RELATIVES None known

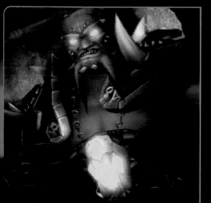

"The end has come! Let the unraveling of this world commence!"

THE DRAENEI

Once like brothers, Kil'jaeden and Velen became enemies when Kil'jaeden accepted Sargeras' offer of untold power. Believing that Velen had betrayed him, Kil'jaeden hunted him for millennia. Those eredar who rejected Sargeras' offer fled with Velen, renaming themselves draenei—"exiled ones."

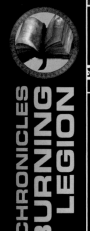

THE BURNING LEGION

The fallen titan Sargeras is both creator and leader of the Burning Legion, a vast, immeasurably powerful demonic army eager to carry out Sargeras' will. The Burning Legion seeks to undo the works of the titans, destroying worlds and setting the universe aflame. It is unknown how many worlds the Burning Legion has destroyed in its bloodthirsty mission.

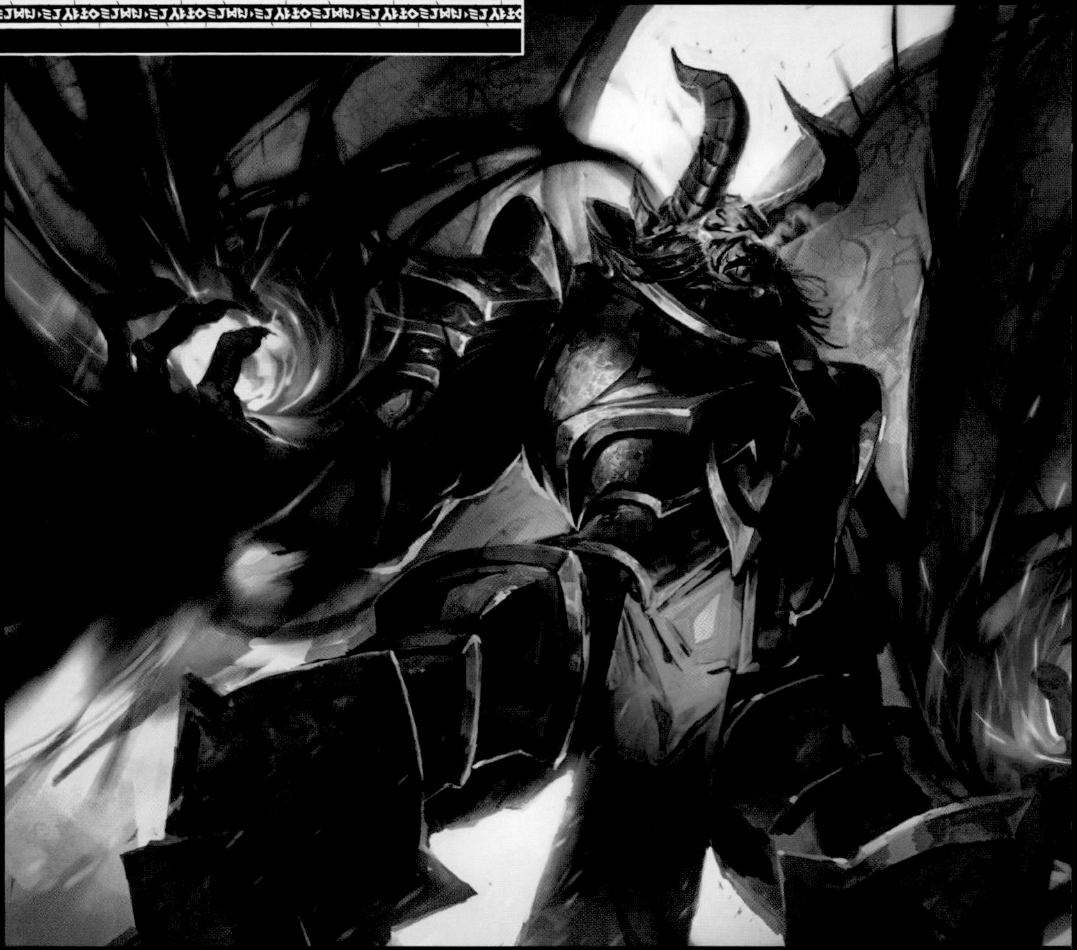

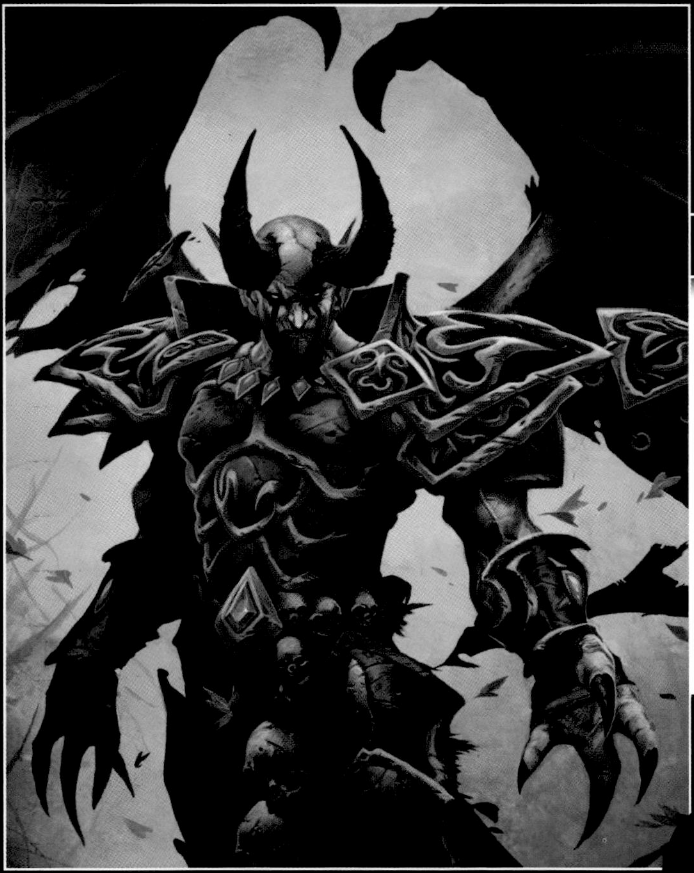

NATHREZIM (DREADLORD)

Cunning, cruel, and dedicated to treachery, the nathrezim and their prowess in manipulation and subterfuge have proven incredibly valuable to the Burning Legion. Intelligent and ruthless, many nathrezim served as commanders of the undead Scourge during the Third War. Masters of manipulation and disguise, the nathrezim are terrifying foes and eminently suited to carrying out the Burning Legion's dark plans.

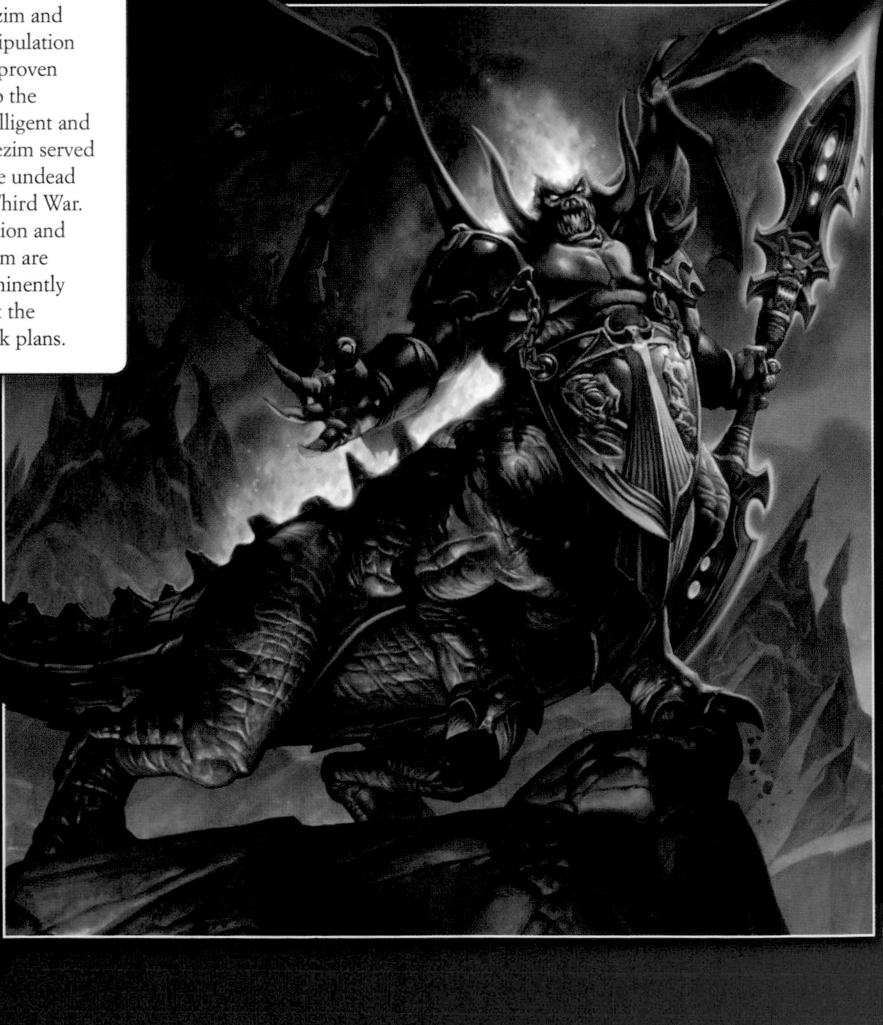

ANNIHILAN (PIT LORD)

The annihilan, or pit lords, were recruited by Kil'jaeden the Deceiver. They are driven by pure rage and bloodlust, with their very blood capable of transmitting their ferocity. Once led by Mannoroth the Destructor, the pit lords are fanatically loyal to the Burning Legion and know nothing of pity or compassion.

INFERNAL

Infernals are similar to constructs or golems, created through malevolent fel energy and fury. They are barely capable of following orders, existing only to destroy before their forms dissipate. They are summoned and used by demons of the Burning Legion to crush their enemies, sow chaos, and even raze cities.

EREDAR (WRATHGUARD)

Once a race of noble and enigmatic spellcasters, the eredar chose to follow Sargeras in return for immeasurable power and prestige. Also called man'ari, or "unnatural beings", these formerly benevolent masters of magic now act as some of the most powerful weapons in the Burning Legion's arsenal. The wrathguard are members of the eredar that act as honor guard for leaders of the Burning Legion.

SHIVARRA (SHIVAN)

Little is known about the shivarra, or shivan. While some are terrifying fighters, most shivarra serve the Burning Legion as priestesses or masters of entropy. As devout believers in Sargeras' vision, they work to focus and inspire the rest of the Burning Legion's forces.

FEL ORC

Fel orcs are members of the orcish race who have been completely consumed by madness and bloodlust. Engineered by the Burning Legion, fel orcs are created by the continual consumption of pit lord blood. This results in a blood haze, uncontrollable bloodlust, and physical changes as well—bright red skin, sharp spines, and reddened eyes signify a fel orc as much as its maddened lust for destruction.

FELGUARD

Felguards are the rank-and-file troops within the Burning Legion, conscripted from the mo'arg species. These warriors can carve through armies, searching for weaknesses within the ranks. They then converge upon a hapless target, breaking into their foes, leaving only blood in their wake.

AYAAD (SUCCUBUS)

While there are many sayaad, or succubi, that loyally serve the Burning Legion, there are also those that serve only themselves or can be impressed by a warlock master. They are known as agile fighters with command of the mystic arts—particularly the ability to magically charm their targets.

FEL REAVER

Fel reavers are huge war machines created by mo'arg engineers. They are immense giants, powered by an internal power core of fel flame. The fel reavers act as sentries or sentinels, crossing great distances, and they attack enemies of the Burning Legion on sight. Many unknowing explorers have been crushed under the boot of a fel reaver.

THE WAR OF THE ANCIENTS

The War of the Ancients proved a defining event in the history of Azeroth. It began with the reckless use of arcane magic that focused the attention of the Burning Legion upon Azeroth, and ended with a cataclysmic event that reshaped the entire world.

THE RISE AND FALL OF THE KALDOREI EMPIRE

Thousands of years ago, the world of Azeroth was a single continent, Kalimdor, with a mystical lake of vast magical power at its center, called the Well of Eternity. Night elf—or "kaldorei"—civilization formed around the Well. However, Queen Azshara, leader of the night elves, began manipulating the Well's energies, accompanied by powerful sorcerers dubbed the Highborne. Their reckless use of magic drew the attention of Sargeras, leader of the Burning Legion. Believing that Sargeras would remake Kalimdor into a paradise, Queen Azshara and her supporters opened a portal to bring the Burning Legion to Azeroth, and then moved the portal to the Well of Eternity. The Legion invaded the world and, as it slaughtered the night elf populace under the eyes of its uncaring queen, a resistance movement grew, leading to the War of the Ancients. Three heroes, the twins Malfurion and Illidan Stormrage and priestess Tyrande Whisperwind, emerged within the resistance, which was joined by many powerful supporters, including the ancient demigods of Azeroth and the dragonflights, all hoping to safeguard their world.

Queen Azshara was loved by her people, revered for her charismatic leadership, arcane mastery, and beauty. But Azshara believed in only one thing: the pursuit of a world that mirrored her own perfection. Sargeras promised this to Azshara, and she pledged her fealty and empire to the Burning Legion.

A fateful trio came to the defense of their people. Malfurion Stormrage was a young druid, with a developing connection to nature. His twin brother, Illidan Stormrage, preferred manipulating the powers of the arcane, and their childhood friend, Tyrande Whisperwind, was a priestess of Elune and committed to the world's protection.

Much of the destruction in the kaldorei Empire was caused by two powerful leaders in Sargeras' armies, Hakkar the Houndmaster and Mannoroth the Destructor.

BATTLES AND BETRAYALS

War raged between the night elven resistance and the Burning Legion, and disaster struck as Neltharion, Aspect of the black dragonflight, revealed his long-hidden madness. Taking the name Deathwing, he attacked the other dragonflights, forcing them to retreat. Even worse, Illidan, enraged by Tyrande's choice of Malfurion over him, betrayed Malfurion's plan to destroy the Well of Eternity to Queen Azshara. She ordered her Highborne sorcerers to bring Sargeras himself into Azeroth. As Sargeras prepared to burst through the portal, Malfurion's forces attacked. Meanwhile, Illidan stole vials of water from the Well, claiming its magic as his own. With battle joined between the defenders of Azeroth and the Legion, the ensuing chaos disrupted the spell, collapsing the portal and destroying the Well of Eternity.

Jarod Shadowsong led the night elven forces and their allies against the Burning Legion. A gifted commander, Jarod tenaciously held ground with minimal losses until the demon lord Archimonde joined the battle. Archimonde turned his attentions on Jarod, nearly killing the night elf, but the demon lord and the rest of the Legion's forces were sucked back into the Twisting Nether, and Jarod escaped with his life.

| MALORNE | AGAMAGGAN | ALEXSTRASZA |

The night elves were joined by the demigods and dragonflights of Azeroth—beings that were inherently part of the world or charged with its preservation. Malorne, the White Stag, and Agamaggan, the Great Boar, were two of the great Ancients, immortal creatures of nature, that entered the fray. Alexstrasza the Dragonqueen also led the dragonflights against the Burning Legion, fulfilling her task to protect Azeroth.

THE GREAT SUNDERING

Sargeras had been stopped just as he tried to cross over into Azeroth. When the Well of Eternity imploded, the continent of Kalimdor was flooded, the remaining land forming disparate landmasses, an event known as the Great Sundering. The Well of Eternity formed into a vast whirlpool, the Maelstrom, at the center of Azeroth's oceans. Azshara and her Highborne followers were swallowed by the sea, but accepted a pact with the Old Gods, who transformed them into naga.

With the demons defeated, the combatants retreated to Mount Hyjal to escape the Great Sundering, where Illidan secretly poured several of his vials into a lake, creating a new Well of Eternity. Shocked at Illidan's actions and lack of remorse, Malfurion requested that his brother be imprisoned in the Barrow Dens. To prevent further misuse of the Well, the Dragonqueen, Alexstrasza, planted the World Tree Nordrassil over it. Blessed by the Aspects, the World Tree granted the night elves health, immortality, and a tie to the Emerald Dream, where sleeping druids would help preserve the balance of nature. The night elves took up residence in Nordrassil and the surrounding forests, determined to never again allow the corruption of their race.

NER'ZHUL

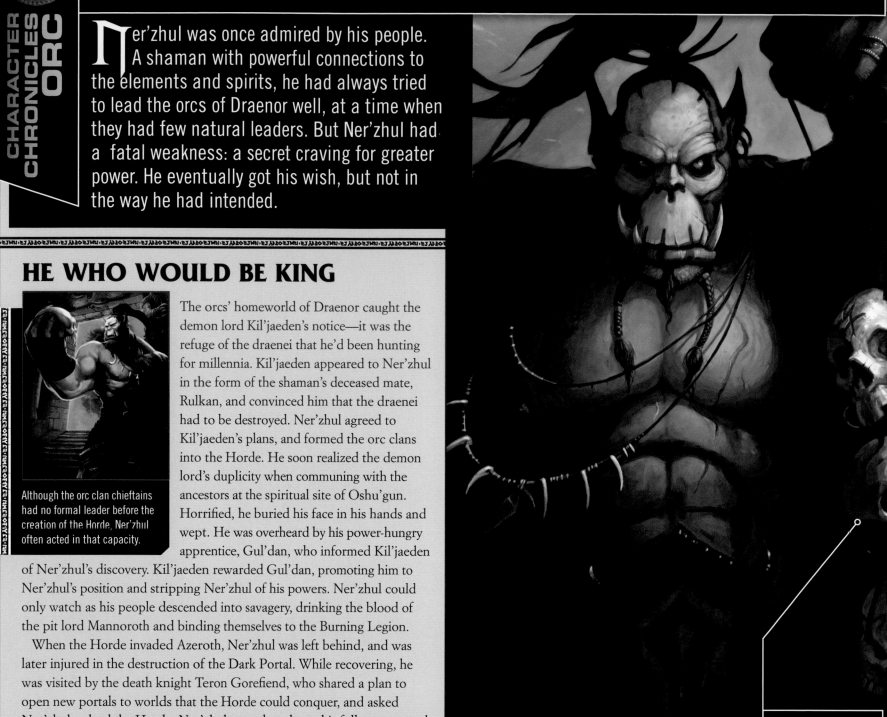

Ner'zhul was once admired by his people. A shaman with powerful connections to the elements and spirits, he had always tried to lead the orcs of Draenor well, at a time when they had few natural leaders. But Ner'zhul had a fatal weakness: a secret craving for greater power. He eventually got his wish, but not in the way he had intended.

HE WHO WOULD BE KING

Although the orc clan chieftains had no formal leader before the creation of the Horde, Ner'zhul often acted in that capacity.

The orcs' homeworld of Draenor caught the demon lord Kil'jaeden's notice—it was the refuge of the draenei that he'd been hunting for millennia. Kil'jaeden appeared to Ner'zhul in the form of the shaman's deceased mate, Rulkan, and convinced him that the draenei had to be destroyed. Ner'zhul agreed to Kil'jaeden's plans, and formed the orc clans into the Horde. He soon realized the demon lord's duplicity when communing with the ancestors at the spiritual site of Oshu'gun. Horrified, he buried his face in his hands and wept. He was overheard by his power-hungry apprentice, Gul'dan, who informed Kil'jaeden of Ner'zhul's discovery. Kil'jaeden rewarded Gul'dan, promoting him to Ner'zhul's position and stripping Ner'zhul of his powers. Ner'zhul could only watch as his people descended into savagery, drinking the blood of the pit lord Mannoroth and binding themselves to the Burning Legion.

When the Horde invaded Azeroth, Ner'zhul was left behind, and was later injured in the destruction of the Dark Portal. While recovering, he was visited by the death knight Teron Gorefiend, who shared a plan to open new portals to worlds that the Horde could conquer, and asked Ner'zhul to lead the Horde. Ner'zhul agreed, and sent his followers to seek out four magic artifacts from Azeroth to help with the task. But the search for power only corrupted him further. Ner'zhul opened portals all across Draenor, then fled through one and left the rest of the Horde behind. Overwhelmed by the strain of magic, Draenor shattered, becoming Outland. Ner'zhul thought he had escaped, but Kil'jaeden was waiting for him on the other side. Kil'jaeden ripped his body to pieces, but used fel magic to preserve Ner'zhul's spirit, torturing him until he swore to obey, and then twisting his soul into the Lich King, ruler of the undead Scourge.

Ner'zhul had the ability to speak with the spirits of the dead.

KEY DATA

NAME Ner'zhul

GENDER AND RACE Male orc

AFFILIATION (Old) Horde

STATUS Deceased

TITLES Elder Shaman, Warchief, Lich King

RELATIVES
Rulkan (mate, deceased)

THE LICH KING
Ner'zhul's spirit was imprisoned in a cask that was hurled to Azeroth and came to be called the Frozen Throne. Hungry for freedom and revenge, he bound the human prince Arthas Menethil to his service. When Arthas shattered the Frozen Throne and placed the Lich King's helm on his head, their two spirits became one—there was now only the Lich King.

"I am the Horde, and I will survive. Choose me, or choose death!"

GUL'DAN

Gul'dan was an ambitious student of the shaman Ner'zhul, on the orc homeworld of Draenor. When Kil'jaeden, loyal servant of the Burning Legion, offered him greater power in exchange for his loyalty, Gul'dan accepted the bargain, becoming the first orc warlock. He established the Shadow Council and became one of the most feared orcs in the race's history.

When members of a species known as the arakkoa tried to strike back at the Horde, Gul'dan used his powerful magic to obliterate them. Today, only their spirits remain in the ruined camps of Sketh'lon.

KEY DATA

NAME Gul'dan

GENDER AND RACE Male orc

AFFILIATION (Old) Horde

STATUS Deceased

TITLES Betrayer of the Orcs, Darkness Incarnate, The Destroyer of Dreams

RELATIVES Unknown

"I am darkness incarnate. I will not be denied."

THE DESTROYER OF DREAMS

As an apprentice shaman to Ner'zhul, the orcs' spiritual leader, young Gul'dan showed strong mastery over the elements. When Kil'jaeden tricked Ner'zhul to recruit the orcs for a war against the demon's draenei enemies, Gul'dan was intrigued. Ner'zhul later discovered the deception, but his apprentice sensed an opportunity and warned Kil'jaeden. As Ner'zhul refused to enslave his people to the Burning Legion, Kil'jaeden promoted Gul'dan to take Ner'zhul's place, teaching him fel magic. Now a potent warlock, Gul'dan took control of the Horde and established the Shadow Council, a group of warlocks who used their dark magic and influence to manipulate the orc clans. Gul'dan and the Shadow Council gave the blood of the pit lord Mannoroth to the orcs, corrupting them and binding them to the Burning Legion. With the Horde under the Burning Legion's control, the orcs slaughtered nearly all of the draenei. The human sorcerer Medivh, possessed by Sargeras, leader of the Burning Legion, then contacted Gul'dan from the distant world of Azeroth, offering him the powers of a god in exchange for sending the Horde to invade. Together, Medivh and Gul'dan opened the Dark Portal, unleashing the orcs on Azeroth and beginning the First War. An attempt to enter the mind of Medivh to find the location of the Tomb of Sargeras (and his promised powers) backfired, and Gul'dan fell into a coma. After he recovered, he sought out the Tomb, using his magic to raise it from the ocean's floor. But upon entering the Tomb, instead of finding the reward he was promised, Gul'dan was torn to shreds by swarms of demons.

While Gul'dan lay in a coma, the orc Warchief Orgrim Doomhammer and his forces turned on the Shadow Council, branding them traitors and slaughtering most of them.

THE SKULL OF GUL'DAN

Gul'dan's skull was a source of immeasurable power. Anyone bearing it could hear a fragment of Gul'dan's soul whispering to them. Ner'zhul used it to open the portals that destroyed Draenor, the human archmage Khadgar used it to destroy the Dark Portal, and eventually, the skull was consumed by the night elf Illidan Stormrage, transforming him into a demon.

THE FIRST WAR AND THE SECOND WAR

The First War began with the arrival of the orcish race on Azeroth. The horrific devastation caused by the Old Horde marked the beginning of a series of conflicts between Alliance and Horde that shaped the world of Azeroth, and continue to this day.

THE FIRST WAR

Thousands of years after the War of the Ancients, the Burning Legion turned their attention to another world—the distant home of the orcs, Draenor. The demon lord Kil'jaeden sought to bring the orcs under the control of the Burning Legion, and ultimately used the power-hungry nature of the orc Gul'dan to manipulate the orc clans. On Azeroth, Sargeras, the fallen titan and leader of the Burning Legion, possessed the powerful human sorcerer, Medivh, the Guardian of Tirisfal. Under Sargeras' control, Medivh used visions to communicate with Gul'dan, orchestrating the construction of the Dark Portal, a gateway between their two worlds. Gul'dan used his influence to declare a warchief, Blackhand, to lead the Horde—but Blackhand was merely a figurehead. Gul'dan and his warlocks, known as the Shadow Council, were secretly in control. With the Dark Portal complete, the Horde invaded Azeroth, and the orcs quickly advanced on the kingdom of Stormwind. Meanwhile, Medivh's apprentice, Khadgar, had realized that something was deeply wrong with his master, and warned Medivh's closest friend, Anduin Lothar, a knight in Stormwind's armies. Together they exposed Medivh's corruption, confronting and killing him.

The Horde army advanced through the Eastern Kingdoms, leaving nothing but devastated countryside in its wake. Soon it marched on Stormwind itself, where Garona Halforcen assassinated King Llane Wrynn, and the kingdom was crushed. Within the Horde, Durotan, leader of the Frostwolf Clan, discovered Gul'dan's treacherous scheming. He informed Blackhand's lieutenant, Orgrim Doomhammer, but shortly afterwards was killed by Gul'dan's assassins. Orgrim, convinced by Durotan's warning, turned on Blackhand, killing him and claiming the role of warchief. But Orgrim was intent on rooting out Gul'dan's treachery. His spies caught and tortured one of Gul'dan's agents, the half-orc assassin, Garona Halforcen. Garona revealed the existence and location of the Shadow Council. Orgrim turned the forces of the Horde on both Shadow Council and Gul'dan, slaughtering the remaining members, but granting Gul'dan mercy.

The survivors of Stormwind, including King Llane's son, Prince Varian, fled. Under the leadership of Anduin Lothar, they crossed the Great Sea to the kingdom of Lordaeron. There, King Terenas Menethil II heeded Lothar's tales of the orcish threat. He united the seven human kingdoms and, with other allies, formed the Alliance of Lordaeron to stand against the coming Horde invasion. For it could only be a matter of time before the Horde rose again.

The fearsome appearance of the orcish Horde was matched by its brutality in battle.

The orcs arrived on Azeroth by traveling through the Dark Portal, a powerful gateway between worlds created by the human sorcerer and Guardian Medivh at the behest of Sargeras, leader of the Burning Legion.

THE SECOND WAR

Orgrim's Horde forces swelled with new reinforcements, including orc recruits from the Dark Portal, members of the enslaved red dragonflight, trolls from the Amani empire, and goblins. Gul'dan swore loyalty to Orgrim, and offered to create new undead warriors, named death knights, to serve the Horde.

Orgrim led two major assaults against the Alliance. The southern offensive in the dwarven lands of Khaz Modan was initially successful, moving deep into dwarven territory. But after a series of savage battles, Alliance forces pushed the Horde back to the bridges of the Thandol Span. From there, the Alliance armies advanced south, forcing the Horde to retreat from Khaz Modan. The Horde kept one foothold, the cursed fortress of Grim Batol, where the red dragonflight had been forced into servitude.

The northern offensive consisted of a naval assault across the Great Sea. Taking advantage of treachery by the human kingdom of Alterac, the Horde besieged Lordaeron. During the siege Gul'dan made his move, withdrawing his followers and leaving to seek the Tomb of Sargeras in order to claim its power. Orgrim and his forces were left to face the Alliance alone. The Alliance pursued the Horde armies south and trapped them at the fortress of Blackrock Spire. Orgrim launched a desperate attack, confronting Lord Anduin Lothar. Lothar and Orgrim fought in an epic battle, and Orgrim slew Lothar. However, Lothar's second-in-command, Turalyon, rallied the Alliance forces and took Orgrim prisoner. The remaining Horde forces made a final stand at the Dark Portal, fighting the bloodiest battle of the war. The Alliance defeated the last of the Horde on Azeroth, and the archmage Khadgar destroyed the Dark Portal, bringing the Second War to an end.

Lord Anduin Lothar led the armies of the Alliance during the Second War.

High General Turalyon was second-in-command to Lord Anduin Lothar. Upon Lothar's death during the assault on Blackrock Spire, Turalyon assumed command of the Alliance forces and defeated the old Horde.

THE THIRD WAR

The Third War marked the Burning Legion's return to Azeroth. With a mighty new tool in the form of the Lich King, commander of the undead Scourge, the Legion sought the powerful waters of the second Well of Eternity in order to destroy Azeroth once and for all.

Thousands of years after the War of the Ancients, the demons of the Burning Legion returned to Azeroth. To survive, the mortal races would have to unite against their common foe.

THE RISE OF THE SCOURGE

Incensed at the refusal by the orc shaman Ner'zhul to deliver the Horde to the Burning Legion, the demon lord Kil'jaeden caught him as he tried to escape Draenor through a portal. Kil'jaeden destroyed Ner'zhul's body and bonded his spirit within a suit of armor, transforming him into the Lich King. Kil'jaeden then encased the Lich King within a block of ice and sent it to Azeroth. On Azeroth, the Lich King used his powers to communicate with the human archmage Kel'Thuzad, ordering Kel'Thuzad to transport grain shipments infected with the plague of undeath to Lordaeron, to raise a monstrous army of undead, called the Scourge. Rumors of the Plague reached the Prince of Lordaeron, Arthas Menethil. Together with the sorceress Lady Jaina Proudmoore, and the paladin Uther the Lightbringer, leader of the Knights of the Silver Hand, Arthas investigated the plague and uncovered Kel'Thuzad's plot. Arthas slew Kel'Thuzad and swore to put an end to his master, the dreadlord Mal'Ganis.

Tracking Mal'Ganis to the city of Stratholme, Arthas discovered that the poisoned grain had already been distributed among its residents. Arthas ordered the city purged: its citizens murdered before the plague could fully take effect. Uther protested this decision, unwilling to slaughter innocent people. Arthas, frustrated with Uther's questioning, disbanded the Knights of the Silver Hand and sent Uther away. Jaina, unable to watch Arthas carry out this horrific deed, left Arthas to carry out his dark task. Butchering his way through the town, Arthas confronted Mal'Ganis, but was unable to slay the dreadlord. Mal'Ganis merely taunted Arthas, and beckoned the prince to follow him to Northrend.

Once a paladin of the Light, Arthas' quest for revenge led him into darkness. Armed with his holy warhammer, Light's Vengeance, he slaughtered the people of Stratholme.

Meanwhile, Jaina was approached by a mysterious prophet, who told her to gather her people and flee to Kalimdor. She agreed, sensing wisdom in the prophet's warning. Arthas traveled to Northrend to find Mal'Ganis, obsessed with putting an end to the dreadlord. Yet instead of Mal'Ganis, Arthas discovered his old mentor, Muradin Bronzebeard, searching for a powerful runeblade called Frostmourne. Muradin spoke of the power of the blade, and Arthas decided to claim it as his own, intent on using Frostmourne to slay Mal'Ganis and fulfill his thirst for vengeance. When the two found Frostmourne, Muradin realized the blade was cursed—yet Arthas, in his single-minded thirst for vengeance, still sought to claim the blade for his own. The ice surrounding Frostmourne shattered, gravely wounding Muradin. Arthas claimed Frostmourne and slew Mal'Ganis, but the blade claimed his soul, forever binding him to the service of the Lich King and the Scourge.

Prince Arthas returned to Lordaeron and murdered his father, King Terenas Menethil II. His next task was to resurrect Kel'Thuzad by using the Sunwell, a fount of unimaginable arcane power used by the high elves. Leading his Scourge army across the kingdom, he razed the forests of Quel'Thalas, defeating the high elf ranger-general Sylvanas Windrunner and raising her soul as a banshee. Once Arthas reached the Sunwell, he used its powers to resurrect Kel'Thuzad as a monstrous lich. With Kel'Thuzad resurrected, Arthas then stole the Book of Medivh, a powerful artifact, from the mage capital of Dalaran. Kel'Thuzad used the book to summon the demon lord Archimonde, loyal and powerful servant of Sargeras, who immediately crushed Dalaran. The combined forces of the Burning Legion and Lich King seemed unstoppable.

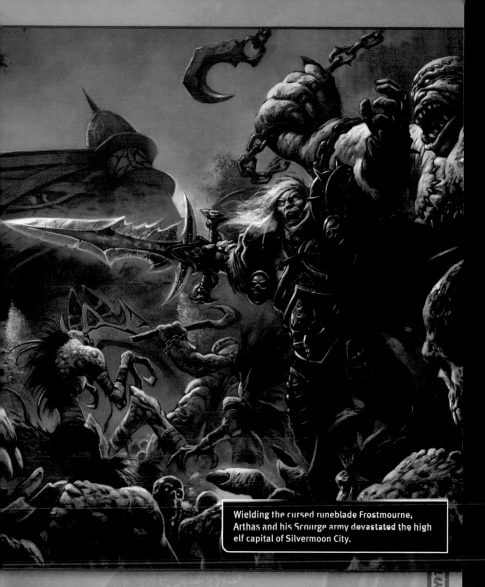

Wielding the cursed runeblade Frostmourne, Arthas and his Scourge army devastated the high elf capital of Silvermoon City.

HOPE IN KALIMDOR

The orc Warchief Thrall was the son of Durotan, slain chieftain of the Frostwolf clan. Found as an infant by the human Aedelas Blackmoore, and raised as a gladiator, Thrall had subsequently escaped, liberating the rest of the orcs from human internment camps, where they had been held after the Second War. Before Lordaeron's fall, the mysterious prophet visited Thrall in a dream, instructing him to lead the Horde across the sea to Kalimdor, where they would find their destiny. Warchief Thrall chose to heed the prophet's warning, traveling to Kalimdor and recruiting more races to the Horde, including the Darkspear trolls and the tauren. Naming the land they arrived on Durotar, after Thrall's father, the orcs began to settle into their harsh desert surroundings. Yet Thrall's closest friend, Grom Hellscream, encountered night elves in the forests of Ashenvale to the north while building a new settlement. He was tricked into once more drinking the blood of the pit lord, Mannoroth, and in his bloodlust, slew the demigod, Cenarius, who was sacred to the native night elves.

Meanwhile, Thrall traveled to Stonetalon Peak, encountering the human forces of Jaina Proudmoore on the way. As the two prepared for combat, the mysterious prophet appeared, warning the two leaders of the Burning Legion's approaching invasion. Thrall and Jaina were told they needed to work together, as the Legion was already making its influence known. When Thrall returned to the orcs, he discovered Grom's corrupted state and the truth behind the prophet's words. Together, Thrall and Grom sought to slay Mannoroth and cleanse Grom, and the orcish race, of the blood-curse once and for all. Grom managed to strike a killing blow, but sacrificed his life in the process. In his final moments, the blood haze lifted from Grom's eyes, and the orcish race was freed.

ETERNITY'S END

Faced with the overwhelming might of the Burning Legion, the night elf leader Tyrande Whisperwind woke her beloved, Archdruid Malfurion Stormrage, from his slumber within the Emerald Dream. Together, they worked to awaken his legion of sleeping druids. Yet Tyrande, after locating a long-forgotten prison, also sought to release Malfurion's twin brother Illidan from imprisonment. Malfurion protested, certain his brother could not be trusted, but Illidan sought to prove himself to Tyrande by fighting the Scourge corruption in Felwood. There, he encountered and fought Arthas. While neither won the battle, Arthas, impressed with Illidan's power and sensing an opportunity, told the night elf of the immense power of the Skull of Gul'dan. Illidan consumed the skull and transformed into a demon, quickly defeating the dreadlord Tichondrius. Yet Malfurion was appalled at his brother's reckless obsession with power and his monstrous transformation. Malfurion banished Illidan from the forests of Kalimdor, and Illidan departed.

The mysterious prophet appeared to Malfurion in a dream, summoning the druid and his beloved to a meeting with Thrall and Jaina. With the assorted leaders of the races gathered, the prophet revealed his identity—the Guardian Medivh, seeking redemption for the acts committed while he was under Sargeras' influence in the First War. He bade the leaders to work together and combat Archimonde at the peaks of Hyjal, hoping to save Azeroth from certain destruction. At the behest of the Prophet Medivh, night elf, human, and Horde forces agreed to join together to fight back against the Burning Legion.

As the unlikely alliance of races worked together, Archimonde reached the World Tree Nordrassil at the peaks of Hyjal, intent on claiming the immense powers of the second Well of Eternity, hidden beneath the roots of the tree, for the Burning Legion. Yet just as it seemed the Legion would be victorious, Malfurion blew the Horn of Cenarius, calling the spirits of nature to gather around Nordrassil, and causing the tree to explode. The force of the blast obliterated Archimonde and badly damaged the World Tree, ending the night elves' immortality. Yet the Third War concluded on a victorious note: the mortal races of Azeroth had once more banded together and defeated the Burning Legion's attempts to wreak havoc on the world. The Prophet Medivh, having redeemed himself for his grievous acts while under the influence of Sargeras, vanished.

The Battle of Mount Hyjal was the final bloody conflict of the Third War. Archimonde the Defiler was destroyed, and the Burning Legion defeated, but at a terrible price.

ASCENSION OF THE LICH KING

The Third War was over, but the Lich King's growing power had not gone unnoticed by his creator, Kil'jaeden. Fearing he would soon be too powerful to control, Kil'jaeden sought out Illidan Stormrage and promised the demonic former night elf untold power if he would destroy the Lich King. Illidan agreed.

LEGACY OF THE DAMNED

Allied with naga leader Lady Vashj and her serpentine followers, Illidan sought out the Tomb of Sargeras on the Broken Isles. Within the Tomb lay an immeasurably powerful artifact, the Eye of Sargeras. With the Eye, Illidan hoped to destroy the Lich King and claim his reward. However, Illidan was pursued by his former jailor, the night elf Warden Maiev Shadowsong. Although she was unable to stop Illidan from obtaining the Eye of Sargeras, she relentlessly followed the Betrayer to the Eastern Kingdoms, accompanied by Illidan's brother Malfurion and night elf High Priestess Tyrande. There, she encountered Prince Kael'thas Sunstrider, leader of the blood elves—the high elf survivors of the Scourge attacks and the Sunwell's destruction. Kael'thas was trying to protect his remaining people from the Scourge, but agreed to assist Maiev and Tyrande in their efforts to capture Illidan. Together, they tracked Illidan down to the ruins of Dalaran, where he sought to use the Eye and destroy the Lich King. His efforts were thwarted, and Illidan fled to Outland, hoping to escape Kil'jaeden's wrath.

Maiev followed Illidan to Outland, and soon captured her quarry. However, Illidan was later rescued by Lady Vashj and another—Prince Kael'thas Sunstrider. Although his forces had sought to help the Alliance, they had been treated harshly by the xenophobic human Lord Garithos and given humiliating and seemingly impossible tasks. Lady Vashj had appeared and offered her assistance to Kael'thas. Kael'thas agreed, but his actions were seen as treason by Garithos, who imprisoned Kael'thas and his people in Dalaran. Freed by Lady Vashj, Kael'thas was told that Illidan could help the blood elves with the addiction to magic that had plagued them since the Sunwell's destruction. Together, Illidan, Lady Vashj, and Kael'thas conquered Outland.

Arthas returned to Northrend to defend the Lich King, battling the forces of Illidan, the blood elves under Prince Kael'thas, and the naga of Lady Vashj.

> "THE FROZEN THRONE IS MINE, DEMON. STEP ASIDE..."
>
> ARTHAS MENETHIL

WAR IN NORTHREND

Illidan's triumph was marred by the reappearance of Kil'jaeden. Angered at his failure, Kil'jaeden ordered Illidan to return to Azeroth and kill the Lich King, or face the eternal wrath of the Burning Legion. Arthas, meanwhile, had returned to Lordaeron after Archimonde's fall. Although Illidan's attempt to destroy the Lich King with the Eye of Sargeras had failed, it had an unintended side effect—it had weakened the Lich King's hold over the Scourge. Because of this, the banshee Sylvanas Windrunner had regained her free will, reclaimed her body, and sought to destroy Arthas. She gathered other free-willed Scourge to her side, calling them "Forsaken." She was nearly successful in killing Arthas, but he managed to escape with the help of the lich Kel'Thuzad, and made his way to Northrend. Left to her own devices, Sylvanas took over Lordaeron. She destroyed the dreadlords that watched over the city for the Burning Legion, leaving only one, Varimathras, to serve her. Together Sylvanas and her army of Forsaken quickly claimed the former capital city as their own.

Having escaped the wrath of Sylvanas, Arthas traveled to Northrend, beckoned by the Lich King. Yet the armies of Prince Kael'thas awaited him, seeking revenge for the destruction of the Sunwell. Arthas escaped with the help of the undead spider-like nerubians and their leader, Anub'arak, eventually reaching the foot of Icecrown Glacier. There, he was met by Illidan Stormrage. The two engaged in a vicious battle, but Arthas proved victorious, leaving a gravely-injured Illidan behind as he began his ascent up the icy peaks. Illidan was found and taken back to Outland by Lady Vashj and Prince Kael'thas to recover.

As Arthas began his ascent, the voices of those he had slain or betrayed whispered in his ears. At the peak stood the Frozen Throne, prison to his dark master. With one swing of Frostmourne, Arthas shattered the throne and set free the armor of the Lich King. He took the helm and placed it upon his head, merging his consciousness with that of Ner'zhul. Arthas Menethil had become one with the Lich King, and took his seat upon the Frozen Throne. There, he waited, biding his time and building his forces until the moment came to strike Azeroth anew.

Illidan Stormrage met Arthas Menethil in single combat at the foot of Icecrown Glacier. Their clash was an epic struggle. Finally, Arthas sliced open Illidan's chest with Frostmourne. Leaving Illidan for dead, Arthas took the Frozen Throne as his.

Few have fallen into darkness as completely as the former Prince of Lordaeron, Arthas Menethil. From noble beginnings, Arthas' calculated decisions led him to corruption and despair. He slaughtered those he loved, and many curse his name to this day. As the Lich King, he ruled over a land as bleak as his heart, and his story is a warning to those seeking revenge at any cost.

ARTHAS MENETHIL (THE LICH KING)

"I've damned everyone and everything I've ever loved in his name, and I still feel no remorse. No shame. No pity."

LICH KING OF THE SCOURGE

The horrors of fighting against the undead started Arthas' journey into darkness. His friends were powerless to prevent his corruption.

Arthas Menethil was the Prince of Lordaeron and a paladin of the Silver Hand. When his people were struck down by a plague that turned them into undead Scourge, Arthas discovered its source: tainted grain developed by the Lich King himself. In an attempt to stop the plague from spreading, Arthas burned the city of Stratholme and killed its residents, an act that revealed Arthas' true nature. Arthas then sought to kill the dreadlord Mal'Ganis, who commanded the Scourge forces in Lordaeron. Pursuing Mal'Ganis to Northrend, Arthas found a weapon that could slay him, the cursed runeblade Frostmourne. However, the moment Arthas' fingers touched Frostmourne, the sword claimed his soul. Although he vanquished Mal'Ganis, Arthas was now bound to serve the Lich King. Commanding an undead army, Arthas returned to his homeland, crushing the kingdoms of Lordaeron and Quel'Thalas.

Following the Third War, the Lich King called Arthas back to Northrend; the demon hunter Illidan Stormrage was closing in, intent on destroying Arthas' master. Before Illidan could strike at the Lich King, Arthas defeated him. Arthas then ascended the Frozen Throne and placed the helm of the Lich King upon his own head, their two entities becoming one. In the ensuing years, Arthas, now completely the Lich King, gathered a new army of Scourge and servants. It took the combined forces of the Alliance, Horde, and Ashen Verdict under Tirion Fordring to finally put an end to Arthas. His death ended years of torment.

BROUGHT INTO DARKNESS
As a death knight, Arthas wielded necromantic powers. Cruelly, he often raised former enemies to serve him in death. Kel'Thuzad, leader of the Cult of the Damned under Mal'Ganis, was raised as a lich. Sylvanas Windrunner was turned into a banshee. Even the corpses of dragons were raised as mighty frost wyrms, including Sindragosa, formerly the prime consort of the Aspect of the blue dragonflight, Malygos.

THE DEATH OF A KING
When Arthas returned to Lordaeron wielding the runeblade Frostmourne, he returned a hero. Bells caroled his arrival to the throne room, and his father, Terenas Menethil II, joyfully greeted him. But Terenas' joy soon turned to horror when his beloved son raised Frostmourne and murdered him, taking the crown as his own. The Scourge claimed Lordaeron, and the country was plunged into chaos.

BETRAYER OF TRUST
Those closest to Arthas witnessed the young prince's descent into darkness first-hand. He killed Uther Lightbringer, his mentor in the Order of the Silver Hand, when the paladin tried to put an end to Arthas' madness. His friend Muradin Bronzebeard was badly injured as he watched Arthas claim the runeblade Frostmourne as his own. And Jaina Proudmoore, once courted by Arthas, could only watch in horror as the last vestiges of his humanity slipped away.

The helm of the Lich King is a potent artifact. It forces the undead Scourge to obey the wearer's will.

KEY DATA

NAME Arthas Menethil

GENDER AND RACE Male human (undead)

AFFILIATION Scourge

STATUS Deceased

TITLES The Lich King, Prince of Lordaeron, Paladin of the Silver Hand

RELATIVES Terenas Menethil II (father, deceased); Lianne Menethil (mother, deceased); Calia Menethil (sister)

Located in the heights of Icecrown, the Frozen Throne is the seat of the Lich King, also serving as his prison.

When Arthas found the runeblade Frostmourne, this was carved upon its dais: *"Whosoever takes up this blade shall wield power eternal. Just as the blade rends flesh, so must power scar the spirit."*

Infamous in night elf history, Illidan Stormrage showed an early obsession and unerring skill with magic that would ultimately shape his destiny. Throughout his life, he fought both for and against his own people, as well as the Burning Legion and many others, eventually gaining notoriety as "the Betrayer." The relentless pursuit of power drove Illidan to seeming madness, his body twisted into demonic form.

ILLIDAN STORMRAGE

"My blind eyes can see what others cannot— that sometimes the hand of fate must be forced."

FRIEND AND FOE

Illidan sought power to win Tyrande's love, but power couldn't save him from those he betrayed.

Illidan Stormrage grew up with his twin brother Malfurion. Seeking the attentions of their friend, the young priestess Tyrande Whisperwind, and lacking his brother's druidic skill, Illidan pursued arcane power. In a fit of jealousy, Illidan supported Queen Azshara and the Burning Legion during the War of the Ancients. The destruction of the Well of Eternity, a fount of magical energy, ended the War, but Illidan stole some of its water. Despite the havoc the Well had brought to the night elves, Illidan created a new Well. This act, and his obsession with forbidden magic, led to his imprisonment by Malfurion. Illidan was watched over for millennia by his jailor Maiev Shadowsong. When the Burning Legion returned to Azeroth in the Third War, High Priestess Tyrande Whisperwind freed Illidan, hoping for his help. Still infatuated with Tyrande, Illidan agreed. Yet Illidan's power lust continued. He consumed the Skull of Gul'dan, transforming himself into a demon. After the Legion's defeat, Illidan fled to the shattered world of Draenor, now called Outland. He and his allies—the naga Lady Vashj, the blood elf Prince Kael'thas Sunstrider, and the Broken Akama—overthrew Outland's demonic leader, Magtheridon, but Illidan's trials continued. The demon lord Kil'jaeden, servant of the Burning Legion, told him to destroy the Lich King, rebellious ruler of the Scourge, or face eternal torment. Illidan confronted the Lich King's champion, Arthas Menethil, on the frozen peaks of Icecrown. Defeated and left for dead, Illidan was rescued by his allies. Ruling Outland from his stronghold, the Black Temple, Illidan was eventually slain by Maiev Shadowsong, with help from a group of heroes.

IMPRISONMENT

When Illidan created a second Well of Eternity using water from the original, Malfurion and Tyrande were horrified; its magic could only be a source of destruction. Illidan was unrepentant and the night elf commander, Jarod Shadowsong, ordered Illidan's death. At Malfurion's request, Illidan was imprisoned instead; his jailer was Jarod's sister Maiev Shadowsong (pictured left) who hated Illidan for having injured Jarod.

FURTHER SACRIFICES

Much to Maiev's displeasure, night elf priestess Tyrande Whisperwind freed Illidan to fight the Burning Legion. Scourge champion Arthas Menethil confided that Illidan could gain great power through the Skull of Gul'dan. (Illidan little knew that the Scourge were using him as a pawn against the Burning Legion.) With this newfound power, he was successful against the Legion… but not so lucky when it came to at last confronting the Scourge.

LORD OF OUTLAND

The vengeful Maiev Shadowsong pursued Illidan to Outland, but the blood elf Prince Kael'thas Sunstrider and the naga Lady Vashj (pictured left) came to his aid, capturing Maiev. Illidan established his empire in Outland. Akama, a sage of the Broken and Illidan's former ally, helped Maiev escape and continue her hunt.

KEY DATA

NAME Illidan Stormrage

GENDER AND RACE
Male demon (former night elf)

AFFILIATION Adversarial

STATUS Deceased

TITLES The Betrayer, Lord of Outland

RELATIVES Malfurion Stormrage (brother);
Tyrande Whisperwind (sister-in-law);
Shandris Feathermoon (adopted niece)

As a "reward" for his loyalty, Sargeras burnt out Illidan's amber eyes, allowing him to see all forms of magic.

Along with his new sight, Sargeras gifted Illidan with arcane tattoos that enshrouded both of his shoulders, permeating the night elf with Sargeras' dark magic.

Illidan wielded the Twin Blades of Azzinoth, which he took from a powerful doomguard of the Burning Legion that he slew over 10,000 years ago. They could be combined to form a single devastating weapon, or divided and brandished as a pair. Illidan mastered them and defeated such monstrosities as Magtheridon, the former Lord of Outland.

DEATH OF THE BETRAYER

After being freed by Akama, Maiev rushed to find Illidan. She came upon him at the top of the Black Temple, where he was engaging a band of adventurers. Maiev entered the fray, and following a violent struggle, Illidan lay dying. But with his final words he tainted Maiev's victory: "the huntress is nothing without the hunt."

WRATH OF THE LICH KING

Tirion Fordring of the Argent Crusade wields Ashbringer.

After years of silence, the Lich King made his first move from the icy peaks of Northrend, launching full-scale attacks on both Stormwind City and Orgrimmar. Faced with a new threat, both Alliance and Horde sent forces to Northrend.

The armies of the Alliance and Horde besieged Angrathar the Wrathgate, the southern entrance to the Lich King's fortress of Icecrown Citadel.

BATTLE OF THE WRATHGATE

The Alliance Vanguard was led by Highlord Bolvar Fordragon, and the Horde Warsong Offensive led by Overlord Garrosh Hellscream. They were not alone in their retaliation—the Argent Dawn merged with the Knights of the Silver Hand to form the Argent Crusade, spearheaded by Highlord Tirion Fordring, and they were joined by Highlord Darion Mograine and the Knights of the Ebon Blade, a group of rebellious death knights that had turned on the Lich King.

It seemed that the Alliance and Horde were united against the Lich King, but the relative peace between the two factions would not last. When the armies converged at Angrathar the Wrathgate, Highlord Bolvar Fordragon and the orc Warlord Saurfang the Younger battled the Scourge together. Yet the Lich King proved too powerful a foe. He struck down Saurfang, and chaos erupted as the Forsaken Grand Apothecary Putress treacherously unleashed a terrible plague on all—Scourge, Alliance, and Horde. As the Lich King retreated, the Dragonqueen Alexstrasza and her red dragonflight intervened, using their flames to keep the plague from spreading.

After the Third War, the Lich King spent years assembling a new army of undead Scourge and recruiting new allies. The vrykul, Val'kyr, and even the trolls of Zul'Drak were forced to serve in the terrifying new onslaught.

BATTLE FOR THE UNDERCITY

Putress and the dreadlord Varimathras traveled back to the Undercity, took over the Forsaken capital, and ousted the Forsaken leader Sylvanas Windrunner. Warchief Thrall led the Horde attack to put an end to Varimathras and take back the city, but the human King Varian Wrynn was incensed at Bolvar's loss, and staged an attack of his own. Putress and Varimathras were defeated, but Horde and Alliance forces then clashed. Needless bloodshed was avoided by the intervention of Lady Jaina Proudmoore, who teleported the Alliance troops back to Stormwind. However, the Battle for the Undercity cast a pall over the war against the Lich King; Alliance and Horde now fought each other as viciously as they attacked the Scourge.

Sylvanas Windrunner longed for the opportunity to finally have her vengeance against the Lich King.

A NEW LICH KING

It was the efforts of the Argent Crusade and the Knights of the Ebon Blade that finally brought champions of both Alliance and Horde to Icecrown Citadel, where the Lich King was ultimately slain. Yet the spirit of Arthas' father, King Terenas, revealed the terrible truth: there must always be a Lich King. Tirion Fordring reluctantly claimed the Lich King's helm, but before he could place it on his head he was stopped by Highlord Bolvar Fordragon. The flames of the red dragonflight had reanimated Bolvar after Angrathar, though he was horrifically charred beyond recognition. He had been captured and tortured by the Lich King, yet refused to yield. Bolvar now volunteered to take the helm of the Lich King and his seat upon the Frozen Throne, acting as jailor of the damned for eternity. With this last sacrifice, the war ended, but the tensions between the Alliance and Horde remained.

Highlord Bolvar Fordragon became the next Lich King. His unflinching will keeps the Scourge in check... for now.

Neltharion, Aspect of the black dragonflight was once known as the Earth-Warder. Driven mad by the Old Gods, he took the name Deathwing. Failing in his goal to enslave the other dragonflights, he aimed to bring about the Hour of Twilight, unmaking all creation. Though he possessed the power to shatter the world, in the end he fought alone, facing his fellow Aspects and their allies. He fell from the skies into the Maelstrom, utterly destroyed by the Dragon Soul, never to rise again.

DEATHWING (NELTHARION)

"My hatred burns through the cavernous deeps. The world heaves with my torment… But at last… all will burn beneath the shadow of my wings."

THE DESTROYER

Neltharion created the Dragon Soul under the Old Gods' guidance during the War of the Ancients. The object's power tore him apart, turning him into the evil creature known as Deathwing.

MORTAL FORM
During the Second War, Deathwing used the form of Lord Daval Prestor, hoping to bring down the Alliance of Lordaeron from within—he nearly became king of the human nation of Alterac. Following in their sire's footsteps, Deathwing's children would later assume the forms of Lady Katrana Prestor (Onyxia), who worked to manipulate King Varian Wrynn, and Lord Victor Nefarius (Nefarian).

The titans gave Neltharion, Aspect of the black dragonflight, custody of the earth and land, but he fell victim to the corrupting whispers of the Old Gods. Lost in paranoia and rage, he became known to the mortal races as Deathwing. He forged the Dragon Soul artifact, retained sole mastery of it, and tricked the other Aspects into adding their power to it. He then betrayed his brethren, attacking and forcing them into hiding. Eventually, the Dragon Soul found its way to the orc warlock Nekros Skullcrusher, who used it to enslave Alexstrasza and the red dragonflight. Attempting to solidify his dominion, Deathwing manipulated the human mage Rhonin to arrive at Nekros' fortress of Grim Batol with the hope of seizing Alexstrasza's eggs, but the end result was Deathwing's defeat. Rhonin destroyed the Dragon Soul, Alexstrasza was freed, and the Aspects united to drive off Deathwing. For decades Deathwing recovered in the realm of Deepholm, but he finally reemerged, bringing about the Cataclysm, which ripped the lands of Azeroth apart. Yet Deathwing's might was not absolute, and the Aspects again joined to defeat him. The Dragon Soul was retrieved through time and, powered by the other Aspects and the orc shaman Thrall, obliterated Deathwing.

HOUR OF TWILIGHT
Deathwing's suicidal plan was to bring about the Hour of Twilight, the moment when the Old Gods are freed from their imprisoned slumber and end all life on Azeroth. The Aspects, imbuing the Dragon Soul with their power, stopped him. Standing in Neltharion's place as Aspect of Earth, Thrall cast the final blow against Deathwing.

FATE OF THE BLACK DRAGONFLIGHT
The black dragonflight has long been the enemy of the other flights, who killed any they happened to find. Deathwing hid many of his eggs in Draenor, but when the planet broke apart, nether energies released from the destruction twisted and warped the eggs into nether drakes. When Deathwing launched his last attack on Azeroth, the black dragons followed their leader. Deathwing's son Wrathion (right) appears to be the only black dragon left alive on Azeroth.

Deathwing's corruption and the Dragon Soul's power nearly tore his body apart.

During the Cataclysm, one of Deathwing's first acts was to nearly destroy the city of Stormwind. His path of devastation would forever change the face of Azeroth.

To keep the Dragon Soul's immense power from destroying him, Deathwing had goblin smiths forge adamantium plates for his body, seen most prominently on his lower jaw.

KEY DATA

NAME Neltharion (Deathwing)

GENDER AND RACE
Male black dragon

STATUS Deceased

AFFILIATION Adversarial

TITLES The Destroyer, Aspect of death, The Worldbreaker, Aspect of the black dragonflight, Earth-Warder (former)

RELATIVES Sintharia (consort, deceased); Nefarian (son, deceased); Onyxia (daughter, deceased); Sabellian (son); Wrathion (son)

LIFE AND DEATH

As the guardian of Life, Alexstrasza was Deathwing's mortal enemy. He sought for countless years to enslave her, and Alexstrasza fought him tirelessly. Their struggle decided the course of existence: an end in cascading flame or a new beginning for Azeroth.

THE CATACLYSM

After his defeat at Grim Batol, the black dragon Deathwing hid within Deepholm, the earthen region of the Elemental Plane. The Twilight's Hammer cult, a group loyal to the Old Gods and intent on bringing Armageddon to the world, forged new plates to hold his torn body together. Once recovered, Deathwing burst forth from the Maelstrom. The seas rose, tidal waves struck, and the very land itself buckled and broke with the force of his emergence.

Deathwing's reemergence caused massive destruction throughout Azeroth. Earthquakes tore open the ground, volcanoes spewed ash and lava, and gigantic tidal waves devastated large areas.

RESISTANCE DIVIDED

Meanwhile, the Alliance and Horde had to deal with the devastation caused by Deathwing's appearance. Warchief Thrall stepped down to concentrate his efforts on the elemental unrest as a shaman, appointing Garrosh Hellscream in his stead as Warchief of the Horde. Hellscream immediately sought to claim land and resources for the Horde, clashing with the Alliance every step of the way. The two factions fought relentlessly even as both sides worked to defeat Deathwing's minions. Ragnaros the Firelord, Al'Akir the Windlord, Cho'gall, leader of the Twilight's Hammer cult, the black dragons Nefarian, Onyxia, Sinestra—all fell under the might of the mortal heroes.

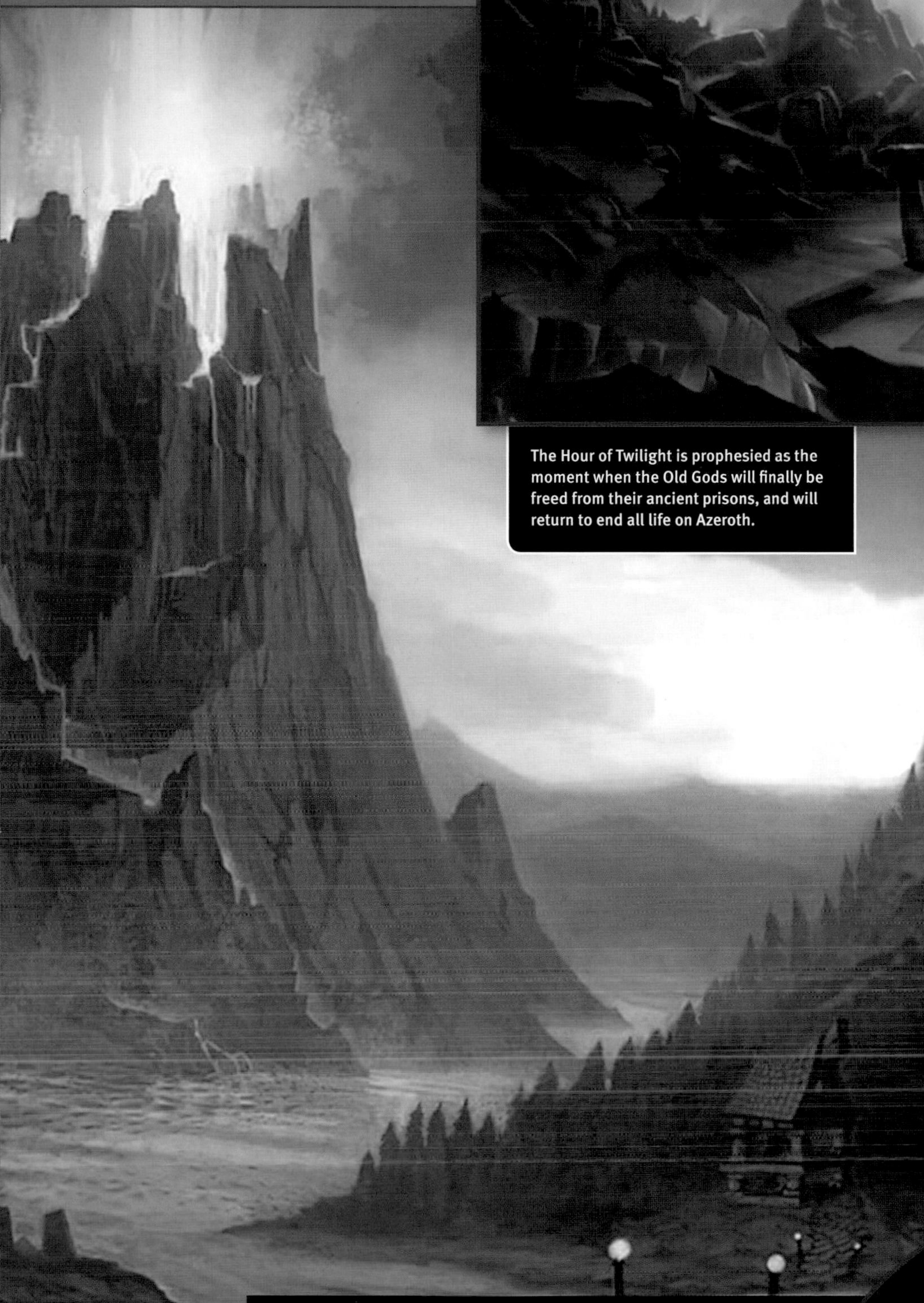

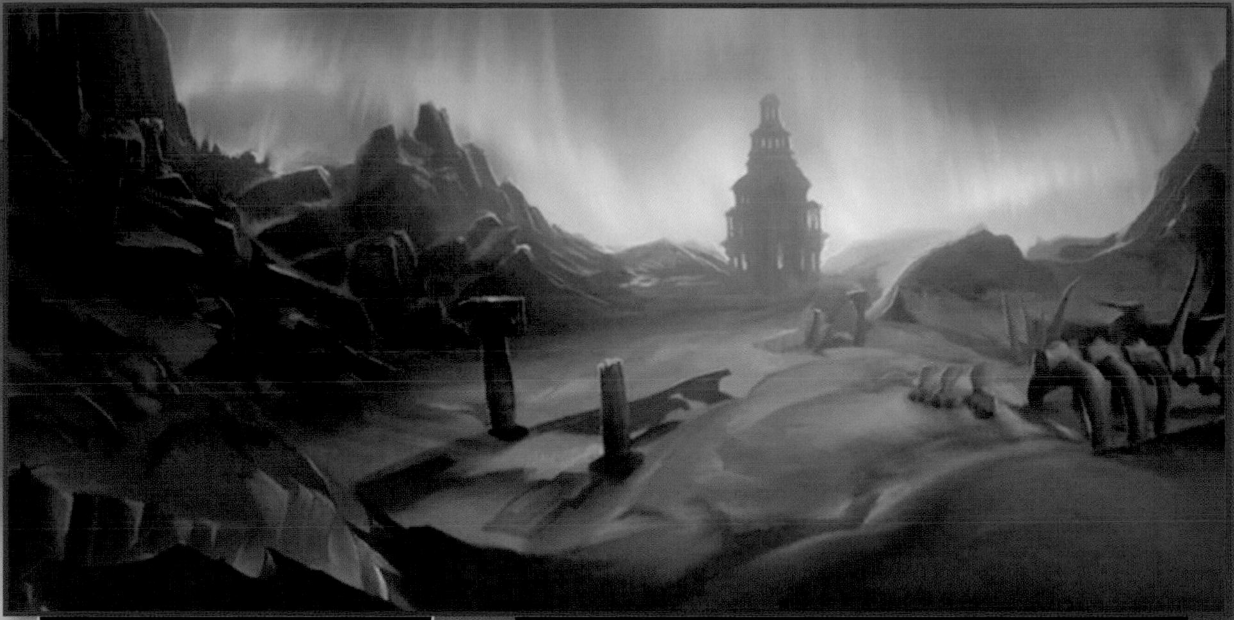

The Hour of Twilight is prophesied as the moment when the Old Gods will finally be freed from their ancient prisons, and will return to end all life on Azeroth.

DEATHWING'S BANE

Yet it soon became clear that Deathwing was too powerful for any single entity to stop, and that he would shortly bring about the prophesied Hour of Twilight: All life would be obliterated, and the Old Gods would reign supreme. To prevent this, a group of champions was sent back in time by Nozdormu, the Aspect of the Bronze Dragonflight. They retrieved the legendary Dragon Soul artifact from the time of the War of the Ancients, to use as a weapon against Deathwing. The Aspects then merged their powers within the artifact, with the orc shaman Thrall temporarily taking Deathwing's place as representative of the element of Earth and wielding the Dragon Soul with mortal hands.

DEATH OF THE DESTROYER

Through the combined powers of all four Dragon Aspects, the actions of Thrall, and the defenders of Azeroth, Deathwing was finally slain over the raging waters of the Maelstrom. But the attack drained the last powers of the Aspects, turning them mortal. By halting the Hour of Twilight and defeating Deathwing, the Aspects had fulfilled their ancient purpose. The Age of Mortals had begun—it was now the charge of Azeroth's mortal races to safeguard their world themselves.

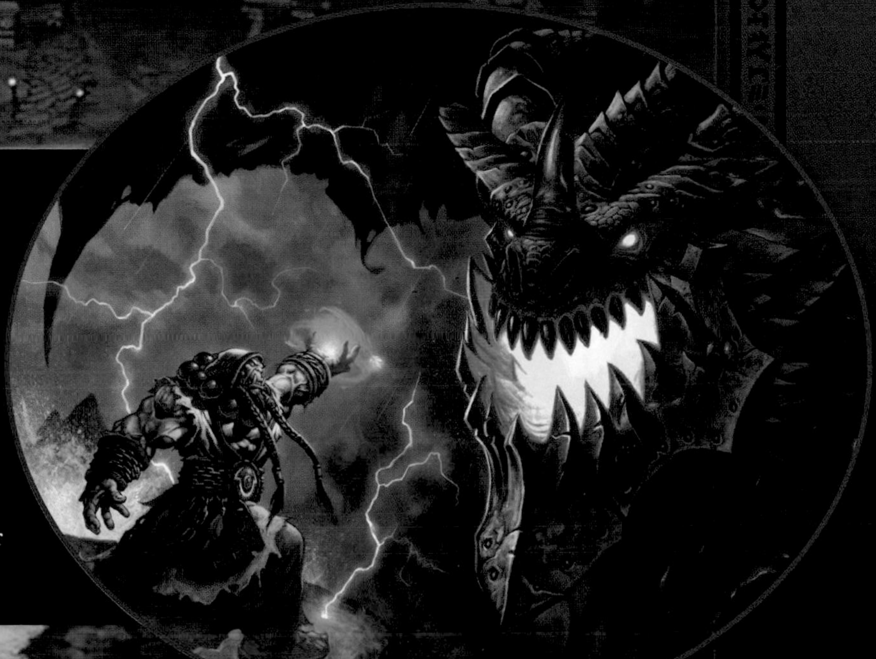

INVASION OF PANDARIA

Following the Cataclysm, tensions between the Alliance and Horde finally erupted into all-out war between the two factions. Yet the bloodthirsty military tactics of Warchief Garrosh Hellscream were overshadowed by the discovery of a beautiful land, once thought merely a legend: Pandaria.

THE FALL OF THERAMORE

After Deathwing's defeat, the Horde, led by Warchief Hellscream, began a new military campaign to wipe out the Alliance and claim the continent of Kalimdor for their own. Hellscream sought to begin his campaign of conquest and bloodshed by destroying the port town of Theramore, led by Lady Jaina Proudmoore. Theramore was vaporized by a powerful mana bomb, and the leader of the Kirin Tor, Rhonin, sacrificed his life to save Jaina. She then took his place, leading the Kirin Tor and the city of Dalaran, and eventually throwing the support of the once-neutral city-state behind the Alliance.

The port town of Theramore was obliterated by the Horde. The once-proud city now lies in ruins, devastated by a powerful mana bomb.

In the wake of Deathwing's defeat, the Horde continued its campaign of brutal conquest, escalating the war with the Alliance.

DISCOVERY OF PANDARIA

Open warfare raged between the two factions. As Alliance and Horde clashed on the open sea, they discovered the lost continent of Pandaria, home of the reclusive pandaren race. Both Alliance and Horde forces immediately began to fight over the land and the right to claim it, with disastrous results. The insidious sha, beings that fed and grew stronger on negative emotion, burst forth all across the continent, causing a chain reaction of attacks that nearly devastated the pandaren race. The insectoid mantid swarmed over the great Serpent's Spine wall, driven by the sha of Fear. Worst of all, the Mogu—ancient creatures who once enslaved the pandaren race thousands of years ago, began a new uprising with the assistance of their ancient allies, the Zandalar tribe of trolls. The Zandalari sought to rebuild their fallen Empire by allying with the mogu and helping them resurrect the Thunder King, the most terrible and powerful Emperor of the Mogu Dynasty.

AN UNCERTAIN FUTURE

In the midst of chaos, Warchief Hellscream sought to claim the land for the Horde, using an ancient artifact wielded by the mogu—the Divine Bell—to harness the powers of the sha and bolster his armies. His efforts were thwarted, but the human Prince Anduin Wrynn was severely injured as a result. Garrosh continued his reckless campaign of destruction, but his ruthless leadership began to splinter the Horde—while some were loyal to Hellscream and his plans, others thought the Warchief had gone too far. Left to his own devices, Hellscream would surely bring the Horde to ruin—and unlikely as it seemed, the Horde would have to look to the Alliance for help in bringing about the Warchief's defeat.

> "TO ASK WHY WE FIGHT, IS TO ASK WHY THE LEAVES FALL...."
>
> CHEN STORMSTOUT

Warfare continued on the shores of the new continent, Pandaria. The effects of the war had disastrous consequences for the land and its people, the pandaren.

THE PRISON OF YOGG-SARON

Deep within the halls of Ulduar lies an ancient evil that forever seeks to be free of its imprisonment. Here lies Yogg-Saron, known to some as the Lucid Dream, to others as the Beast with a Thousand Maws, or simply, the God of Death. For countless ages, this Old God has been shackled in this prison, whispering dark words in the minds of mortals. For those adventurers brave and foolish enough to descend into its lair, only madness and horror await.

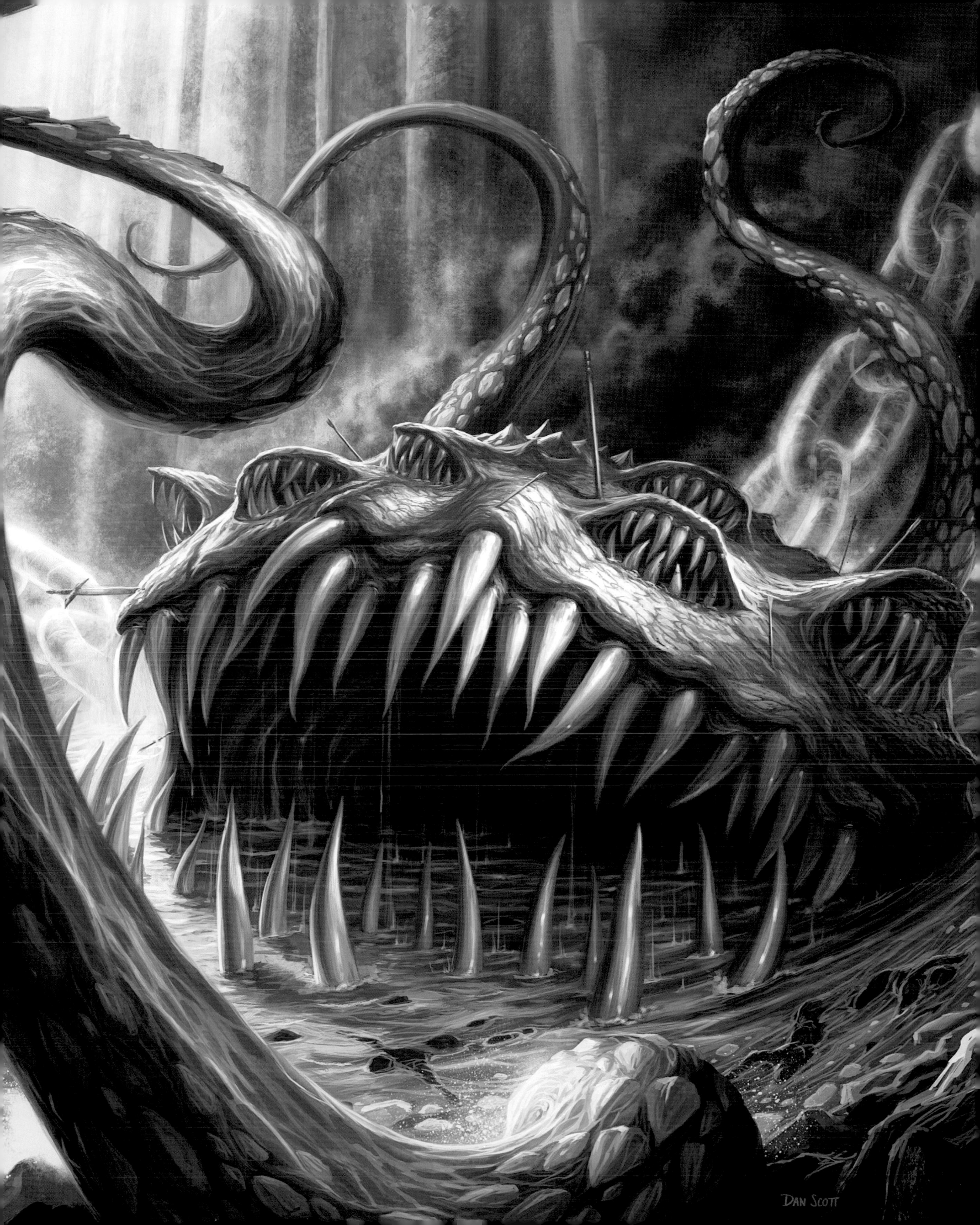
DAN SCOTT

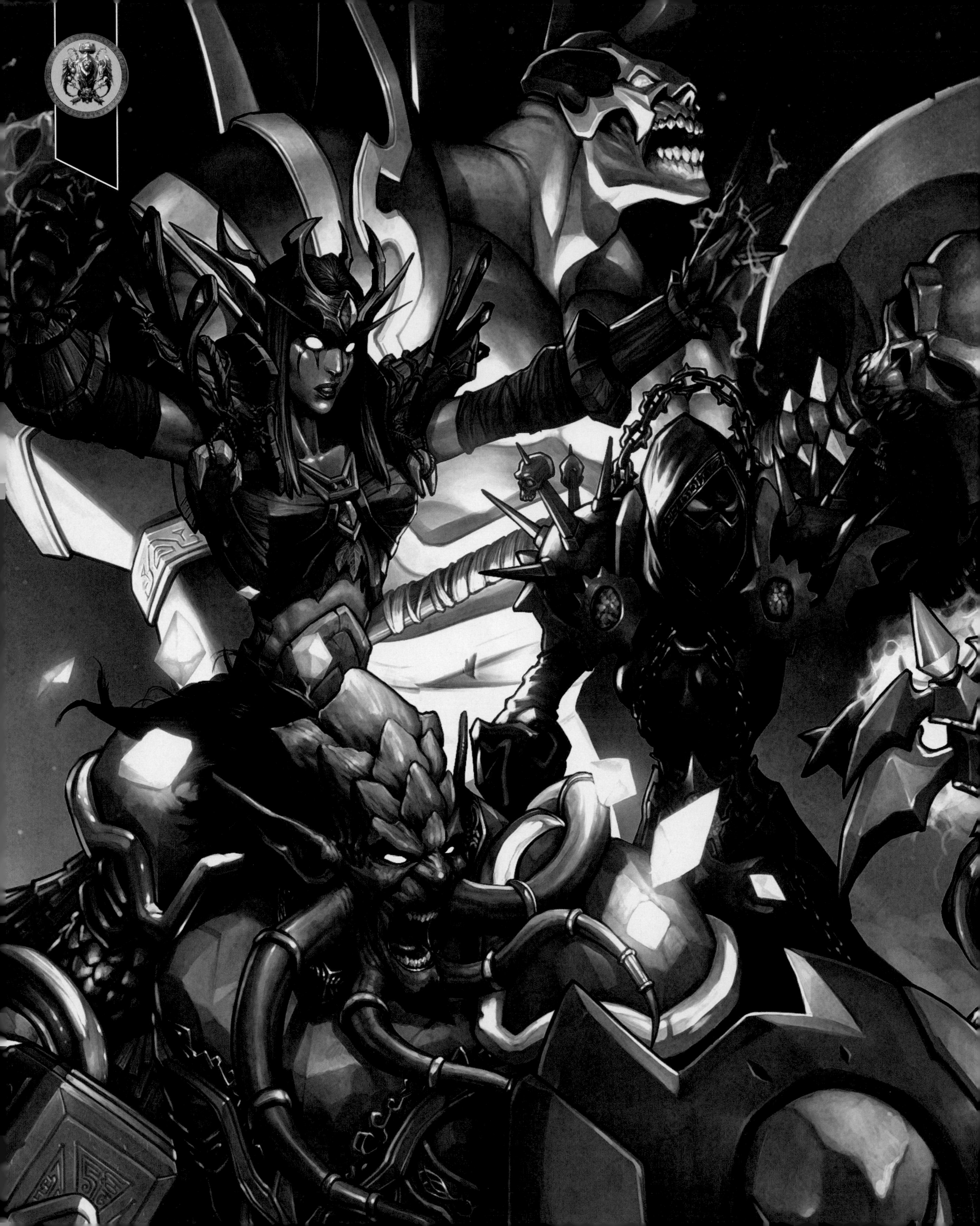

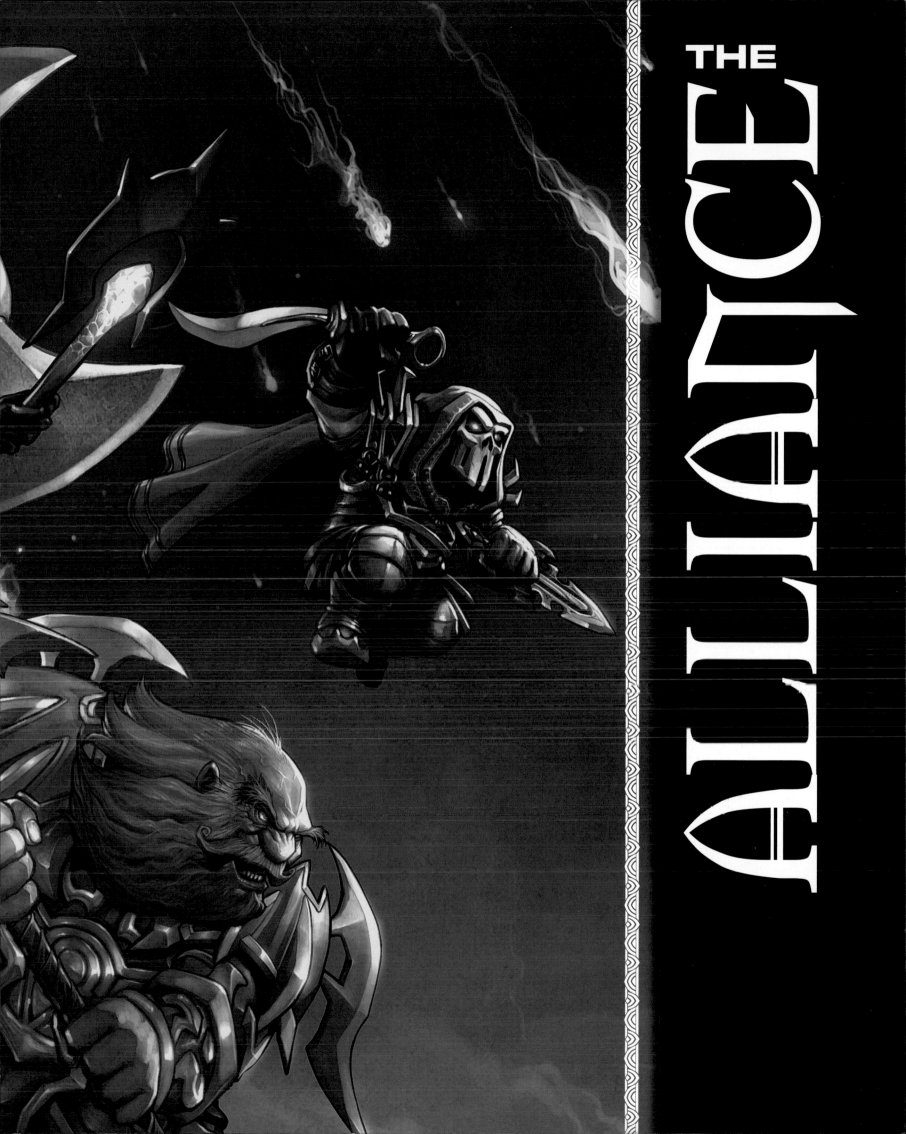

THE ALLIANCE

THE ALLIANCE

The Alliance is a united group of diverse mortal races and cultures that share a common goal: to preserve order on Azeroth. The humans, night elves, dwarves, gnomes, draenei, and worgen stand against any form of darkness, from the orcish Horde to the demonic Burning Legion, seeking to envelop the world. Their leaders are champions of justice, hope, knowledge, and honor.

A HISTORY OF HONOR

The Alliance is an evolution of the original Alliance of Lordaeron, formed to combat the threat of the old Horde during the Second War. While the Alliance of Lordaeron was initially a human-centric partnership, the Alliance of today has grown far larger and more diverse, including a multitude of races from Azeroth and beyond. The Alliance stands as a united front to support and defend the light of the world. Shared values form the bond that has kept the Alliance together throughout its many travails.

> "THE ALLIANCE CONSISTS OF POWERFUL CULTURES AND GROUPS BOUND NOT BY DESPERATION OR NECESSITY, BUT BY THEIR DEEP COMMITMENTS TO ABSTRACT CONCEPTS LIKE NOBILITY AND HONOR"
>
> **ALGALON THE OBSERVER**

HUMANS

The human kingdom of Stormwind, in the temperate lands of the Eastern Kingdoms, forms the backbone of the Alliance. Led by King Varian Wrynn, the humans of Stormwind are a tenacious and courageous group. The people of Stormwind are survivors; they have fought back against overwhelming odds, rebuilding the kingdom after its destruction in the First War, and again after the dragon Deathwing's assault. Yet even more than sheer tenacity, the true strength of the human race lies in its willingness to work with others and seek diplomatic solutions. This ability to look beyond their own interests and see others' points of view has enabled the humans to form lasting alliances with other races.

DWARVES

The dwarves have been staunch allies and friends to the humans and gnomes for many years. The dwarven capital of Ironforge is located in the snowy peaks of the Eastern Kingdoms, carved into the heart of the mountain of Khaz Modan. The strength of the dwarven race is tempered by a keen curiosity about their past, and many dwarves possess as much zest for exploring their roots as they do for battle. They also have a strong work ethic and are highly skilled craftsmen, especially adept at metalwork. The three dwarf clans—Bronzebeard, Wildhammer, and Dark Iron, have recently come together as an uneasy union, led by the Council of Three Hammers.

GNOMES

The gnomes share the land of Dun Morogh in the Eastern Kingdoms with the dwarves, and the two races often work together for mutual benefit. Gnomes possess some of the most inventive and ingenious minds on Azeroth, continually taking strides in technological advancement in everything from transport to warfare. Although brilliant, the gnomes found that brilliance tested when their race was betrayed from within—they were nearly wiped out, and their home city of Gnomeregan was rendered uninhabitable. But the insightful leadership of High Tinker Gelbin Mekkatorque, combined with gnomish ingenuity, has led to the beginning of Gnomeregan's eventual reclamation. Whatever the future holds for the Alliance, the gnomes will rush toward it filled with optimism, creative fervor, and loyalty to their allies.

NIGHT ELVES

The night elves are one of the oldest races in Azeroth, with a rich and impressive history. The night elves are currently led by High Priestess Tyrande Whisperwind and Archdruid Malfurion Stormrage. The night elf race has spent millennia in seclusion, but in their addition to the Alliance they have proven themselves to be formidable allies. The capital city of the night elves is Darnassus, nestled high in the branches of the World Tree Teldrassil, located off the northwestern edge of Kalimdor. Although far from most Alliance territories, the night elves maintain a strong presence within the Alliance. Their experience, wisdom, and fierce dedication to the preservation of the natural world has made them esteemed and valued allies.

DRAENEI

Draenei, or "Exiled Ones," are a part of the eredar race that abandoned their homeworld of Argus after the arrival of Sargeras, refusing to give in to the corruption that claimed the rest of their kind. Led by Prophet Velen, the draenei fled, eventually settling on a distant world they named Draenor. When the Burning Legion came to Draenor, the draenei were forced to flee once more. Their ship, the Exodar, crash-landed in Azeroth off the northern coast of Kalimdor. After seeking out the Alliance, Prophet Velen decided to pledge the draenei to their cause, having heard previous tales of the Alliance's battles against the Burning Legion. Dedicated to upholding the Light and defeating whatever evil that may darken the universe, the draenei have proven themselves strong allies of the Alliance in their own right.

WORGEN

The human kingdom of Gilneas abruptly pulled its support from the Alliance of Lordaeron after the Second War. Gilneas' leader, King Genn Greymane, wanted to keep his kingdom isolated, going so far as to construct the Greymane Wall to seal Gilneas off from the rest of the world to keep it safe. Yet not all of Gilneas agreed with King Greymane's decision, and as the country was thrown into civil revolt, vicious wolf-like creatures known as worgen began to overrun the kingdom. Many of the Gilneans soon found themselves falling victim to a mysterious curse and transforming into worgen themselves, becoming the very creatures that terrorized them. The problems of the Gilneans spiraled out of control as armies of the Forsaken attacked the weakened kingdom, and the world itself was split by the Cataclysm. Forced to abandon their kingdom, the Gilneans were rescued by the night elves, who offered refuge and a new home in the Howling Oak located in Darnassus. Realizing the error of his ways, King Greymane once more swore the allegiance of his people to the Alliance.

THE ALLIANCE OF LORDAERON

The Alliance of Lordaeron was originally united and led by the human King Terenas Menethil II, in order to combat the forces of the Old Horde during the Second War. It comprised the seven human kingdoms as well as other allies—the Bronzebeard and Wildhammer dwarves, the gnomes of Gnomeregan, and the high elves of Quel'Thalas. Although the Alliance of Lordaeron was victorious, it soon began to crumble in the aftermath of the Second War. However, memories of past allegiances and idealism ultimately inspired the new Alliance of the present day.

LORDAERON

The end of the First War was marked by the death of the human King Llane Wrynn and the fall of his kingdom, Stormwind. The survivors of the orcish assault fled north and arrived in Lordaeron as refugees. The refugees' leader, Regent Lord Anduin Lothar, told King Terenas of the threat that the Old Horde posed to all kingdoms. King Terenas used his political skills to bring together the seven human kingdoms, and later the dwarves, the gnomes, and the high elves. The united forces of the Alliance of Lordaeron put an end to the orcish threat and ended the Second War with a resounding victory. King Terenas continued to lead the Alliance as it began to fall apart. During the Third War, the kingdom of Lordaeron fell to the Scourge, and King Terenas was murdered by his son, Arthas.

> "THINGS LOOK BLEAK NOW, BUT CALM WILL FOLLOW THE STORM AS SURELY AS PEACE WILL FOLLOW WAR."
> ANDUIN LOTHAR

THE SEVEN KINGDOMS

The seven human kingdoms formed most of the Alliance of Lordaeron's military forces, but each kingdom had its own ambitions, and there was a great deal of skepticism and rivalry among them. The seven kingdoms were Lordaeron, Stormwind, Kul Tiras, Stromgarde, Gilneas, Dalaran, and Alterac.

Stormwind remains a strong force in the present day Alliance, however the fortunes of the other kingdoms varied. Gilneas pulled its support from the Alliance of Lordaeron after the Second War, but has rejoined the Alliance after being attacked by the Horde. Stromgarde is but an echo of the mighty kingdom it once was, although its citizens still fight in the Arathi Highlands, hoping to restore it to its former glory. The city of Dalaran, home to the magi of the Kirin Tor, was nearly destroyed in the Third War. The Kirin Tor subsequently restored their city and relocated it to Northrend to combat the Lich King. Under the guidance of Lady Jaina Proudmoore, the Kirin Tor and Dalaran have renewed their old union with the Alliance. The kingdom of Alterac was ruled by a corrupt noble, Aiden Perenolde. During the Second War, the Perenolde family was ousted from the kingdom. Many favored giving the throne to Lord Daval Prestor. However, Lord Prestor—who was the black dragon Deathwing in human guise—disappeared, and currently Alterac lies in ruins. The nation of Kul Tiras has also fallen silent since their leader, Daelin Proudmoore, and his men perished in a Horde assault on the city of Theramore shortly after the Third War.

The brutal battles of the Second War inflicted terrible casualties on the armies of the seven human kingdoms.

THE DWARVES AND GNOMES

Two major Dwarven clans eventually pledged their support to the Alliance of Lordaeron: the Bronzebeard clan, based in Ironforge, and the Wildhammer Clan, based in Aerie Peak. There had once been intense rivalry and even open warfare between these clans, but they agreed that the Horde was even more dangerous. Today, Ironforge and Aerie Peak remain staunch advocates of the Alliance, and both Wildhammer and Bronzebeard clans have united with the Dark Iron to rule the dwarven kingdoms via the Council of Three Hammers.

The gnomes, originally allies of Ironforge, served the Alliance of Lordaeron well during the Second War, providing valuable technology to aid their cause. They formally joined the Alliance as a sovereign nation after the Third War, hoping to reclaim their capital city of Gnomeregan from a trogg invasion.

The dwarves of Ironforge and gnomes of Gnomeregan were vital to the Alliance during the Second War, supplying its armies with weapons, siege engines, and mechanical contraptions.

THE ELVEN KINGDOM

Quel'Thalas, home of the high elves, was at best a reluctant member of the Alliance. King Anasterian Sunstrider only agreed to join because of an ancient pledge made to Anduin Lothar's ancestors. At the end of the Second War, King Anasterian believed that his country had suffered unnecessarily, and pulled his support from the Alliance of Lordaeron. Quel'Thalas was nearly destroyed by the Scourge during the Third War, and King Anasterian was killed, leaving his son, Prince Kael'thas Sunstrider, to lead. Kael'thas renamed his people sin'dorei, or blood elves, as a tribute to those that had fallen in the Third War. The blood elves were later committed to the Horde by their Regent Lord, Lor'themar Theron. Yet some high elves remained outside of Quel'Thalas, disgusted by the actions of their brethren, and to this day still support the Alliance.

The King of Stormwind, Varian Wrynn shows strength, cunning, and determination in defending his lands and people. His journey has been marked by pain and suffering, but this does not deter him from confronting all who would stand against him or his kingdom. As the leader of the Alliance, Varian will not rest until his people are safe, whatever the cost.

VARIAN WRYNN

"A gladiator's life is simple: You win and live... or lose and die. A king's life is more complex. The only truth for a king is that there are no easy answers."

A KING RESTORED

As a child, Varian witnessed the Horde's destruction of his homeland and the brutal murder of his father, King Llane, at the hands of the assassin Garona Halforcen.

As heir to Stormwind's throne, Varian's rise to king began in tragedy. The savage orc armies of the old Horde decimated his father King Llane Wrynn's kingdom in the First War. Young Varian witnessed his father's death, Llane's heart cut out by the half-orc assassin Garona. After the Alliance of Lordaeron's victory in the Second War, Varian was crowned and soon married. But his beloved wife Tiffin was tragically killed, leaving Varian to care for their infant son, Anduin. Years later, Varian was kidnapped in an elaborate scheme orchestrated by the black dragon Onyxia. Onyxia used a spell to brutally divide the king into two aspects of his personality: one a fierce warrior, the other an easily manipulated pawn.

The warrior Varian, washed ashore in Kalimdor without his memories, was forced to serve in gladiatorial combat by the orc Rehgar Earthfury. Earning the name Lo'Gosh, the "Ghost Wolf," for his ferocity in the ring, Varian soon escaped. After discovering his true identity, slaying Onyxia, and uniting his two selves, Varian has reclaimed his rightful place as king, but the scars of his past remain. Varian has vowed to crush all threats to his family, kingdom, and the Alliance. Only when all of the Alliance's foes are purged will Varian enjoy peace.

A MOMENT OF PEACE
For a brief time, young king Varian Wrynn and his wife, Tiffin Ellerian, raised their son Anduin together in peace. Varian loved his wife deeply, and her death haunts him still. Part of him wonders if she would still love the man he has become.

A CHAMPION OF WAR
Varian's nickname, Lo'Gosh, is the tauren name for the Ancient Goldrinn. The great ghost wolf Goldrinn was known for his savage ferocity and unyielding will. The nickname was given to Varian after spectators witnessed his ferocity in gladiatorial combat.

THE KING RETURNED
Once again ruler of Stormwind, Varian now fights with renewed vigor to rid the world of the evils that threaten the Alliance. He is determined to be a strong role model for his son, showing Anduin what it means to live a life dedicated to truth, honor, and duty.

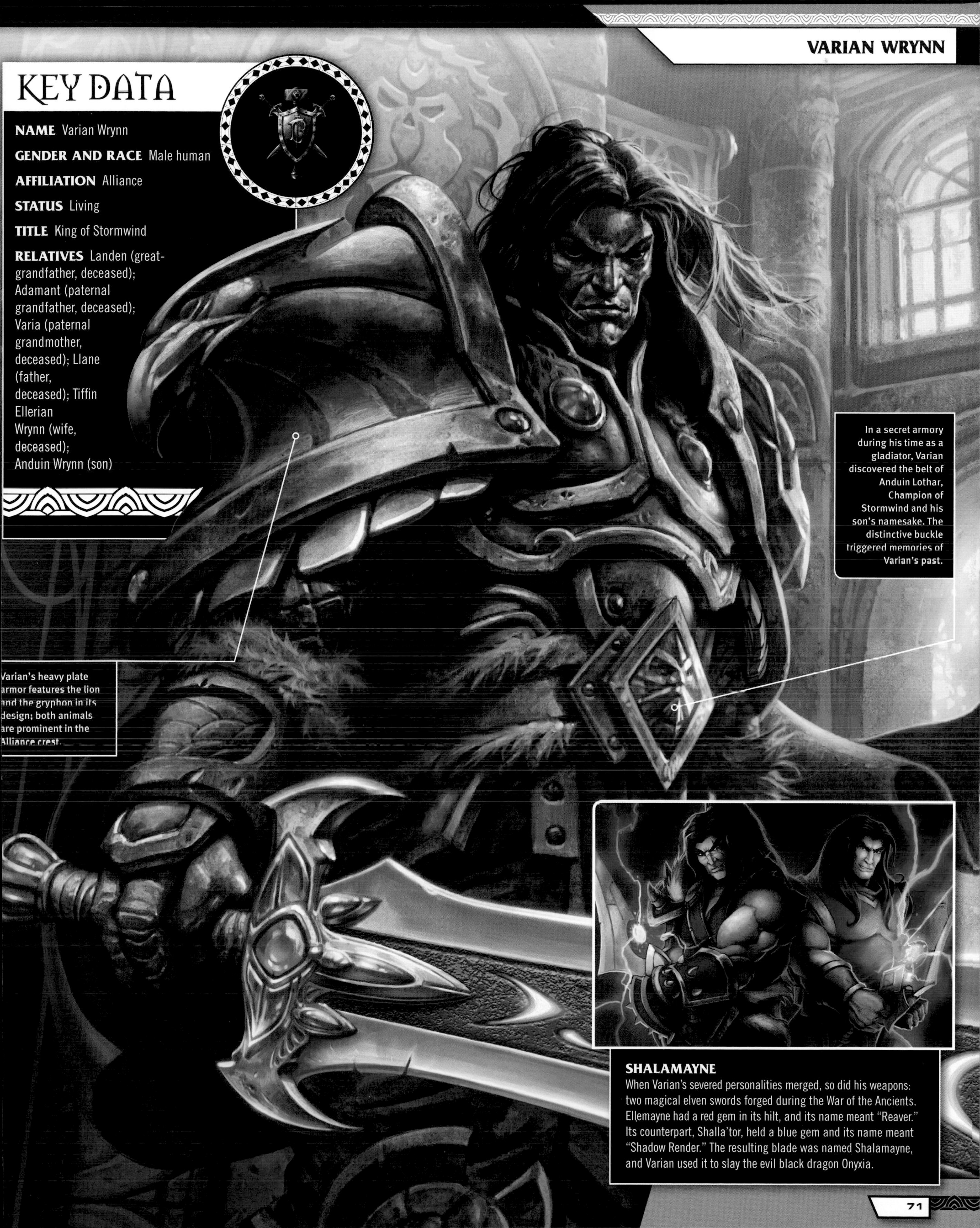

KEY DATA

NAME Varian Wrynn

GENDER AND RACE Male human

AFFILIATION Alliance

STATUS Living

TITLE King of Stormwind

RELATIVES Landen (great-grandfather, deceased); Adamant (paternal grandfather, deceased); Varia (paternal grandmother, deceased); Llane (father, deceased); Tiffin Ellerian Wrynn (wife, deceased); Anduin Wrynn (son)

In a secret armory during his time as a gladiator, Varian discovered the belt of Anduin Lothar, Champion of Stormwind and his son's namesake. The distinctive buckle triggered memories of Varian's past.

Varian's heavy plate armor features the lion and the gryphon in its design; both animals are prominent in the Alliance crest.

SHALAMAYNE

When Varian's severed personalities merged, so did his weapons: two magical elven swords forged during the War of the Ancients. Ellemayne had a red gem in its hilt, and its name meant "Reaver." Its counterpart, Shalla'tor, held a blue gem and its name meant "Shadow Render." The resulting blade was named Shalamayne, and Varian used it to slay the evil black dragon Onyxia.

HUMANS

The human race stands as a monument to tenacity in the face of adversity. The most notable heroes of the human race are pinnacles of heroism, bravery, and strength. No matter the path they chose to follow, these beacons of heroism act as protectors, role models, and inspirations for their people.

JAINA PROUDMOORE

Lady Jaina Proudmoore is one of Azeroth's most powerful sorcerers. She was among the first to discover the blight of the Scourge with her beloved, Prince Arthas Menethil, and the first to investigate it. She then watched Arthas' descent into darkness with the utmost sorrow. As Lordaeron fell, she heeded the warning of the Prophet Medivh and led the survivors to Kalimdor. Jaina later joined her forces with orcish and night elven armies to defeat Archimonde at the peak of Mount Hyjal in the Third War. Jaina stood as a strong advocate for diplomacy and peace between the two factions, working in tandem with the orc Warchief Thrall to try and achieve that goal. But the departure of Thrall and the destruction of Theramore at Warchief Garrosh Hellscream's hands shattered her faith and sent her to Dalaran, to take her place as leader of the Kirin Tor. As leader, Jaina has recently directed Dalaran and the Kirin Tor to abandon their neutral leanings and again stand proudly at the Alliance's side.

"I must stay ever vigilant against forces outside of our control if I'm to ensure my people remain safe and happy."

KEY DATA

TITLES Leader of the Kirin Tor, Ruler of Theramore
STATUS Living
AFFILIATION Alliance
RELATIVES Daelin Proudmoore (father, deceased); Derek Proudmoore (brother, deceased)

ANDUIN WRYNN

The only child of King Varian Wrynn, Anduin was crowned the temporary King of Stormwind at age ten—with the assistance of Regent Lord Bolvar Fordragon and Lady Katrana Prestor—when his father was kidnapped. Precocious and wise beyond his years, Anduin Wrynn was among the first to sense something amiss with Prestor, who in truth was the black dragon Onyxia in human guise. Over the years, Anduin has developed a thirst for peace and diplomacy, preferring level-headed thinking and discussion over brute force and war. He has also demonstrated an innate and powerful affinity for the Light and pressed the Prophet Velen to take him as a pupil, despite his father's violent objections. In Pandaria, Anduin appears to be working on his own, helping those in need and never wavering in his firm belief that the Light's guidance will ultimately lead to peace and prosperity for all.

KEY DATA

TITLE Crown Prince of Stormwind
STATUS Living
AFFILIATION Alliance
RELATIVES Llane Wrynn (grandfather, deceased); Varian Wrynn (father); Tiffin Ellerian Wrynn (mother, deceased)

ANDUIN LOTHAR

BOLVAR FORDRAGON

KEY DATA

TITLES Highlord, Lich King, High General of the Valiance Expedition, Regent of Stormwind
STATUS Deceased
AFFILIATION Alliance
RELATIVES None known

Highlord Bolvar Fordragon served as Regent of Stormwind after King Varian Wrynn's disappearance. Later, he was sent to Northrend to serve as High General of the Valiance Expedition. Thought to have been killed by the plague at the Battle of the Wrathgate, Bolvar was saved but charred beyond recognition by the flames of the red dragonflight. Caught and tortured by the Lich King, Bolvar's resolve never wavered. After the Lich King's death, Bolvar took his place, using his remarkable will to keep the Scourge in check.

AEGWYNN

KEY DATA

TITLES Supreme Commander of the Alliance of Lordaeron
STATUS Deceased
AFFILIATION Alliance of Lordaeron
RELATIVES Ancestors of the Arathi bloodline (deceased)

Often referred to as the Lion of Azeroth, Anduin Lothar was one of the greatest warriors in human history. As a Knight Champion in the First War, Lothar was instrumental in the defeat of the sorcerer Medivh. His heroic efforts continued when he lead the survivors of Stormwind's destruction to Lordaeron after the First War, standing as temporary Regent Lord of Stormwind, warning King Terenas of the orcish threat, and inspiring the formation of the Alliance of Lordaeron. He proudly served as the Supreme Commander of the Alliance armies during the Second War, and although he perished at the hands of Horde Warchief Orgrim Doomhammer, his influence and inspiration bolstered the Alliance armies on to victory even after his demise.

TURALYON

General Turalyon, a paladin, was Anduin Lothar's second-in-command during the Second War. After Lothar's death, Turalyon inherited command of the Alliance armies, capturing Warchief Orgrim Doomhammer. Under his command, the Alliance of Lordaeron triumphed, ending the Second War. Later, he led the Alliance Expeditionary Force beyond the Dark Portal, where they discovered the dark plans of the orc shaman Ner'zhul. To save Azeroth, Turalyon and the archmage Khadgar destroyed the Dark Portal, stranding themselves. Turalyon and his companion, the high elf Alleria Windrunner, are currently missing. Their son, Arator, still searches for them to this day.

KEY DATA

TITLES High General of the Alliance Expedition, Supreme Commander of the Alliance of Lordaeron, Knight of the Silver Hand
STATUS Unknown
AFFILIATION Alliance of Lordaeron
RELATIVES Arator the Redeemer (son)

KEY DATA

TITLES Guardian of Tirisfal, Magna, Chamberlain
STATUS Deceased
AFFILIATION Independent (Neutral)
RELATIVES Nielas Aran (lover, deceased); Medivh (son); Med'an (grandson)

The sorceress Aegwynn was a Guardian of Tirisfal, an elite position chosen by a secret sect of the Kirin Tor. Charged with defending world from the threat of the Burning Legion, Aegwynn successfully encountered and defeated the Avatar of its leader, Sargeras. Unbeknownst to Aegwynn, the spirit of Sargeras lived on inside of her, eventually passing to her son, Medivh, in order to use him as a dark vessel. During the First War, Medivh opened the Dark Portal under Sargeras' command, but was subsequently killed Lord Anduin Lothar. Aegwynn revived Medivh after his death, allowing him to act as Prophet in the Third War. Later, she was discovered by Lady Jaina Proudmoore and brought to Theramore to act as both chamberlain and advisor. Aegwynn's final act was to sacrifice her life for her grandson, Med'an.

HUMANS

10ff## MEDIVH

KEY DATA

TITLES The Prophet, The Oracle, Accursed, Magus
STATUS Unknown
AFFILIATION Independent (Neutral)
RELATIVES Aegwynn (mother, deceased); Nielas Aran (father, deceased); Garona Halforcen (lover); Med'an (son)

Medivh was the son of Aegwynn, Guardian of Tirisfal, and Archmage Nielas Aran. Unknowingly possessed by the spirit of Sargeras, leader of the Burning Legion, Medivh killed his father and went into a coma when he came into his power at age 14. Twenty years later, he awoke under the control of Sargeras and opened the Dark Portal, a doorway between Azeroth and Draenor, allowing the orcish invasion that began the First War. During this time, he fathered a child with Garona Halforcen; their son Med'an was born in secrecy. Medivh was killed by his apprentice Khadgar and Anduin Lothar, ending Sargeras' control. Medivh was later brought back from death by his mother, who expended most of her power in the process. Taking the guise of a prophet, Medivh orchestrated the Third War's victory, using his influence to bring together human, night elf, and orc armies to defeat Archimonde at the Battle of Mount Hyjal. He then disappeared; his whereabouts remain unknown.

UTHER THE LIGHTBRING

Uther the Lightbringer was the first paladin of the order of the Knights of the Silver Hand. A great hero of the Second War, he exemplified the noble ideals of his order, which he tried to impart to his beloved pupil, Prince Arthas Menethil. But Arthas betrayed everything the Light stood for, murdering his own father, King Terenas Menethil II. Uther stood guard over Terenas' ashes in Andorhal, where he was confronted and killed by Arthas. Uther's body was buried near Andorhal, but his spirit still counsels those who would stand against evil.

KEY DATA

TITLES Supreme Commander of the Paladin Order, The Lightbringer
STATUS Deceased
AFFILIATION Alliance of Lordaeron
RELATIVES None known

KHADGAR

The sorcerer Khadgar was apprentice to Medivh. Khadgar discovered that Medivh was possessed by Sargeras, and sought to destroy him. With the help of Anduin Lothar, he succeeded—but paid a terrible price. His life was drained by Medivh during the battle, aging him in moments. Khadgar was instrumental in destroying the Dark Portal at the end of the Second War, and later joined the Alliance Expeditionary Force to Draenor. After the Dark Portal closed once again, stranding him, Khadgar found his way to Shattrath City. Years later, he returned to Azeroth and joined the Council of Six, and now resides in Dalaran with the Kirin Tor.

KEY DATA

TITLE Archmage of the Kirin Tor
STATUS Living
AFFILIATION Alliance
RELATIVES None known

KING TERENAS MENETHIL II

A wise and beloved ruler, King Terenas Menethil II was the leader of Lordaeron during the First and Second Wars. He was instrumental in bringing about the Alliance of Lordaeron. Terenas was killed by his son, Arthas, during the Third War. His remains were housed in an urn and guarded by paladins in the city of Andorhal. Yet Terenas would find no rest; the urn was later stolen by Arthas and used to transport the necromancer Kel'Thuzad's remains to Quel'Thalas, where Kel'Thuzad would be reborn as a lich.

KEY DATA

TITLES King of Lordaeron, Leader of the Alliance of Lordaeron
STATUS Deceased
AFFILIATION Alliance of Lordaeron
RELATIVES Lianne (wife; deceased), Calia (daughter), Arthas (son; deceased)

KING LLANE WRYNN I

King Llane Wrynn was the beloved ruler of Stormwind during the First War, fighting against the orc Horde and leading Stormwind against Warchief Blackhand. Trusting, respectful, and kind, King Llane was advisor and friend to many, including Anduin Lothar, the sorcerer Khadgar, and young Horde agent Garona Halforcen. Yet Llane's kindness led to his downfall; compelled by her master, the warlock Gul'dan, Garona murdered Llane in full sight of his young son, Varian.

KEY DATA

TITLE King of Stormwind
STATUS Deceased
AFFILIATION Independent
RELATIVES Landen (grandfather, deceased); Adamant (father, deceased); Varia (mother, deceased); Varian (son); Tiffin (daughter-in-law, deceased); Anduin (grandson)

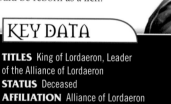

ALEXANDROS MOGRAINE

Alexandros Mograine was a paladin and Knight of the Silver Hand. Mograine both wielded and earned the nickname Ashbringer for the ashes of Scourge that fell beneath his might. He and his wife, Elena, had two sons, Renault and Darion. Renault eventually betrayed and killed his father, and Alexandros was reanimated as a death knight by the lich Kel'Thuzad. His spirit was freed by Darion, at the cost of Darion's life and soul.

KEY DATA

TITLES The Ashbringer, Highlord, Scourge of the Scourge, Knight of the Silver Hand
STATUS Deceased
AFFILIATION Independent
RELATIVES Elena (wife, deceased); Renault (son, deceased); Darion (son, deceased)

RENAULT MOGRAINE

Renault Mograine joined the Scarlet Crusade (which was secretly led by dreadlord Balnazzar of the Burning Legion) as a paladin. At Balnazzar's request, Renault took his father Alexandros' sword, Ashbringer, and murdered him. Renault's treachery corrupted the Ashbringer, and trapped Alexandros' spirit in the blade. Later, Renault's brother Darion acquired the Ashbringer. When Darion confronted Renault, Alexandros' spirit appeared and killed Renault for his betrayal.

KEY DATA

TITLES Scarlet Commander
STATUS Deceased
AFFILIATION Adversarial
RELATIVES Alexandros (father, deceased); Elena (mother, deceased); Darion (brother, deceased)

DARION MOGRAINE

Darion Mograine became a death knight after he plunged the corrupted sword Ashbringer into his own chest, freeing the trapped spirit of his father, Alexandros. Once a servant of the Lich King, Darion rebelled, and gave Highlord Tirion the Ashbringer. The Ashbringer was purified by Tirion's hand, and Darion's force of rebels became the Knights of the Ebon Blade, instrumental in Arthas' final demise.

KEY DATA

TITLES Leader of the Knights of the Ebon Blade
STATUS Deceased
AFFILIATION Independent (neutral)
RELATIVES Alexandros (father, deceased); Elena (mother, deceased); Renault (brother, deceased)

TIRION FORDRING

Tirion Fordring was one of the first five Knights of the Silver Hand. After the Second War, he was stripped of his title for defending the orc Eitrigg. Exiled, Tirion lived as a hermit for many years, until he discovered his son Taelan's involvement with the Scarlet Crusade. Taelan was then murdered by the Scarlet Crusade for attempting to defect. Heartbroken, Tirion reformed the Knights of the Silver Hand, and later, the Argent Crusade. Tirion's connection to the Light allowed him to cleanse the corrupted sword Ashbringer. He wielded the Ashbringer and confronted the Lich King atop Icecrown Citadel, slaying him with the help of heroes of Azeroth. He now leads the Argent Crusade to reclaim lands once tainted by the Scourge.

KEY DATA

TITLES Supreme Commander of the Argent Crusade, Highlord of the Silver Hand, Lord of Mardenholde Keep
STATUS Living
AFFILIATION Independent (neutral)
RELATIVES Karandra (wife, deceased); Taelan (son, deceased)

DANATH TROLLBANE

Danath Trollbane served as the military commander of Stromgarde and tactical advisor to General Turalyon during the Second War. He then accompanied Turalyon through the Dark Portal as part of the Alliance Expeditionary Force. After the Dark Portal closed, he was trapped in Outland. Danath now leads Honor Hold, the Alliance bastion in Hellfire Peninsula, but his people in Stromgarde anxiously await his return.

KEY DATA

TITLES Master of Honor Hold, Tactical Advisor to General Turalyon, Captain of the Stromgarde Militia
STATUS Living
AFFILIATION Alliance of Lordaeron
RELATIVES Liam Trollbane (grandfather, deceased); Thoras Trollbane (uncle, deceased); Galen Trollbane (cousin, undead)

RHONIN

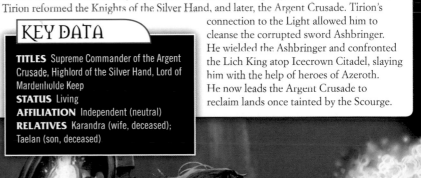

Former leader of the Kirin Tor, Rhonin's exploits are the stuff of legend. He was instrumental in destroying the Demon Soul and freeing the Dragonqueen Alexstrasza, as well as traveling back in time to assist with the War of the Ancients. He sacrificed his life to save Jaina Proudmoore when Theramore was destroyed by the Horde, leaving behind his wife Vereesa Windrunner and twin sons, Giramar and Galadin.

KEY DATA

TITLE Leader of the Kirin Tor
STATUS Deceased
AFFILIATION Independent (Neutral)
RELATIVES Vereesa Windrunner (wife); Giramar and Galadin (twin sons); Alleria Windrunner (sister-in-law); Arator Windrunner (nephew); Sylvanas Windrunner (sister-in-law)

STORMWIND CITY

Stormwind City is the capital of the Kingdom of Stormwind, the largest human nation in Azeroth. Stormwind City has been rebuilt and improved several times over the years. It was destroyed by the armies of the Old Horde during the First War, and later devastated by Deathwing's attack during the Cataclysm. Today, Stormwind City stands as a triumphant symbol of human tenacity and strength, a monument to Alliance ideals.

STORMWIND KEEP
This mighty castle is King Varian Wrynn's seat of power, where he resides with his son, Prince Anduin.

SEAT OF THE ALLIANCE
Stormwind City is home to residents from all over the world. The large Dwarven District hosts both dwarves and gnomes, and there is also a small night elf population. Stormwind City also has transport routes connecting to Kalimdor as well as outposts in Northrend. The Eastern Earthshrine has mystical portals that allow nearly instantaneous travel to locations across Azeroth and beyond.

HEROES OF HISTORY
Statues of Alliance Expedition members, the great heroes who traveled to Draenor and sealed the Dark Portal, guard the main entrance to Stormwind City. Thane Kurdran Wildhammer and Archmage Khadgar are on the left; Force Commander Danath Trollbane and Ranger-Captain Alleria Windrunner take up the right. General Turalyon, the expedition's leader, secures Stormwind's entrance.

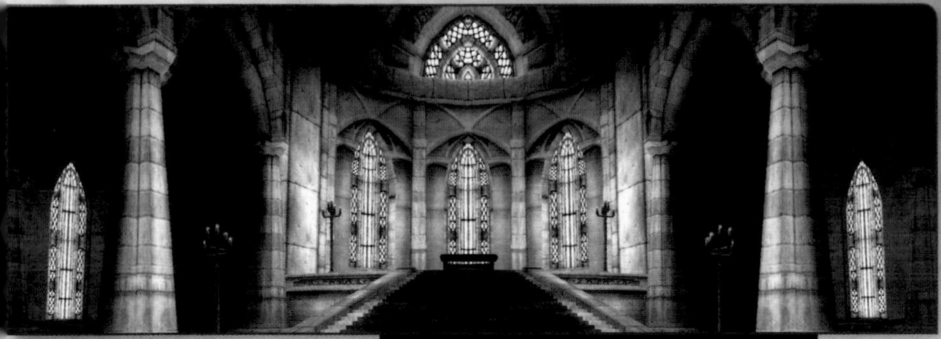

THE CATHEDRAL OF LIGHT
The Cathedral of Light towers over the city center. It stands as a home to high-ranking members of the Church of the Holy Light, and all those that choose to follow the philosophical ways of the Light's teachings.

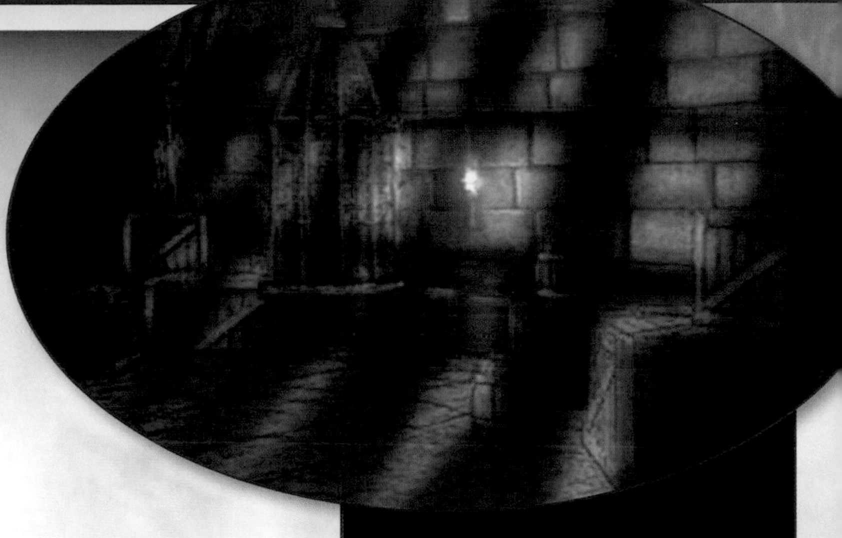

THE STORMWIND STOCKADE
The Stormwind Stockade is a large prison system located beneath the Canals in the center of the city. Prison revolts have been a common occurrence, despite Warden Thelwater's best efforts to keep the prisoners contained.

DEATHWING'S ATTACK
During the Cataclysm, Deathwing attacked Stormwind City. The avenues were bathed in flame and ash, and the great black dragon carved his mark into the capital, completely destroying portions of the city. Afterward, King Varian Wrynn embarked upon a large scale renovation, expanding the Dwarven District, opening access to Stormwind City's outskirts, and fortifying Stormwind Keep.

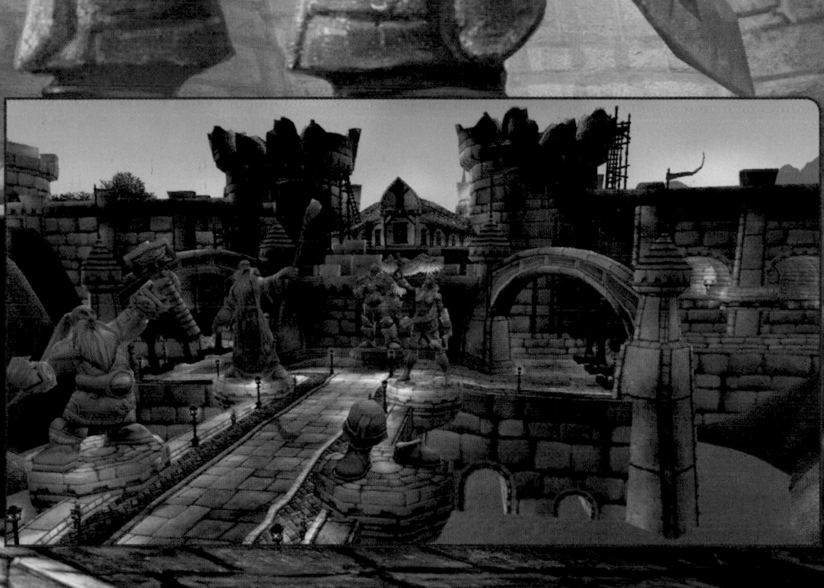

The Bronzebeard nation of Khaz Modan was plunged into disarray by the sudden crystallization of its king, Magni Bronzebeard. Now Ironforge is governed by representatives of its three most powerful clans: Bronzebeard, Wildhammer, and Dark Iron. This arrangement will come to an end if the heir presumptive, Dagran Thaurissan II, achieves his majority and takes control of the kingdom.

COUNCIL OF THREE HAMMERS

"Welcome to our home beneath the mountain."

THE STRIKE OF HAMMER TO ANVIL

Magni Bronzebeard gave the gnomes refuge in Ironforge when they lost their home, Gnomeregan. He supported King Varian Wrynn and mentored his son, Anduin. Magni's loss nearly shattered the dwarven clans, but the formation of the Council of Three Hammers has preserved a tentative peace, for now.

Dwarves consider their clans vital to their personal identities. However, in an earlier time, the clans were united under the guidance of a high king. When the last high king, Modimus Anvilmar, died, the clans fractured. The Bronzebeard clan finally took control, banishing the Wildhammer and Dark Iron clans from Ironforge. Although tensions eventually eased slightly between the Bronzebeards and Wildhammers, the blood feud with the Dark Irons only deepened. When Magni Bronzebeard ascended to the throne, he used the support of his brothers, Muradin and Brann, to make overtures toward the Wildhammer clan, with some success. The Dark Irons, however, struck out by kidnapping the king's daughter, Moira. Emperor Dagran Thaurissan, Lord of the Blackrock Mountains, unexpectedly showed Moira respect and compassion, and she soon fell in love with the Emperor, marrying him and bearing his only son. After a ritual that Magni conducted turned the king into diamond, Moira returned to Ironforge. She brought her newborn son Dagran, the heir to two kingdoms, with her. The Council of Three Hammers now governs the dwarven lands.

HOME AND FORTRESS

The dwarven city of Ironforge serves as both capital city and fortress. Carved into the heart of the Khaz Modan mountain, Ironforge was a source of great contention between the three clans. High King Modimus Anvilmar was the united ruler of all, but when he died, his eldest son was not yet old enough to lead. Left without a proper ruler, Ironforge quickly descended into chaos as Bronzebeard, Wildhammer, and Dark Iron all fought for the right to rule the mountain fortress, beginning the War of the Three Hammers.

HEART OF THE MOUNTAIN

When the elements arose in distress prior to the Cataclysm, King Magni Bronzebeard sought to use an ancient tablet to commune with them. The plan backfired when Magni literally became one with the mountain, his body transformed to glittering diamond. Today, King Magni still rests beneath the heart of Ironforge.

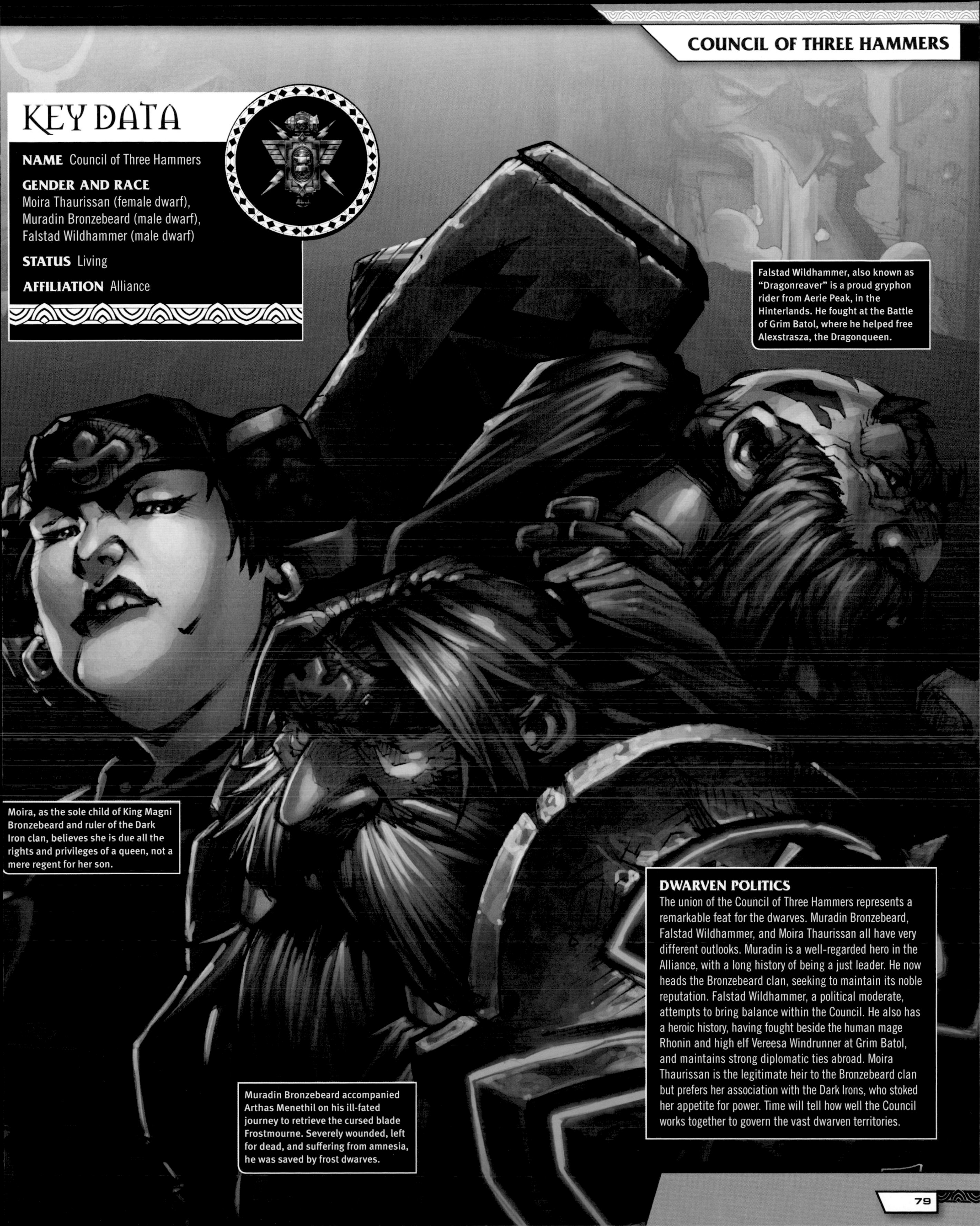

KEY DATA

NAME Council of Three Hammers

GENDER AND RACE
Moira Thaurissan (female dwarf),
Muradin Bronzebeard (male dwarf),
Falstad Wildhammer (male dwarf)

STATUS Living

AFFILIATION Alliance

Falstad Wildhammer, also known as "Dragonreaver" is a proud gryphon rider from Aerie Peak, in the Hinterlands. He fought at the Battle of Grim Batol, where he helped free Alexstrasza, the Dragonqueen.

Moira, as the sole child of King Magni Bronzebeard and ruler of the Dark Iron clan, believes she is due all the rights and privileges of a queen, not a mere regent for her son.

Muradin Bronzebeard accompanied Arthas Menethil on his ill-fated journey to retrieve the cursed blade Frostmourne. Severely wounded, left for dead, and suffering from amnesia, he was saved by frost dwarves.

DWARVEN POLITICS

The union of the Council of Three Hammers represents a remarkable feat for the dwarves. Muradin Bronzebeard, Falstad Wildhammer, and Moira Thaurissan all have very different outlooks. Muradin is a well-regarded hero in the Alliance, with a long history of being a just leader. He now heads the Bronzebeard clan, seeking to maintain its noble reputation. Falstad Wildhammer, a political moderate, attempts to bring balance within the Council. He also has a heroic history, having fought beside the human mage Rhonin and high elf Vereesa Windrunner at Grim Batol, and maintains strong diplomatic ties abroad. Moira Thaurissan is the legitimate heir to the Bronzebeard clan but prefers her association with the Dark Irons, who stoked her appetite for power. Time will tell how well the Council works together to govern the vast dwarven territories.

DWARVES

Dwarves are a strong and hardy people with a zest for combat, exploration, and many a fine ale. The dwarven race is one that is steeped in tradition. While the monarchs of the past are honored, so, too, are the explorers that continue to search for answers surrounding the mysterious origins of the dwarven race.

MAGNI BRONZEBEARD

KEY DATA

TITLES Lord of Ironforge, King of Khaz Modan
STATUS Unknown
AFFILIATION Alliance
RELATIVES Muradin (brother); Brann (brother); Moira Bronzebeard (daughter); Dagran Thaurissan II (grandnephew)

King Magni Bronzebeard was the eldest of the three Bronzebeard brothers, and the King of Ironforge, beloved by his people. Magni was also an accomplished weaponsmith—he forged the legendary blade Ashbringer. Magni's interest in the roots of dwarven civilization led to the founding of the Explorers' League, an organization dedicated to researching the history of the dwarven race. Magni had one daughter, Moira, who was kidnapped by the Dark Iron clan and married its leader, Emperor Dagran Thaurissan, to Magni's dismay.

The elemental unrest prior to the Cataclysm deeply troubled King Magni. In an attempt to better understand the unease of the earth, Magni performed a rite to make him "one with the earth." It succeeded, after a fashion. Magni was turned into diamond, indeed becoming one with the earth. Although a funeral was held for the monarch, his ultimate fate is still unknown.

BRANN BRONZEBEARD

Brann Bronzebeard is the youngest brother of King Magni and Muradin Bronzebeard. Years ago, when Magni founded the Explorers' League, Brann left Ironforge to explore the world at his brother's behest. He traveled all over Azeroth, and he documented his adventures along the way. In recent years, Brann has been instrumental in discovering many of the titans' secret strongholds. Brann's innate curiosity and reverence for ancient culture sometimes land him in trouble, but his wit and keen intelligence always save the day.

KEY DATA

TITLE None
STATUS Living
AFFILIATION Alliance
RELATIVES Magni Bronzebeard (brother, fate unknown); Muradin Bronzebeard (brother); Moira Bronzebeard Thaurissan (niece); Dagran Thaurissan II (grandson)

THARGAS ANVILMAR

During King Magni Bronzebeard's rule, the great dwarven warrior Thargas Anvilmar helped protect the kingdom from enemies within and without. On one occasion, Thargas was sent by King Magni to meet with a human warrior named Lo'Gosh and his companions, Valeera Sanguinar and Broll Bearmantle, and escort them back to Ironforge. However, the group was beset by agents of the Defias Brotherhood. Thargas aided the group and then informed Lo'Gosh, revealed to be King Varian Wrynn of Stormwind, that a "different" Varian was ruling Stormwind. On their way to Ironforge, the group was attacked again, this time by the Dark Iron dwarves. After the fight, Thargas found out that his brother, Hjalmar, had been captured. The group traveled to the Thandol Span bridges to rescue Hjalmar. Though Hjalmar sacrificed his life for his brother, the group fought back against the Dark Iron dwarves and also saved Thandol Span from destruction. Thargas later helped King Varian drive the black dragon Onyxia, who had taken the human form of Lady Katrana Prestor, from Stormwind.

KEY DATA

TITLE Defender of Thandol Span
STATUS Living
AFFILIATION Ironforge
RELATIVES Hjalmar Anvilmar (brother, deceased)

MODIMUS ANVILMAR

Long ago, high king Modimus Anvilmar ruled the united dwarf clans from Ironforge. During this period of history, the dwarven race was a united force; although many dwarven clans existed, all worked together under the High King. Modimus was known for his diplomacy, particularly when dealing with the three strongest clans—Bronzebeard, Dark Iron, and Wildhammer. However, he is perhaps most notorious for his death, which sparked a civil war that forever changed dwarven history. Before Modimus' eldest son could be crowned, the three strongest clans began to fight for supremacy and the right to rule Ironforge in the War of the Three Hammers. The Bronzebeard clan won the war and banished both Wildhammer and Dark Iron from the city. While Modimus has long since passed on, he is a revered hero. His descendants continue to play an important part in dwarven history to this day. An immense statue of Modimus can be found watching over the gates of Ironforge.

KEY DATA

TITLE High King
STATUS Deceased
AFFILIATION Kingdom of Khaz Modan
RELATIVES Hjalmar (descendant, deceased); Thargas (descendant)

HEMET NESINGWARY

Hemet Nesingwary is a dwarven hunter with an inexhaustible drive to find new creatures to stalk. He's been through Stranglethorn Vale, Nagrand, and Sholazar Basin in pursuit of greater and greater game to bring down. It's said that Hemet even took a hot air balloon to Pandaria! Adventurers far and wide have bumped into this legendary dwarf or his son, Hemet Nesingwary, Jr., who follows in his footsteps. He's written great tales (mostly about his own exploits), with *The Green Hills of Stranglethorn* being his most notable work.

KEY DATA

TITLE Greatest Hunter in all of Azeroth
STATUS Living
AFFILIATION Independent (Nesingwary Expedition)
RELATIVES Hemet Nesingwary, Jr. (son)

DAGRAN THAURISSAN

Emperor Dagran Thaurissan ruled the Dark Iron dwarves of Blackrock Mountain with a combination of charisma, sorcery, and iron will. He was a direct descendant of Sorcerer-Thane Thaurissan, who led the Dark Iron clan to defeat in the War of Three Hammers. As with all Dark Iron dwarves, Dagran was a loyal servant of Ragnaros the Firelord. After kidnapping King Magni's daughter, Moira Bronzebeard, Dagran treated her with the respect due her position, and even kindness and affection. Moira soon fell in love with Dagran, marrying him and later bearing his son, Dagran Thaurissan II. In time, Magni Bronzebeard asked a team of adventurers to assault Blackrock Mountain and retrieve Moira. They killed Dagran, earning Moira's enmity. His son, however, remains the acknowledged heir to the throne of Ironforge.

KEY DATA

TITLE Emperor of Blackrock
STATUS Deceased
AFFILIATION Adversarial
RELATIVES Thaurissan (ancestor, deceased); Modgud (ancestor, deceased); Moira Bronzebeard Thaurissan (wife); Dagran Thaurissan II (son)

KURDRAN WILDHAMMER

Formerly the high thane of the Wildhammer clan, Kurdran Wildhammer rose to infamy during the Second War owing to his impressive aerial combat on the back of his beloved gryphon mount, Sky'ree. Kurdran was a member of the Alliance expeditionary force sent through the Dark Portal, leaving Falstad Wildhammer to take his place as high thane in Aerie Peak. Once thought lost beyond the Dark Portal, Kurdran was discovered leading Wildhammer Stronghold in Shadowmoon Valley. He returned to Azeroth some time after the Dark Portal was reopened and, for a time, took a seat on the Council of Three Hammers, before realizing Falstad was far more suitable for the task. Kurdran returned to the Twilight Highlands, where he now serves as ruler of Highbank and high commander of the Alliance assault force against the Twilight's Hammer cult.

KEY DATA

TITLES Ruler of Highbank, High Thane of the Wildhammer Clan, Gryphon Master of the Aerie Peak
STATUS Living
AFFILIATION Alliance
RELATIVES None known

IRONFORGE

The ancient city of Ironforge has long been the dwarves' seat of power. The massive fortress, carved into the peaks of Khaz Modan, reflects dwarven values: hearth, home, industry, and a keen reverence for history. Though Ironforge has long been a source of contention between the dwarven clans, the mountain citadel remains a bastion of Alliance power.

THE HIGH KING'S STATUE

Ironforge was once ruled by High King Modimus Anvilmar, whose statue stands at the entrance. When he died, a civil war broke out amongst the dwarf clans. The Bronzebeard clan won the war, and both Wildhammer and Dark Iron clans were banished from Ironforge. The Bronzebeards ruled over Ironforge for many years, until a ritual involving an ancient tablet inadvertently turned King Magni Bronzebeard to diamond. Now all three clans have returned, and the Council of Three Hammers rules Ironforge.

CITY OF THE DWARVES

Dwarven craftsmanship and gnomish ingenuity have made Ironforge famous for its industry and as an Alliance center of commerce. The city is a series of concentric rings, with the smaller levels deeper underground. The Council of Three Hammers meets within the High Seat. The crystalline body of the former king of Ironforge, Magni Bronzebeard, rests below the High Seat, within the Assembly of Thanes. The Hall of Explorers, a testament to the dwarven reverence for history and exploration houses a massive library and a museum of artifacts found by the Explorers' League.

TINKER TOWN

Gnomes and dwarves have been staunch allies and friends for millennia. When Gnomeregan was rendered uninhabitable, gnomish refugees found shelter within Ironforge. An entire section of the city, called Tinker Town, was set aside for their use. Although many gnomes have now relocated to New Tinkertown near Gnomeregan, there are those that still call Ironforge home.

FORLORN CAVERN

THE MYSTIC WARD

HALL OF EXPLORERS

THE GREAT FORGE

TINKER TOWN

THE DEEPRUN TRAM

THE COMMONS

THE MILITARY WARD

THE GATES OF IRONFORGE

DEEPRUN TRAM

Deeprun Tram, an engineering marvel, connects Ironforge with Stormwind City. The dwarves are also known for using gryphons as flying mounts, providing vital passage to allies.

THE GREAT FORGE

The Great Forge dominates the capital's center. The Great Anvil rests at the center, used to craft many a fine weapon. Canals of lava from deep within the mountain heat this massive foundry.

Gelbin Mekkatorque epitomizes the gnomish ideal: a creative mind, a desire for technological progress, and compassion toward others. Elected to the position of High Tinker, Gelbin represented his people during their darkest time, the loss of Gnomeregan, their capital city. With assistance from his allies, Gelbin fights on to take back the city, looking with hope toward the future.

GELBIN MEKKATORQUE

"It is our loyalty to our friends that provides our truest, greatest strength... It is a power that numbers cannot match."

A BRILLIANT DEFENDER

Gelbin assembled troops to take back the rightful home of the gnomes. This mission was called Operation: Gnomeregan.

Gelbin Mekkatorque grew up as a remarkable inventor. His many works included the first mechanostrider and the Deeprun Tram between the cities of Stormwind and Ironforge. Gelbin developed many of his inventions alongside his classmate and closest friend, Sicco Thermaplugg. As a result of his intelligence, ingenuity, and astonishing array of useful inventions, Gelbin was elected High Tinker of Gnomeregan. This infuriated Sicco, who thought that he should have the position instead. Yet he kept his feelings secret and acted as Gelbin's top advisor in Gnomeregan. When the troggs invaded Gnomeregan before the onset of the Third War, Gelbin turned to Sicco Thermaplugg for assistance. Thermaplugg provided a brutal but decisive solution: release toxic gas in the lower levels of the city to eliminate the troggs.

The plan was enacted and Sicco had his revenge. The radiated gas rose to fill the entire city, killing most of the gnome populace along with the troggs. Gelbin and the few survivors were forced to flee, taking refuge in Ironforge. This left Gnomeregan to be occupied by a diseased, violent population of irradiated gnomes and troggs, led by the insane Sicco Thermaplugg. With support from his friends in the Alliance, Gelbin vowed to retake the city. Although they made a valiant effort, it was not completely successful. Today, Gelbin continues to work diligently at reclaiming Gnomeregan for his people. Filled with optimism and hope, and knowing that the gnomes can surmount any catastrophe, he is resolute in his desire to assist the Alliance.

MASTER OF INVENTION

As a young genius, Gelbin's inventions included the first mechanostrider, the gyromatic micro-adjustor, the repair bot, and even a prototype of the dwarven siege engine. His most impressive feat was developing the Deeprun Tram, which revolutionized large-scale transport.

THE FALL OF GNOMEREGAN

Under Gelbin's orders, the gnomes released a toxic gas into their city in a failed attempt to stop the trogg invasion. The gas horribly mutated anything left alive in Gnomeregan, and Gelbin took personal responsibility for the consequences.

THE BETRAYER CONFRONTED

During the reclamation of Gnomeregan, Gelbin confronted Thermaplugg inside the city. In the ensuing battle, Gelbin's inventiveness won. Thermaplugg's legs were severed in the encounter when Gelbin re-engineered one of Thermaplugg's own traps against him. Gelbin left the wounded Thermaplugg to the troggs, believing it a fair punishment for his crimes.

Sicco Thermaplugg gave Gelbin his mithril-rimmed spectacles in his youth, as a graduation gift.

Gelbin's weapon is called Wrenchcalibur. Its complex series of runes, cogs, pistons, and levers allow it to serve as a mace, providing a focus for Gelbin's sharp, tactical mind.

KEY DATA

NAME Gelbin Mekkatorque

RACE Male gnome

AFFILIATION Alliance

TITLE High Tinker

STATUS Living

RELATIVES None known

GNOMEREGAN RECLAIMED?
Although unable to fully reclaim Gnomeregan, Gelbin and his troops were able to claim a vital foothold in their former home, dubbing it New Tinkertown.

GNOMES

The gnomes of Azeroth have an insatiable drive for learning, innate curiosity, and passion for knowledge. Many of them are explorers or collectors, and their expertise in technology has made them important contributors in a variety of endeavors. Their discoveries will continue to play an important role in Azeroth's future.

FIZZCRANK FULLTHROTTLE

Fizzcrank Fullthrottle designed and managed the Fizzcrank Airstrip in the Borean Tundra in Northrend to assist in the war against the Lich King. Fizzcrank encountered a problem with the pump station. The obstruction was revealed to be an ancient, gnome-like mechanical creature. It called itself Gearmaster Mechazod and claimed to be one of the first gnomes. In gratitude for his rescue, Mechazod began "rewarding" the gnomes by transforming the station's personnel into mechagnomes. Adventurers were sent to deal with the menace, and Mechazod was disassembled. But the very fact of Mechazod's existence unsettled Fizzcrank's view of gnomish history and evolution.

KEY DATA

TITLE Member of Valiance Expedition
STATUS Living
AFFILIATION Alliance
RELATIVES None known

MILLHOUSE MANASTORM

The Arcatraz, part of Tempest Keep, functioned as a naaru prison for a myriad of dangerous and destructive beings, but Millhouse Manastorm found himself there as a victim of circumstance. Millhouse's natural curiosity led him to Arcatraz, and he was imprisoned near Harbinger Skyriss, a devotee of the Old-Gods. It was perhaps this proximity to an agent of the Old Gods that led to his next move—joining the Twilight Cult, working on their operations in Deepholm. He was thought killed in the Stonecore after being knocked off a precipice, but he survived and went on to become a gladiator in the Brawler's Guild. He chooses only the rarest of opponents to fight.

KEY DATA

TITLE Member of the Twilight's Hammer Cult
STATUS Living
AFFILIATION Independent/Adversarial
RELATIVES None known

J.D. COLLIE

The crystal pylons of Un'Goro Crater bear unmistakable traces of the titans. J.D. Collie, part of Marshal Expeditions to Un'Goro, has embarked on an extensive investigation of the pylons, which are power crystals growing throughout the crater. She collected her research in a manual that illustrated how to use the unique crystals of Un'Goro Crater for beneficial purposes. J.D.'s expertise in the field may help shed new light on the titans and their creations.

KEY DATA

TITLE None
STATUS Living
AFFILIATION Independent (Neutral)
RELATIVES None known

CRUSADE ENGINEER SPITZPATRICK

Crusade Engineer Spitzpatrick joined the Argent Crusade in an effort to use his engineering expertise against the forces of the Scourge. During the war against the Lich King in Northrend, he assisted with the construction of the Argent Vanguard, the forward base used by the Argent Crusade against the Lich King's fortress of Icecrown Citadel.

KEY DATA

TITLE Crusade Engineer
STATUS Living
AFFILIATION Independent
RELATIVES None known

SILAS DARKMOON

A friendly and passionate entertainer, Silas Darkmoon created the Darkmoon Faire, the greatest show on Azeroth. It is found on Darkmoon Island, which can be accessed by portal in Elwynn Forest and Mulgore. Under the supervision of Silas, the Faire is not only entertainment for the discerning traveler, it is home to a motley assortment of people, a refuge for the wayward souls of the world. Silas is very protective of the family he has built with the Darkmoon Faire. Violence on Faire grounds will not be tolerated—and those unfortunate few that cross Silas or his makeshift family may find that their fate is much darker than Silas' genial nature would suggest.

KEY DATA

TITLE Leader and Founder of the Darkmoon Faire
STATUS Living
AFFILIATION Independent (Neutral)
RELATIVES None known

GNOMEREGAN

Dense green smoke still veils t[he] marvels that gnomish technology created long ago.

Located in the frozen fields of Dun Morogh, Gnomeregan is the capital city of the gnomes. Although the gnomes lost the city years ago as a result of treachery and radiation, parts of it have since been reclaimed. High Tinker Gelbin Mekkatorque continues to work tirelessly with his people to reclaim the rest of the city and restore it to its former glory.

GNOMEREGAN INTERIOR

For generations, Gnomeregan fostered the technological pursuits of its people. Prior to the Third War, an evil, primitive race of humanoids called troggs invaded Gnomeregan. In desperation the gnomes released toxic radiation into the city. It was meant to only destroy the troggs, but irradiated the entire city instead. Most of its citizens were killed or transformed into violent, diseased creatures, known as leper gnomes.

NEW TINKERTOWN

Gnomish survivors have recently taken back the surface and a small part of Gnomeregan. Their base is called New Tinkertown, in honor of the shelter the refugees received in the dwarven city of Ironforge. Though these citizens are dedicated to restoring their capital, there are still gnomes that choose to practice their engineering skills in the safety of Ironforge.

Mutated, violent, and deranged leper gnomes still wander the halls of Gnomeregan, attacking any who enter.

As co-ruler of the night elves and High Priestess of the moon goddess Elune, Tyrande Whisperwind has tirelessly protected her people. In her youth, her closest companions were the twin brothers Illidan and Malfurion Stormrage. While both loved Tyrande, her heart lay with Malfurion alone. She is dedicated to her goddess, her people, and her beloved.

TYRANDE WHISPERWIND

"Raw power is no substitute for true strength...."

CHOSEN OF THE MOON

While the demigod Cenarius, Ancient of Nature, taught Malfurion Stormrage the ways of the druid, Tyrande followed a different calling as a priestess of the moon goddess, Elune.

Tyrande spent her early years in the company of the twin brothers Illidan and Malfurion Stormrage, but each of them chose a different path to follow when they came of age. Tyrande became a priestess, while Malfurion became a druid under the demigod Cenarius' tutelage. Illidan's path led first to the arcane arts… and then to a darker fate. During the War of the Ancients against the Burning Legion, Tyrande was told of High Priestess Dejahna's death, and that she had named Tyrande as her successor.

Although Tyrande was fond of both Stormrage twins, she fell in love with Malfurion, Illidan's destructive addiction to power turning her away. Ultimately, Illidan's actions against all of creation—including the betrayal of his closest allies and creation of a second Well of Eternity—led to his imprisonment by Malfurion. But Tyrande later freed him during the Third War, hoping that he would join the fight against the Burning Legion's second demonic invasion. Although Tyrande could not redeem Illidan, Archimonde, Lord of the Burning Legion, was defeated, and Azeroth saved. Illidan ultimately departed to the distant world of Outland, and Malfurion entered the ethereal realm of the Emerald Dream, leaving Tyrande alone to guard her people. Tyrande then became aware of a new threat: corruption within the Emerald Dream. She led a force into the Nightmare-plagued realm, to eliminate the infection and rescue her beloved. Today, Malfurion and Tyrande are wed, and their union guides the night elves in strength and wisdom.

LIFELONG LOVE
The love story of Malfurion and Tyrande is one of the greatest romantic tales from Azeroth. Attended by Alliance, Horde, and dragon representatives, their marriage celebration transcended political and racial tensions, and was an event that gave joy and hope to all.

COMPASSION BETRAYED
Illidan loved Tyrande deeply and never accepted the fact that she chose Malfurion over him. His later acts justifiably earned him the title of Illidan the Betrayer and cost him any chance of compassion from Tyrande.

CHILD OF THE HEART
When she was a young adult, Shandris Feathermoon's family and home were destroyed by the Burning Legion. Tyrande watched over her and guided her, becoming her adopted mother. Now Shandris does the same for her people as general of the Sentinels, the army of the night elf nation.

Due to her position and the love her people show her, Tyrande has always been worried that she could become like Queen Azshara—a corrupt, ego-driven tyrant.

KEY DATA

NAME Tyrande Whisperwind

GENDER AND RACE
Female night elf

STATUS Living

AFFILIATION Alliance

TITLES High Priestess of Elune,
Co-ruler of the Night Elves

RELATIVES Malfurion Stormrage
(husband); Illidan Stormrage
(brother-in-law, deceased);
Shandris Feathermoon
(adopted daughter)

Tyrande has worn many different forms of armor over the years, from plate armor to priestess robes. Despite her formidable nature, she has taken arms only to protect others.

TRUSTED COMPANIONS
Ash'alah, a nightsaber, is Tyrande's ally and battle mount. Ash'alah has been with Tyrande since before the War of the Ancients. A large, snowy spirit owl named Dori'thur also frequently accompanies Tyrande.

Malfurion Stormrage is one of the most respected heroes in Azeroth. As an Archdruid of the Cenarion Circle, he has fought tirelessly to defend the world against evil, whether it arises from the demonic Burning Legion, the corruption of the Emerald Dream, or the machinations of his own twin brother, Illidan. Together, Malfurion and his beloved Tyrande Whisperwind guide the night elven people to a brighter future.

MALFURION STORMRAGE

"Standing in the way of nature is heresy. Even when nature's force is a destructive one."

A FAMILY DIVIDED

Malfurion became the first druid of the night elves, having learned the druidic arts from Cenarius, the demigod guardian of nature.

Malfurion Stormrage spent his youth with his love Tyrande Whisperwind and twin brother Illidan. While studying under the demigod Cenarius to become a druid, he recognized the dangers that the Burning Legion posed when they first invaded Azeroth. His actions during the ensuing War of the Ancients ended with the Legion's defeat, the destruction of the Well of Eternity—the source of arcane magic on Azeroth—and Illidan's secret creation of a new Well at Mount Hyjal. Dismayed by Illidan's sacrilege, Malfurion requested that his brother be imprisoned. Malfurion then entered into the mystical world of the Emerald Dream. He sought to learn from it, and the dragon Aspect Ysera, how best to guide and heal the world. For centuries at a time his body slept while his consciousness protected this mystical realm.

Millennia after he first entered the Dream, Malfurion was awakened by Tyrande only to find the Burning Legion once more ravaging the land. He reunited with Tyrande, stopped the Legion and its leader, Archimonde, at the Battle of Mount Hyjal, and then later returned to his slumber. Within the Emerald Dream, Malfurion became imprisoned by the Nightmare, a terrible corruption of the Dream, but was eventually able to escape and finally end its threat. Once again fully awakened, he and Tyrande settled back into life in Darnassus, where they were married under the boughs of Teldrassil, the World Tree. After the devastating Cataclysm that ripped the face of the world, Malfurion moved to defend the sacred summit of Mount Hyjal from yet another foe: the Elemental Fire Lord, Ragnaros.

A DREAM OF LOVE
Tyrande Whisperwind (pictured here with Ash'alah, her Frostsaber mount and companion) was Malfurion's childhood friend. Their shared reverence for nature and desire to care for the world brought them together. It was Tyrande's efforts and love that finally broke Malfurion free from the Nightmare in the Emerald Dream, allowing the two to finally wed. Today, they jointly rule the night elves as husband and wife.

HIS BROTHER'S KEEPER
Although he loved his twin brother, Malfurion's feelings toward Illidan were complex. Illidan was responsible for many dark deeds, and Malfurion's relationship with him was colored with anger, sorrow, and regret.

NORDRASSIL'S FALL
In the final moments of the Third War, Malfurion sacrificed the World Tree Nordrassil to put an end to the demon lord Archimonde. Malfurion used the Horn of Cenarius to call spirits of nature to the tree. The tree detonated, destroying Archimonde but being badly damaged itself. This act sacrificed the night elves' immortality, but saved the world.

KEY DATA

NAME Malfurion Stormrage

GENDER AND RACE
Male night elf

AFFILIATION Alliance, Cenarion Circle

STATUS Living

TITLES Archdruid, Shan'do,
co-ruler of the night elves

RELATIVES Illidan Stormrage (twin brother,
deceased); Tyrande Whisperwind (wife); Shandris
Feathermoon (adopted daughter)

In night elf culture, Malfurion's
antlers are regarded as a sign of
great druidic potential. Very few
night elves possess them.

Malfurion has accepted druidic
pupils, including Broll Bearmantle
and Fandral Staghelm. Many refer to
him as Shan'do, which means
"honored teacher."

During his time in the Emerald
Dream, Malfurion underwent
additional transformations; his body
now possesses attributes of a bird,
a cat, and a bear.

CENARION CIRCLE
Malfurion established the Cenarion
Circle as an organization to teach
and guide new druids. Today, the
Cenarion Circle embraces druids
from many different races and paths.

NIGHT ELVES

The night elven race has a long and storied history on Azeroth, pre-dating the War of the Ancients, which resulted in the Sundering that split Kalimdor into the continents known today. Although individual night elves may have faltered, for thousands of years the race has stood strong against any who would threaten their world and the lands they revere.

BROLL BEARMANTLE

KEY DATA

TITLE Druid of the Cenarion Circle
STATUS Living
AFFILIATION Independent/Alliance
RELATIVES Anessa (daughter, deceased); Telandria (cousin)

Broll was born with antlers, a sign that he was marked for a greater destiny, but he never felt that he lived up to his promise. He fought in the Third War, where he lost his only daughter, Anessa. Distraught, Broll left night elven society, eventually ending up as a gladiator slave. During that time, he met two people who would become his closest companions: a human warrior named Lo'Gosh and a blood elf named Valeera Sanguinar. When Lo'Gosh was revealed to be part of King Varian Wrynn, separated by the black dragon Onyxia, Broll helped Varian kill Onyxia, restore himself to completeness, and reclaim his throne. Broll then returned to the night elves, where he discovered new, vast amounts of untapped inner power and helped to save Malfurion Stormrage and Ysera, Aspect of the green dragonflight, from the Emerald Nightmare—thus finally fulfilling the greater purpose for which he'd been destined since birth. Later, Broll joined with Malfurion to keep Fandral and his master, Ragnaros the Firelord, from destroying the lands near Mount Hyjal. Broll now serves his people as a well-respected druid and works as a member of the new Council of Tirisfal.

FANDRAL STAGHELM

KEY DATA

TITLES Majordomo of Ragnaros, Archdruid of the Flame, Archdruid
STATUS Deceased
AFFILIATION Independent (later Adversarial)
RELATIVES Valstann (son, deceased); Leyara (daughter in law, deceased); Istaria (granddaughter, deceased)

In his youth, Fandral Staghelm showed marked proficiency for the druidic arts, and a flair for hot-tempered antagonism—he was prone to frequent arguments with Malfurion Stormrage. He married, then tragically lost his wife as she gave birth to his son, Valstann. Fandral and Valstann were incredibly close as a result, and when Valstann was killed before his father's eyes during the War of the Shifting Sands, Fandral only grew angrier at the world. Shortly after the end of the Third War, Malfurion Stormrage went missing in the Emerald Dream. Fandral, by this time archdruid, ordered the growth of a new World Tree, Teldrassil, in the hopes of regaining the night elves' immortality. Later, it was revealed that Fandral had been corrupted by the Nightmare Lord, and that he was slowly poisoning Malfurion in order to keep him in a state of eternal slumber. After Malfurion escaped the Emerald Dream, Fandral was imprisoned in the Barrow Dens of Hyjal, but later freed by an agent of Ragnaros the Firelord. Ragnaros promised Fandral untold power and made Fandral his new majordomo and head of a new order—the Druids of the Flame. Fandral was later killed by the heroes of the Guardians of Hyjal in the Firelands, Ragnaros' domain.

KUR'TALOS RAVENCREST

As leader of the night elven army during the War of the Ancients, Lord Kur'talos Ravencrest fought against the Burning Legion. He was a charismatic and skilled leader, inspirational to his soldiers on the field of battle, but he distrusted other races and believed that the night elves could defend themselves without help. Although Kur'talos was deeply loyal to Queen Azshara, his queen was secretly working with the Burning Legion. His continued resistance against them angered her, and she had him assassinated. After his death, Kur'talos' unskilled and xenophobic second-in-command, Lord Desdel Stareye, briefly took control of the night elf forces, before being killed by the Burning Legion. Jarod Shadowsong, who had impressed Kur'talos greatly, then took control of the night elf army, upholding the heroism of his former commander.

KEY DATA

TITLES Lord of Black Rook Hold, Leader of the Kaldorei Resistance
STATUS Deceased
AFFILIATION Independent
RELATIVES None known

JAROD SHADOWSONG

Jarod Shadowsong became a hero during the War of the Ancients, although he was never comfortable with the title. He originally served under Kur'talos Ravencrest as a guard, but Kur'talos soon recognized his leadership potential and willingness to fight the Burning Legion. Jarod was assigned to protect the spell casters in the night elf army: Krasus (the red dragon Korialstrasz), Rhonin, and Malfurion and Illidan Stormrage. When Kur'talos was assassinated on Queen Azshara's orders, Jarod was placed under Lord Desdel Stareye, an unreasonable man with no battle skills. After Desdel's death, Jarod took control of the night elven military. He was captured and tortured by Archimonde, but resisted through the pain, which earned him further acclaim. After the War of the Ancients, he left with his wife, Shalasyr, into self-imposed exile. He later returned in the hopes of saving his ailing wife, but Shalasyr passed before Tyrande could save her. Yet this brought him back into contact with his sister, Maiev, with whom he always had a difficult relationship, and Shandris Feathermoon, who cared deeply for him. Jarod now leads the Watchers, which act as a security force. His goal is to hunt down and stop Maiev, before she descends further into insanity.

KEY DATA

TITLES Leader of the Watchers, Military Leader of the Kaldorei Resistance, Guard Captain
STATUS Living
AFFILIATION Alliance
RELATIVES Maiev Shadowsong (sister); Shalasyr (wife, deceased)

MAIEV SHADOWSONG

Once a priestess of Elune and possessing a fierce hatred of the arcane arts, Maiev Shadowsong volunteered to be Illidan Stormrage's jailer upon his imprisonment at the end of the War of the Ancients. In her new role, Maiev established the Watchers, to guard Illidan and prevent his escape.

Thousands of years later, Illidan was freed by High Priestess Tyrande Whisperwind, much to Maiev's fury. Maiev pursued Illidan across Azeroth and beyond, finally capturing him in Outland. Yet Illidan's allies freed him and captured Maiev instead. Her jailor over the next several years was the Broken Akama, who, disillusioned with Illidan's rule, conspired to set Maiev free. Together with a band of adventurers they brought an end to Illidan. Still Maiev was dissatisfied. As Illidan told her with his final breaths, the huntress was nothing without the hunt—without Illidan to pursue. Driven mad from years of imprisonment, the loss of her prey, and an obsessive hatred of the arcane, Maiev returned to Azeroth looking for a new purpose. In a move of sheer insanity, she plotted to capture and kill Malfurion Stormrage, believing him to be cut from the same cloth as his twin and resentful of the possible inclusion of Highborne arcanists in night elven ranks. The assassination attempt was thwarted by Maiev's brother, Jarod, but Maiev escaped. Her current whereabouts are unknown.

KEY DATA

TITLES Leader of the Watchers, Jailer of Illidan Stormrage
STATUS Living
AFFILIATION Independent/Adversarial
RELATIVES Jarod Shadowsong (brother)

SHANDRIS FEATHERMOON

When still only a child, during the War of the Ancients, Shandris Feathermoon's home and family were destroyed by the Burning Legion. She was later found and taken under the wing of Tyrande Whisperwind. After the end of the war, Shandris continued to stand with unwavering devotion by Tyrande's side, becoming an adopted daughter and fierce defender of the high priestess. A skilled warrior and archer, Shandris was eventually promoted to general of the Sentinels, residing in Feathermoon Stronghold in Feralas. Shandris was overjoyed when Tyrande and Malfurion were finally able to wed. She acted as coordinator for those attending the ceremony and was also a witness at the couple's wedding.

Today, Shandris still proudly leads the Sentinels, defending, protecting, and standing strong against any who would threaten the night elves or the Alliance.

KEY DATA

TITLE General of the Sentinel Army
STATUS Living
AFFILIATION Alliance
RELATIVES Tyrande Whisperwind (adoptive mother); Malfurion Stormrage (adoptive father)

DARNASSUS

Nature surrounds the capital of the night elven lands. Darnassus is built around and within the boughs of the World Tree Teldrassil, its branches wide and strong enough to support forests and lakes—one such lake dominates the center of Darnassus. Most of the city's buildings are constructed to provide ample opportunities to commune with the natural world.

THE HOWLING OAK

The night elves helped the people of Gilneas to escape when their kingdom was devastated in the Cataclysm. The refugees—including those afflicted with the worgen curse—now reside in the Howling Oak, an enormous tree. The Howling Oak is located near the Cenarion Enclave, where both worgen and night elf druids train.

CITY OF THE NIGHT ELVES

When the World Tree Nordrassil was damaged at the end of the Third War, the night elves lost their immortality. Teldrassil was grown in a failed attempt to recreate that bond, and its creation was a source of tension between the druids of the Cenarion Circle. Darnassus is one of the Alliance's quietest cities. For thousands of years, the night elves rarely interacted with the outside world, instead choosing a life of seclusion. The inhabitants' natural reticence, combined with the city's remote location, makes Darnassus exceptionally peaceful.

WARRIOR'S TERRACE

The Warrior's Terrace protects Darnassus from violent incursions. Patrollers on nightsaber mounts guard the city's impressive gates. The north portion leads into the Craftsmen's Terrace; the south portion flows into the Tradesmen's Terrace.

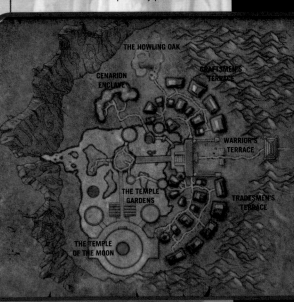

THE HOWLING OAK

CENARION ENCLAVE

CRAFTSMEN'S TERRACE

WARRIOR'S TERRACE

THE TEMPLE GARDENS

TRADESMEN'S TERRACE

THE TEMPLE OF THE MOON

REACHING DARNASSUS

Rut'theran Village sits at the base of Teldrassil. This outpost connects to Darnassus above via a magical portal, and to the outside world and the Kalimdor mainland by docks and hippogryph flights.

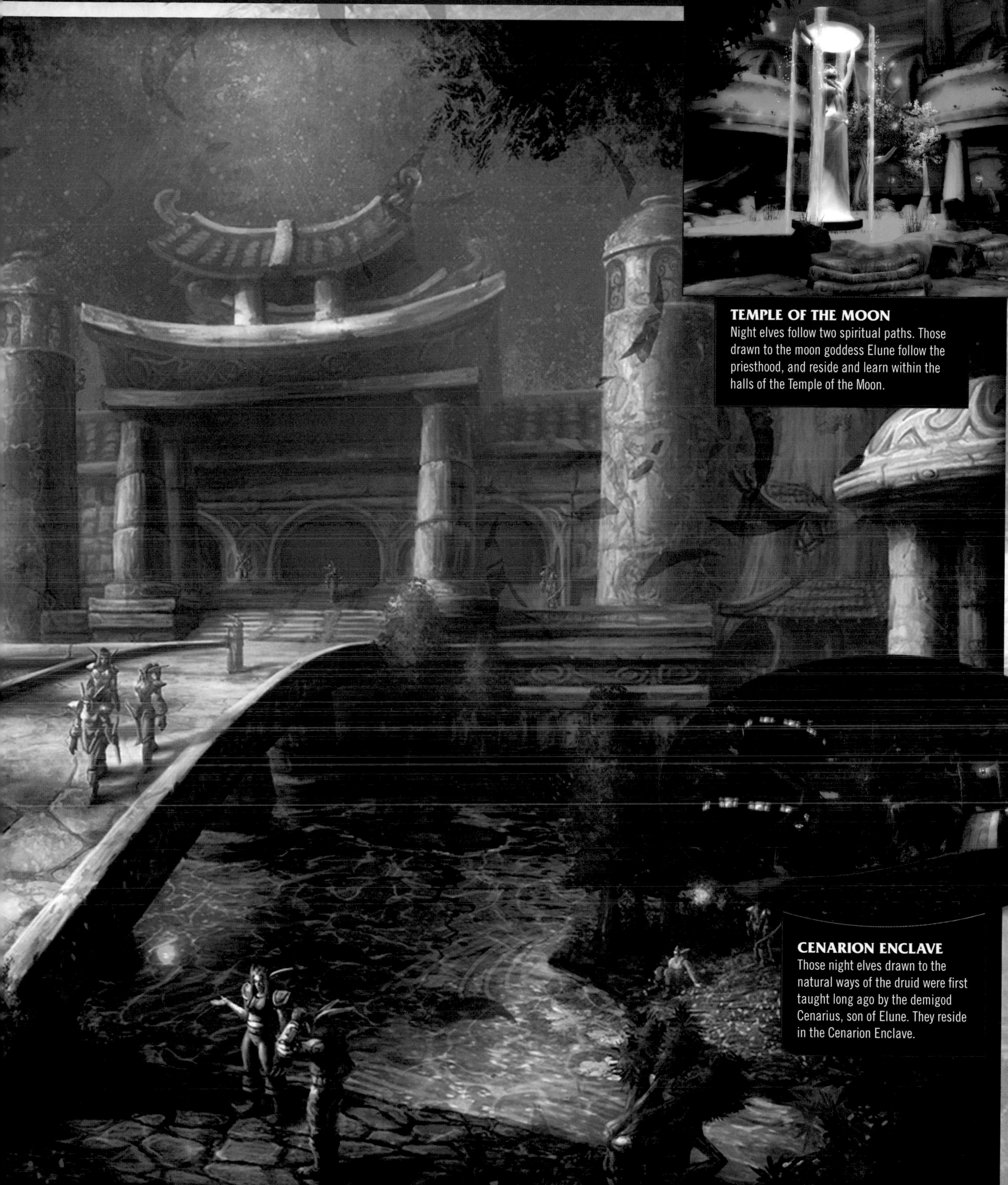

TEMPLE OF THE MOON

Night elves follow two spiritual paths. Those drawn to the moon goddess Elune follow the priesthood, and reside and learn within the halls of the Temple of the Moon.

CENARION ENCLAVE

Those night elves drawn to the natural ways of the druid were first taught long ago by the demigod Cenarius, son of Elune. They reside in the Cenarion Enclave.

Velen has led his people, the draenei, with foresight and wisdom for countless ages. Under his guidance, they fled their homeworld of Argus, seeking safety from the Burning Legion. Now, in the new land of Azeroth, Velen uses his gift of prophecy and his tempered knowledge to safeguard the Alliance from the forces of darkness.

THE PROPHET VELEN

"Where faith dwells, hope is never lost."

A CANDLE IN THE DARKNESS

The naaru are beings made of pure energy, with a deep affinity for the Light. They blessed the draenei with this power to aid them against their mutual sworn enemies, the Burning Legion.

Thousands of years ago, the eredar of Argus lived in tranquillity. The eredar's three strong leaders —Archimonde, Kil'jaeden, and Velen—ruled their people in harmony. But the achievements of the eredar gained the attention of the evil Sargeras, Destroyer of Worlds. When most of the populace turned to darkness under Sargeras' control, becoming demons, Velen (gifted with the power of prophecy) guided his followers off the planet with the help of the naaru. They fled Argus, taking the name draenei, "exiled ones." Their ship took them to a world they would name Draenor, where they encountered the orcs. Under siege by orcish forces controlled by the Burning Legion, Velen and the draenei were forced to take matters into their own hands and flee the world.

They captured an interdimensional transport, the Exodar, and traveled to Azeroth, where the ship crash-landed on Azuremyst Isle. Velen soon encountered members of the Alliance and, having previously heard tales of their virtue, hoped to gain their help against the Burning Legion. Velen now works to save the remnants of his people and guide the Alliance, taking Prince Anduin Wrynn under his wing to study the Light.

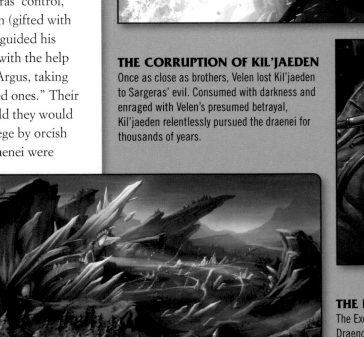

PROPHET OF THE LIGHT
Velen's gift of Sight warned him of the dangers of joining Sargeras. Granted a vision by K'ure—one of the naaru, a race of powerful beings dedicated to grace and altruism—Velen led his people off Argus.

THE CORRUPTION OF KIL'JAEDEN
Once as close as brothers, Velen lost Kil'jaeden to Sargeras' evil. Consumed with darkness and enraged with Velen's presumed betrayal, Kil'jaeden relentlessly pursued the draenei for thousands of years.

THE EXODAR
The Exodar is the ship that took the draenei from Draenor to Azeroth, where it crashed upon Azuremyst Isle. It has since been repaired, and is now fully capable of leaving Azeroth at any time. It currently serves as a gathering place and functional city for the draenei.

The Exodar Life-Staff serves as a focal point for Velen's magic and provides light to all who seek it.

KEY DATA

NAME Velen

GENDER AND RACE Male eredar

STATUS Living

AFFILIATION Alliance

TITLES Great Prophet, Ageless One

RELATIVES Unknown

Velen is gifted with the Sight, allowing him to see prophetic visions of the future. He also holds a deep spiritual connection to the Light, taught to him and his people by the enigmatic naaru.

A powerful variety of priest robe is named after Velen—Velen's Robes or Velen's Regalia—highlighting his great connection to the Light.

NOBLE CALLING

Once, Velen's driving goal was to combat the Burning Legion above all else. But, through his conversations with Prince Anduin Wrynn, he has reevaluated his beliefs. To Velen, every life is sacred and worthy of protection and care. The draenei's mission is now to heal the world.

DRAENEI

The draenei are former members of the eredar race who fled their homeworld of Argus rather than submitting to the corruption of the Burning Legion. They were assisted by the naaru, a race of sentient energy beings who blessed the draenei with Light-given knowledge and power. Heroes of the draenei stand as bastions of Light and purity, masters of arcane magic, intent on defending the world from the horrors of the Burning Legion.

VINDICATOR MARAAD

While living on Draenor, Maraad's sister was captured by orcs. Maraad never abandoned her memory, and discovered the existence of his niece—the assassin Garona Halforcen. Maraad searched for Garona for years, eventually arriving at Theramore and rescuing her. He worked on gaining her trust, eventually revealing her past and explaining that he was her uncle. Later, Maraad became one of the founding members of the New Council of Tirisfal. He was also instrumental in teaching Garona's son, Med'an, in the ways of the Light. In the war against the Lich King, Maraad served as a Vindicator in the Alliance Expedition. After the war's end, Maraad returned to the Exodar and discovered a group of human refugees seeking the Prophet's guidance. A riot ensued, and Maraad helped heal the injured after the riot was quelled. Maraad currently resides in the Exodar, ever-dedicated to the draenei and the Prophet's will.

KEY DATA

TITLES Member of the Valiance Expedition, Member of the New Council of Tirisfal
STATUS Living
AFFILIATION Alliance
RELATIVES Garona (niece); Med'an (grandnephew)

IRIDI

The draenei priestess Iridi and her close friend were both blessed by the naaru and given twin staves at the end of their training. After traveling to Azeroth together, Iridi's friend was later killed, and her staff stolen by a blood elf named Zendarin Windrunner. Iridi sought to retrieve her friend's staff, and traveled to Grim Batol to do so, where she encountered an unusual group of heroes. Kalecgos, Krasus, Rhonin, and Vereesa Windrunner were all trying to stop the black dragon Sintharia from creating a new Twilight dragonflight. Iridi attempted to free an imprisoned nether dragon named Zzeraku, who was slated to be devoured by Sintharia's ultimate creation, the twilight dragon Dargonax but was unable to. In order to destroy Dargonax, Iridi used all of her power, and that of her naaru-blessed staff, sacrificing her life in the process. She was buried in Outland, her last wish being to see her home once more.

KEY DATA

TITLE None
STATUS Deceased
AFFILIATION Alliance
RELATIVES None known

ISHANAH

Leader of the Aldor, an order of draenei priests, High Priestess Ishanah remained in Outland when Velen and his followers departed to Azeroth. She currently resides in Shattrath City, at the Shrine of Unending Light. As a devout believer in the Light and a venerated holy woman, Ishanah gives guidance and wisdom to her people. She also represents draenei interests in Alliance political matters when Velen is unavailable.

KEY DATA

TITLE High Priestess of the Aldor
STATUS Living
AFFILIATION Alliance
RELATIVES None known

FARSEER NOBUNDO

Nobundo was a paladin vindicator in the days when the orcs of Draenor were corrupted by the Burning Legion. When the draenei capital of Shattrath City came under attack, Nobundo was among its defenders. Yet Nobundo was one of many who were afflicted by a strange haze that the orcish invaders carried with them. Attacked by Grom Hellscream, Nobundo nearly perished as Shattrath City fell, but managed to escape. He and many of the other survivors underwent a physical transformation that cut them off from the Light, twisting their bodies into what the draenei called krokul, or "Broken." These Broken were banished by the draenei for fear that their condition might spread to the healthy. Haunted by nightmares of the horrors he witnessed in Shattrath, Nobundo desperately sought to reconnect with the Light as the other survivors descended into madness, one by one. Nobundo's pleas were at last answered not by the Light, but by the elements, who sought to teach the broken draenei the ways of the shaman, a practice abandoned by the orcs in favor of the dark arts of the Burning Legion. Nobundo worked tirelessly to learn and understand the lessons of the elements, mastering the shaman arts with surprising proficiency. After returning to the draenei, and with the blessing of the Prophet Velen, Farseer Nobundo began to teach his people the ways of the shaman, traveling to Azeroth with Velen and his followers. On Azeroth, Nobundo eventually joined the Earthen Ring, a shaman organization dedicated to studying and preserving the elements. Nobundo was instrumental in helping to heal the world after the Cataclysm, and has represented the draenei in Alliance affairs in Pandaria.

KEY DATA

TITLES Farseer, Emissary of the Elemental Spirits, High Shaman of the Earthen Ring
STATUS Living
AFFILIATION Alliance/Independent
RELATIVES None known

AKAMA

Akama was a priest at the Temple of Karabor on Draenor. When the orc Horde attacked, incited by the influence of the Burning Legion, Akama helped as many survivors as he could to flee to Shattrath City. When Shattrath City also fell, Akama was among those injured by the strange mist that the orcs carried, and he fell into a coma. When Akama awoke, he was cut off from the Light for good, transformed into one of the krokul, or Broken. Akama stealthily followed Nobundo, observing Nobundo's transformation into a shaman. When Akama witnessed Nobundo calling upon the power of the elements, it gave Akama the hope he needed. He began to form his own resistance movement, leading the Broken against any who stood in his way. He fought against the Burning Legion even as the pit lord Magtheridon took control of Outland. While fighting a losing battle against the pit lord, Akama was aided by Illidan's allies, the blood elf Kael'thas Sunstrider and the naga Lady Vashj. Grateful for the assistance, he and his followers, the Ashtongue Deathsworn, allied with Illidan, believing they could finally realize vengeance against the Legion. Nonetheless, Akama harbored doubts about his new master. Although assigned as the jailor of Maiev Shadowsong, Illidan's dedicated enemy, he stealthily worked with her. Eventually, Akama freed Maiev, and together they assaulted the former Temple of Karabor, now serving as Illidan's stronghold, the Black Temple. With Illidan's death, Akama swore to once again fill the halls of the Black Temple with Light.

KEY DATA

TITLES Leader of the Ashtongue Deathsworn, Leader of the Ashtongue Tribe, Jailor of Maiev Shadowsong
STATUS Living
AFFILIATION Independent (Neutral)
RELATIVES None known

THE EXODAR

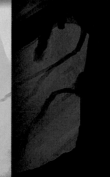

The Exodar is actually a cross-dimensional ship, originally part of Tempest Keep on the shattered world of Outland. The draenei used it to escape from Outland, but after it crash-landed on Azeroth the draenei re-purposed it to serve as their capital city while it was repaired. Filled with a complex array of technological and magical systems, the halls of the Exodar hold wonders beyond most Azerothians' wildest imaginations.

TEMPEST KEEP

The fortress Tempest Keep was created by the naaru, a powerful and benevolent race of inter-dimensional beings composed of pure energy. After the naaru arrived on Outland, Tempest Keep was left largely defenseless. It was later overrun by the blood elf forces of Prince Kael'thas Sunstrider, but the draenei were able to capture one wing of the fortress, the Exodar, using it to escape Outland.

BLESSED BY THE NAARU

The Exodar's power and sturdiness can be seen in how much of the ship remains intact, despite all it has been through. It traversed the Great Dark Beyond, and it withstood a fearsome battle between blood elves and draenei to control it. Although sabotaged by the blood elves, the Exodar largely survived its plummet from the skies into the forests of the Azuremyst Isle, off the coast of Kalimdor.

THE CRYSTAL HALL

SEAT OF THE NAARU

THE VAULT OF LIGHTS

TRADERS' TIER

CRYSTAL HALL
Crystals gathered in the Crystal Hall help to repair the Exodar. The hall is the training ground for many shaman, as well as home to elementals that can be seen only under the influence of Sapta Sight.

SEAT OF THE NAARU
The Seat of the Naaru within the Exodar is the city's central hub. It is the heart of draenei economic trade, and home to the naaru called O'ros.

THE VAULT OF LIGHTS
The Vault of Lights houses a holographic museum. A tour group periodically visits large, translucent displays of various monstrous creatures affiliated with the Burning Legion.

As King of Gilneas, Genn Greymane's unwavering commitment to his people's welfare has proved both a strength and a weakness. Genn and many of his constituents have become afflicted by a terrible curse. He now fights a battle to retain his followers' humanity.

GENN GREYMANE

"For too long I let my fear control me… Look upon me now, and see that which I have kept hidden. Now that you know the truth, I ask each of you… who will fight by my side?"

CONTROLLING THE BEAST WITHIN

Genn Greymane ordered Archmage Arugal to unleash the worgen on the Scourge, but in so doing, sealed the fate of his kingdom.

As a young man, Genn Greymane learned never to rely on others, a lesson he remembered when he became King of Gilneas. Seeing the destruction that the Second War wrought, he stubbornly believed that his people would be far better off without the Alliance of Lordaeron. He withdrew Gilneas and then constructed the massive Greymane Wall, both to protect his people and to isolate Gilneas from the outside world. Later, facing the threat of the undead Scourge assaulting the wall, Genn instructed the human Archmage Arugal to summon feral wolf-men called worgen to fight the Scourge. Though the Scourge were defeated, the worgen persisted, and began to attack the Gilneans as well, posing a new and even greater threat. Those bitten by worgen were cursed to become worgen themselves. The worgen affliction overwhelmed the Gilnean kingdom, and even Genn himself was stricken.

The Gilneans were still in the midst of recovering from a civil war, and the worgen attack forced them to evacuate their capital to the small city of Duskhaven. Yet those afflicted with the curse were not lost; a partial cure allowed sufferers to retain their sanity. Even as the Gilneans worked to overcome the curse and reclaim their capital, Horde forces attacked, and the Cataclysm crumbled the Greymane Wall. With the way into the kingdom reopened, the Horde armies, led by the Forsaken Queen Sylvanas Windrunner, rushed into the city. Genn launched a counterattack, but Sylvanas slew his son Liam. Faced with the loss of Gilneas, Genn accepted the help offered by the night elves, taking refuge in Darnassus and abandoning his beloved kingdom. In the wake of all the Gilneans have lost, Genn has pledged his people to the Alliance anew.

THE GREYMANE FAMILY
Genn and his wife, Mia, gave their children strong values, intelligence, and compassion. Their son, Liam, was killed during the Battle of Gilneas City, taking a poisoned arrow intended for his father. Their daughter Tess is now the kingdom's sole heir.

THE CURSE OF THE WORGEN
The worgen curse began thousands of years ago, when a sect of night elf druids assumed a new form that embodied the ferocious spirit of Goldrinn, the wolf Ancient. In an attempt to temper their fury, the night elves were transformed into worgen. Thousands of years later, a partial cure was found. With the help of an elixir devised by Krennan Aranas, a Gilnean alchemist, and the Ritual of Balance developed by the night elves, cursed Gilneans can now control their rage and retain their sanity while transformed.

THE NORTHGATE REBELLION
Genn's decision to sequester Gilneas was not without its opponents. Lord Darius Crowley (pictured left) violently opposed it, igniting a civil war throughout Gilneas. The rebellion was crushed and Genn imprisoned Crowley for treason. However, Genn later acknowledged his rashness. He freed Crowley and the two put aside their differences for the sake of the country.

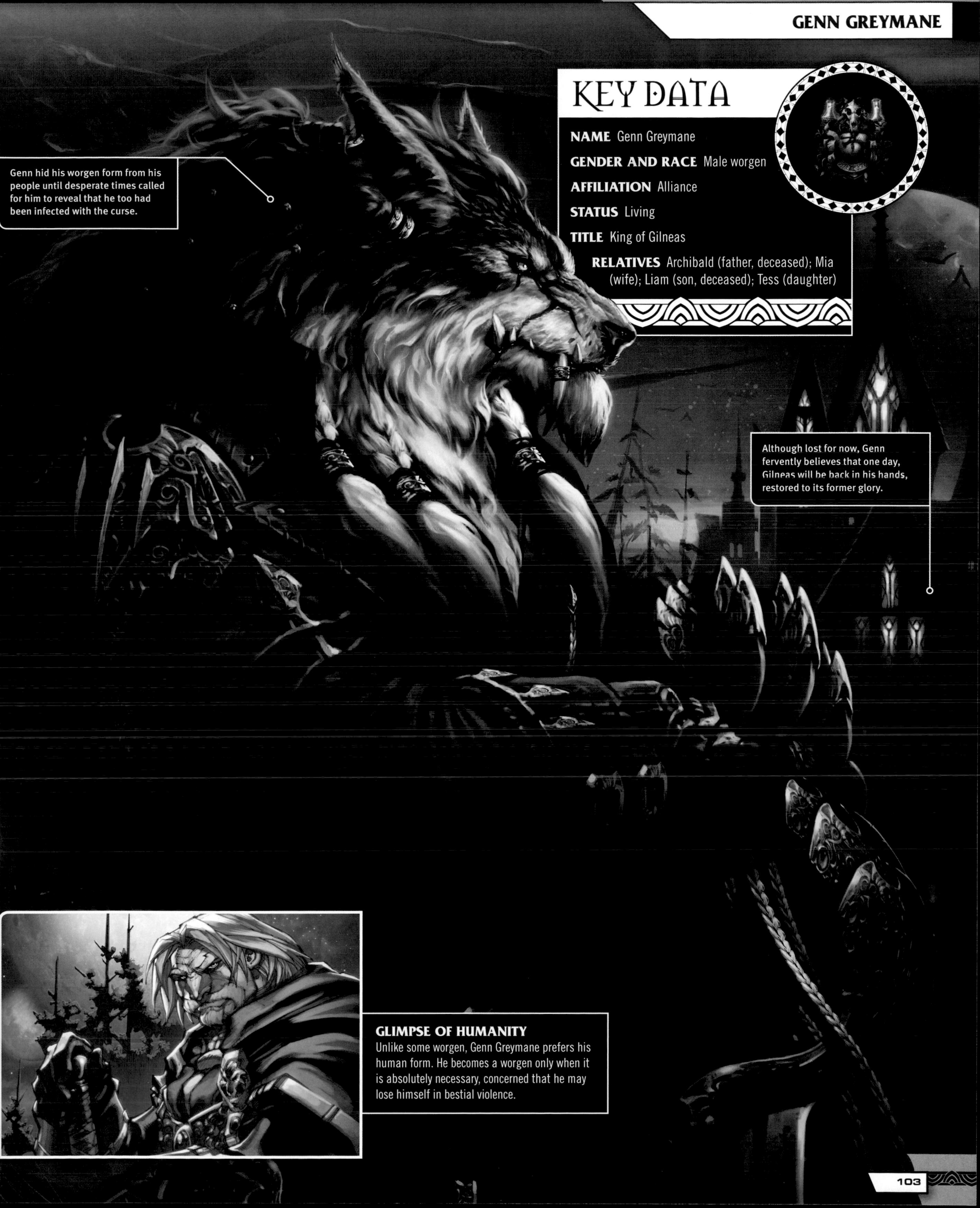

KEY DATA

NAME Genn Greymane

GENDER AND RACE Male worgen

AFFILIATION Alliance

STATUS Living

TITLE King of Gilneas

RELATIVES Archibald (father, deceased); Mia (wife); Liam (son, deceased); Tess (daughter)

Genn hid his worgen form from his people until desperate times called for him to reveal that he too had been infected with the curse.

Although lost for now, Genn fervently believes that one day, Gilneas will be back in his hands, restored to its former glory.

GLIMPSE OF HUMANITY
Unlike some worgen, Genn Greymane prefers his human form. He becomes a worgen only when it is absolutely necessary, concerned that he may lose himself in bestial violence.

WORGEN

The origins of the worgen date back to ancient times, when a renegade band of night elf druids sought to master the form of the wolf, using an artifact called the Scythe of Elune. The scythe was meant to restrain their rage when transformed, but instead they lost all control and became ravening worgen. Thousands of years later, they overran the kingdom of Gilneas, infecting its citizens and turning them into worgen as well.

DARIUS CROWLEY

KEY DATA

TITLES Leader of the Gilneas Liberation Front
STATUS Living
AFFILIATION Alliance, Gilneas, Gilneas Liberation Front
RELATIVES Lorna Crowley (daughter)

During the Second War, Lord Darius Crowley helped convince King Genn Greymane to give the Alliance of Lordaeron the support of Gilneas. As the dust settled from the Second War, Genn removed Gilneas from the Alliance and ordered the construction of the Greymane Wall, cutting off part of Darius' lands. Incensed by Genn's stubborn lack of support, Darius sent a small band of Gilneans to assist Lady Jaina Proudmoore during the Third War. Genn was furious and accused Darius of treason. Following a civil war, known as the Northgate Rebellion, Darius was imprisoned, however Genn later freed Darius and his rebels to assist in Gilneas' defense when the kingdom came under attack by feral worgen. Darius made a valiant stand at Light's Dawn Cathedral, but was attacked and transformed into a worgen himself. He subsequently worked with night elven allies to help other worgen tame their feral spirit. After the Cataclysm, Darius again joined forces with Genn—this time, to defend Gilneas from the Forsaken with the help of his daughter Lorna and the Gilneas Liberation Front. Darius later surrendered the city to the Forsaken in order to save his daughter.

GOLDRINN

Goldrinn is an Ancient, one of several demigods on Azeroth. Also called Lo'Gosh—or "Ghost Wolf" in Taur-ahe—he takes the form of a monstrously powerful white wolf, and embodies ferocity, savagery, and an unyielding will. Goldrinn was worshipped by the Druids of the Scythe, who helped create the Scythe of Elune using one of Goldrinn's fangs and the staff of Elune. They intended to use the scythe to tame their feral spirit, but were instead transformed into bestial, humanoid worgen.

KEY DATA

TITLES Demigod
STATUS Living
AFFILIATION Independent (Neutral)
RELATIVES None known

RALAAR FANGFIRE

Thousands of years ago, Ralaar Fangfire was an accomplished druid, able to transform into wolf or "pack" form. During the War of the Satyr, Ralaar sought to teach others to use pack form in order to win the war, forming the Druids of the Pack. However, Malfurion Stormrage forbade the form's use, citing its vicious nature and instability. Ralaar persisted, working to create the Scythe of Elune to try and temper the volatile nature of the form. Instead, he was transformed into the first of the worgen. He and his followers, now called the Druids of the Scythe, were eventually subdued by Malfurion and the druids of the Cenarion Circle. They were placed into perpetual sleep in the Emerald Dream. Thousands of years later, Ralaar was summoned back into Azeroth, but was killed trying to retrieve the Scythe of Elune.

KEY DATA

TITLES Alpha Prime, Leader of the Druids of the Pack
STATUS Deceased
AFFILIATION Adversarial
RELATIVES None known

LORNA CROWLEY

The daughter of Lord Darius Crowley, Lorna believes strongly in his ideals and echoes his heroism. Lorna remains uninfected by the worgen curse, but is a fierce fighter, distinguishing herself by leading forces of the Gilneas Liberation Front against the Forsaken invaders, helping to retake Gilneas City and destroying a Forsaken camp near the Greymane Wall. Later in the campaign, Lorna was captured by the treacherous Lord Godfrey, who had recently been risen as a Forsaken. Godfrey and the Forsaken leader, Sylvanas Windrunner, threatened to turn Lorna into a Forsaken if her father did not surrender. Darius acquiesced, and he, Lorna, and the remaining Gilneans fled toward Gilneas and escaped.

KEY DATA

TITLE Commander of the Gilneas Liberation Front
STATUS Living
AFFILIATION Alliance
RELATIVES Darius Crowley (father)

IVAR BLOODFANG

Ivar Bloodfang is the leader of the Bloodfang worgen of Silverpine Forest. When the Forsaken invaded Gilneas shortly after the Cataclysm, Lord Darius Crowley sought and successfully gained a tentative alliance with Ivar. The two united to defend Gilneas from the Forsaken armies. However, when Darius surrendered to the Forsaken in order to save his daughter Lorna, Ivar was incensed. Cursing Darius for his weakness, Ivar led his pack back to the contested lands of Gilneas. Currently, Ivar is very close to being a feral worgen. Although clever and willing to form alliances with others, he doesn't hesitate to use violence, brutality, and desperate measures to get what he wants. Although no longer impressed with Darius Crowley, Ivar still assists the Alliance and considers the Forsaken his blood enemies.

KEY DATA

TITLE Leader of the Bloodfang Pack
STATUS Living
AFFILIATION Alliance
RELATIVES None known

ADMIRAL RIPSNARL

James Harrington had a family and a successful naval career until he was infected with the worgen curse. One night, mad with bloodlust, he transformed into a worgen and killed his wife, daughter, and son. Abandoning his former life, James took the name Ripsnarl and fled into Westfall. He subsequently joined forces with the Defias Brotherhood and became one of their principle commanders. He died in the Deadmines, his thirst for blood finally ended.

KEY DATA

TITLE Admiral
STATUS Deceased
AFFILIATION Adversarial
RELATIVES Calissa (wife, deceased); Emme (daughter, deceased); Erik (son, deceased)

TOBIAS MISTMANTLE

An ally of Lord Darius Crowley, Tobias Mistmantle fought alongside Darius at Stoneward Prison. He was later infected with the curse when he and Darius were overrun by the worgen at Light's Dawn Cathedral. After fleeing from the Forsaken, Tobias sought what was left of his family, namely, his bloodthirsty brother, Stalvan. Tobias' efforts to determine the fate of Stalvan started an investigation, with the grim answer revealed at Manor Mistmantle: Stalvan had become an undead monster.

KEY DATA

TITLE None
STATUS Living
AFFILIATION Alliance
RELATIVES Stalvan Mistmantle (brother, deceased)

MARL WORMTHORN

Saddened by the devastation of the Tainted Scar in the Blasted Lands, the worgen druid Marl Wormthorn tried to use his arts to heal the land from its corruption by the Burning Legion. He planted a giant tree, called Maldraz, and focused his power upon it in a trance, hoping that nature could bring balance back to the land. Though Marl's power was impressive, Maldraz could only bring some vitality back to the region. And as the tree grew, it attracted the attentions of the demonic nathrezim, or dreadlords, that inhabited the Tainted Scar. The nathrezim crept into Marl's trance, tearing at his mind and using him as a weapon. Marl's intentions were good, but the nathrezim were too powerful for him. He was finally killed to prevent the Tainted Forest he had created from endangering the lives of others.

KEY DATA

TITLE None
STATUS Deceased
AFFILIATION Adversarial
RELATIVES None known

GILNEAS

Gilneas City, the capital of its kingdom, lies within the Eastern Kingdoms. In the days of the Alliance of Lordaeron, Gilneas was one of the most powerful kingdoms, but years of isolation have taken their toll. The cobblestoned streets and beautifully unique architecture of Gilneas were unlike anywhere else in the world. However, both the disastrous Cataclysm and Forsaken attacks have left the city deserted, for now.

KEEL HARBOR

Keel Harbor was the scene of the final evacuation of survivors from Gilneas. The Great Sea surrounds the Gilneas peninsula on three sides—storms from over the sea are common, and the sun rarely shines.

A DESERTED CITY

Gilneas was invaded by worgen during a desperate attempt to fend off a Scourge incursion. Many Gilneans were bitten and became worgen themselves. Following the Cataclysm and invasion by the Forsaken, the Gilneans fled their homeland. The night elves offered them refuge in Darnassus. Today, all that is left of Gilneas' capital city are partially buried ruins.

THE GREYMANE WALL

To enforce Gilneas' secession from the Alliance after the Second War and maintain the kingdom's isolation, King Genn Greymane ordered the construction of an enormous wall separating Gilneas from the rest of the world. The Greymane Wall toppled during the Cataclysm, revealing Gilneas to the world.

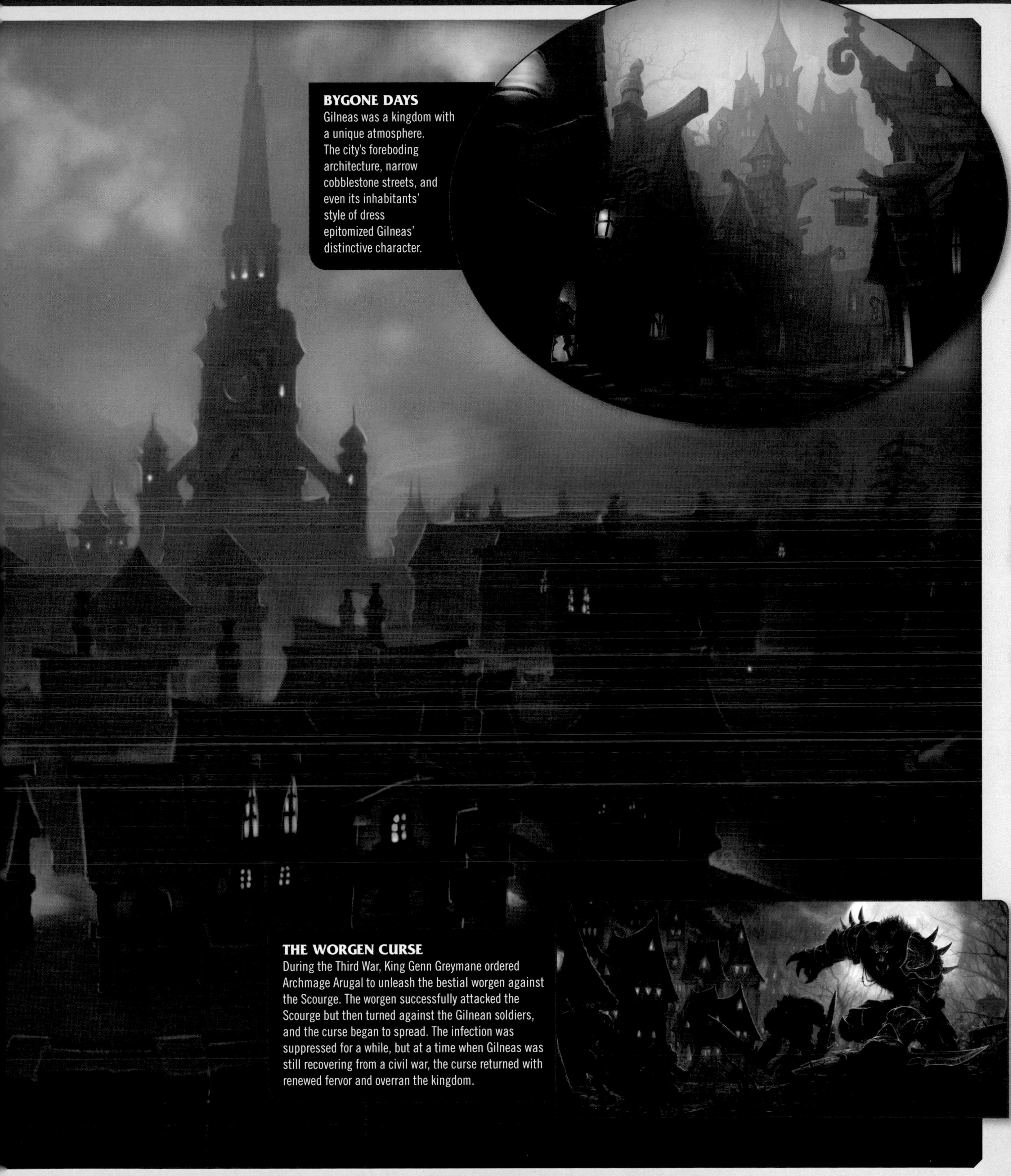

BYGONE DAYS

Gilneas was a kingdom with a unique atmosphere. The city's foreboding architecture, narrow cobblestone streets, and even its inhabitants' style of dress epitomized Gilneas' distinctive character.

THE WORGEN CURSE

During the Third War, King Genn Greymane ordered Archmage Arugal to unleash the bestial worgen against the Scourge. The worgen successfully attacked the Scourge but then turned against the Gilnean soldiers, and the curse began to spread. The infection was suppressed for a while, but at a time when Gilneas was still recovering from a civil war, the curse returned with renewed fervor and overran the kingdom.

ELVEN CONFLICT

Following the War of the Ancients, the night elves banished the surviving Highborne elves from the continent of Kalimdor for continuing to practice arcane magic. After crossing the Great Sea, they founded the kingdom of Quel'Thalas. There they abandoned worship of the moon, diminished in size, and lost the purple hue of their skin, becoming high elves. Millennia later, and the enmity between the night elves and high elves shows no sign of abating, their opposing allegiances acting as a catalyst for their ancient hatred.

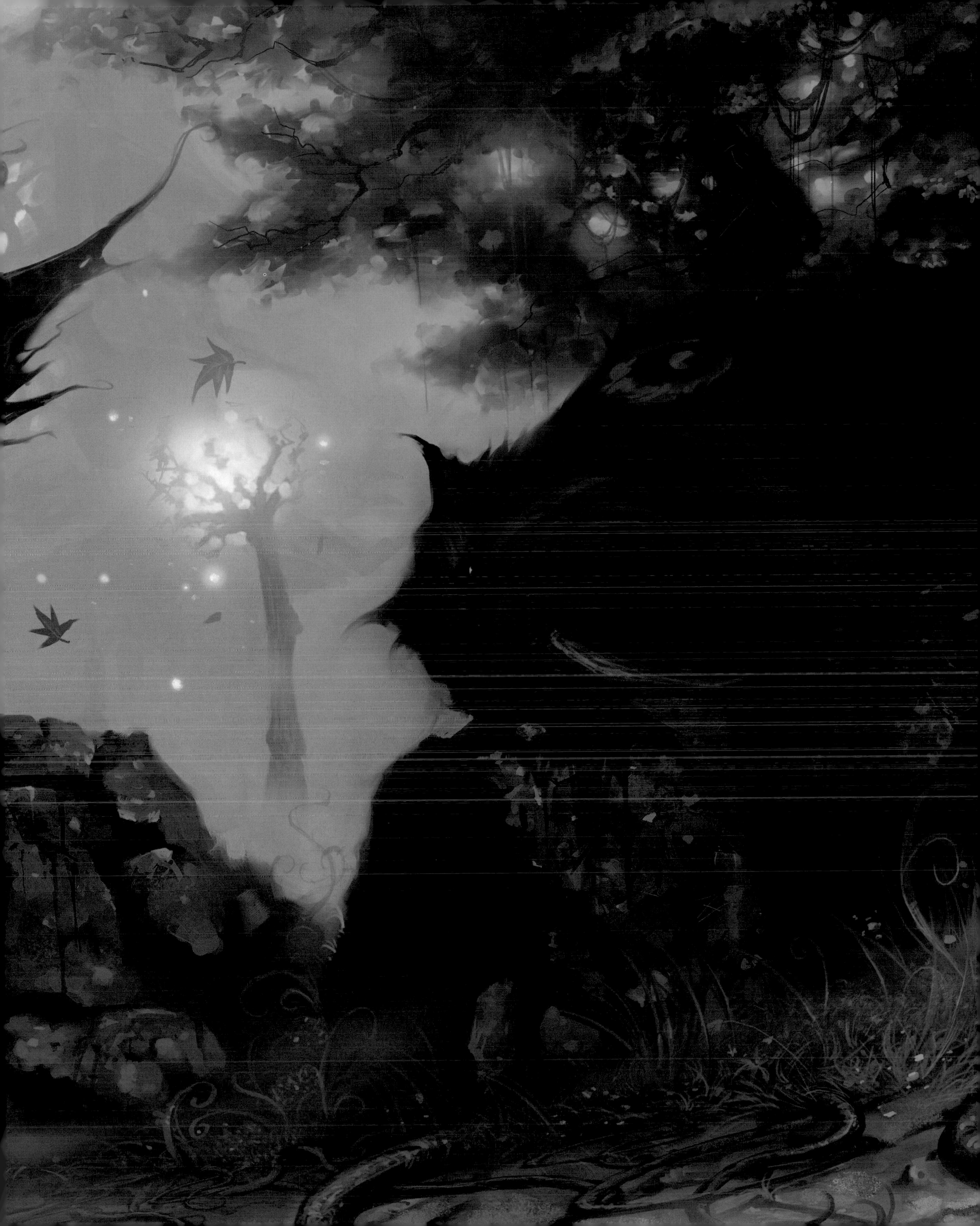

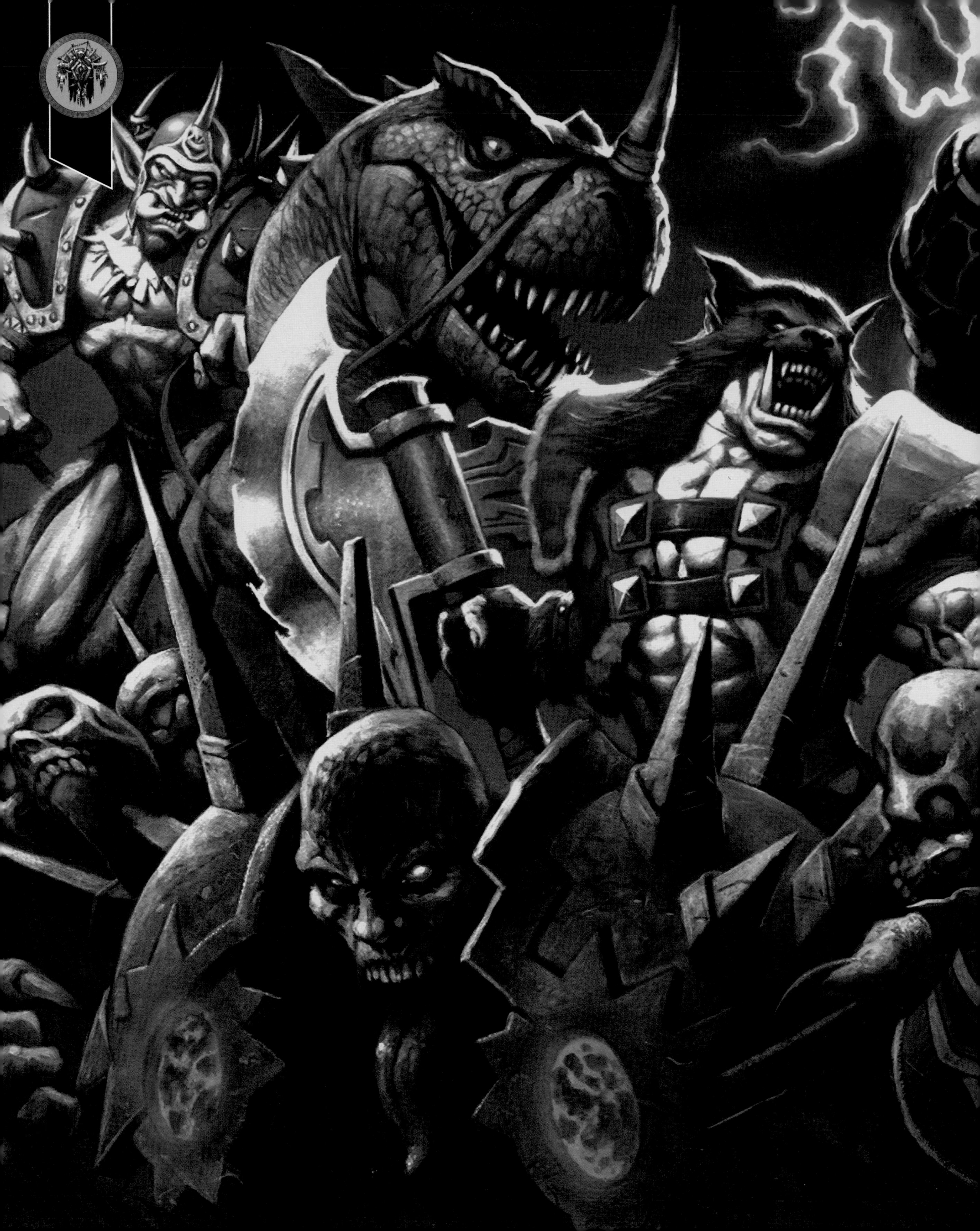

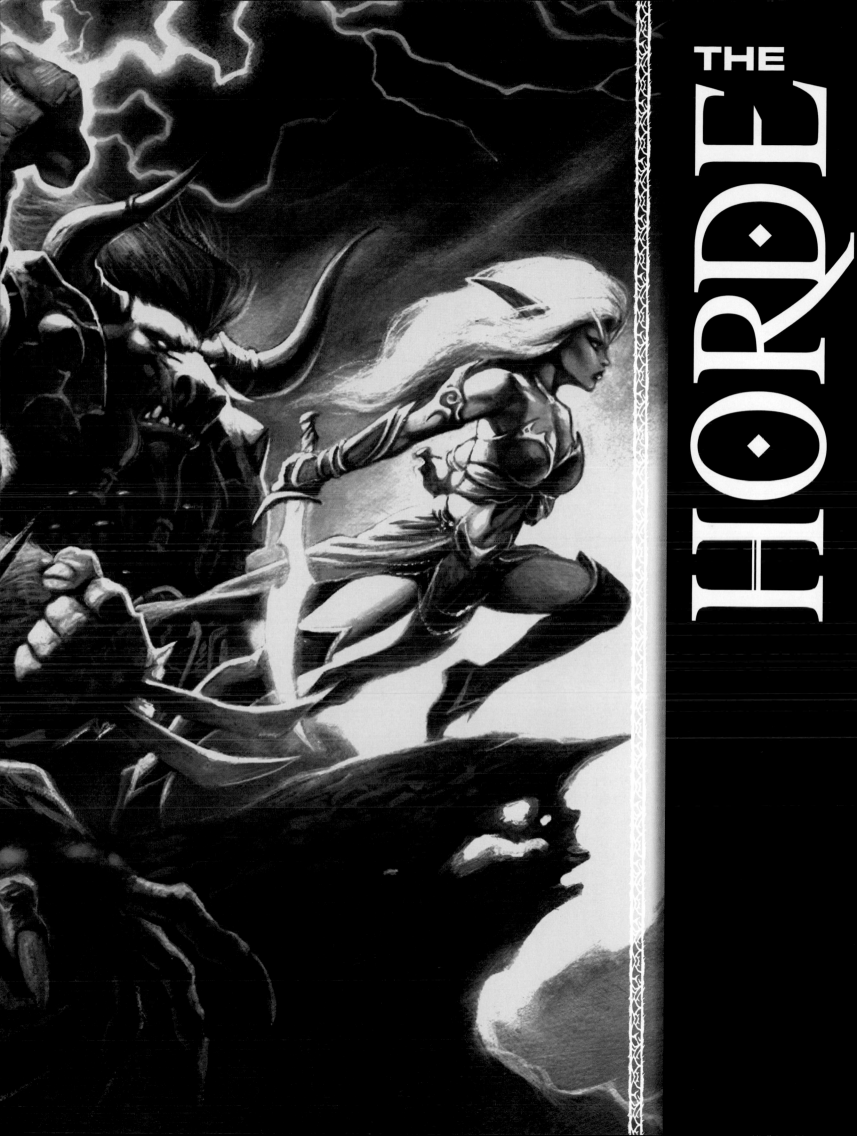

THE HORDE

THE HORDE

The Horde consists of a coalition of disparate races and cultures, working together to achieve prosperity and preserve their independence. While the Horde had its beginnings in Azeroth as an invasion force composed largely of orc clans, it has since grown and prospered with the addition of troll, tauren, Forsaken, blood elf, and goblin members. Honor, glory and a common strength of purpose hold the Horde together, inspiring them to fight for their survival in an unfriendly world.

> "WE FIGHT ON THIS DAY FOR OUR FALLEN BROTHERS AND SISTERS! THOUGH WE FACE GREAT CONFLICT, OUR MIGHT COMBINED SHALL OBLITERATE THOSE WHO WOULD OPPOSE US!"
>
> THRALL

STRENGTH AND SURVIVAL

The old Horde was first formed by the manipulations of the demon lord Kil'jaeden. Later, after being contacted by the sorcerer Medivh, the human Guardian of Tirisfal, the orc clans burst through the Dark Portal from the world of Draenor into Azeroth. Thus began two wars that ended with the defeat and internment of the orcs within Lordaeron. An orc named Thrall eventually freed them from captivity, and as the new warchief, led them across the sea to the continent of Kalimdor. Along the way, Thrall and the Horde made allegiances with other races, all seeking to survive in a harsh world. The varied races of this new Horde have all had their hardships, but the Horde represents a united force to be reckoned with, fighting against a world that forever seems to reject them.

ORCS

Originally led by Thrall, the Horde now takes its orders from orc Warchief Garrosh Hellscream. The primary capital of the Horde is the orc city of Orgrimmar, located in the harsh deserts of Durotar. Known for being both powerful and vicious fighters, the orcish race places particular value on strength both on and off the battlefield. Although orcish history is a long and painful one, the orcs of present day take great pride in their freedom. Under the iron rule of Warchief Hellscream, the orcs seek to crush their enemies and claim the land and resources that Hellscream believes they rightfully deserve.

TROLLS

The Darkspear tribe of trolls were once residents of the jungles of Stranglethorn Vale, cast out by their brethren and relocated to a series of remote islands off the coast. After Thrall helped the Darkspears deal with attacks by both murlocs in the service of the naga, and the Alliance, he offered them a place in the Horde, allowing them to claim a new homeland in the Echo Isles off the coast of Durotar. Led by Vol'jin, the Darkspears share many of the same spiritual beliefs as Thrall, and have proved themselves both cunning and clever allies that are fiercely devoted to the ideals of the Horde.

TAUREN

The tauren race were once nomads that roamed the plains of Kalimdor. Yet their enemies, the centaur, posed a constant threat—one that Thrall offered a solution to. With the Horde standing at their backs, the tauren have settled into their ancestral lands, building the capital city of Thunder Bluff and uniting the assorted tribes in one location. Although a new leader, High Chieftain Baine Bloodhoof quietly commands with respect, honor, and dignity. The tauren race may be one of spirituality, reverence for nature, and respect for elders, but it also possesses powerful warriors that willingly fight when the situation demands it.

FORSAKEN

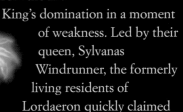

Originally part of the Scourge, the Forsaken broke free from the Lich King's domination in a moment of weakness. Led by their queen, Sylvanas Windrunner, the formerly living residents of Lordaeron quickly claimed the fallen kingdom for their own, dominating much of it. The Forsaken have a tenuous relationship with the Horde; while some look upon them with sympathy, others view them with trepidation. The Forsaken have shown themselves time and time again as a threat to be reckoned with, and their territory provides the Horde with a vital foothold in the Eastern Kingdoms.

BLOOD ELVES

Once members of the Alliance of Lordaeron, the high elves of Quel'Thalas were nearly wiped out by the Scourge invasion during the Third War. The Scourge razed the forests of Quel'Thalas, nearly destroyed the capital city of Silvermoon, and the source of the high elves' power, the Sunwell, was defiled. After their near extinction, Prince Kael'thas Sunstrider renamed the survivors blood elves, in remembrance of those fallen. Although the Sunwell was eventually restored, Kael'thas was revealed to be a traitor, allying himself with the Burning Legion. Yet despite the numerous tragedies of their past, the blood elves continue to stand strong and endure. Now led by Regent Lord Lor'themar Theron, the blood elves tenaciously seek to rebuild and restore their nation's past glory.

GOBLINS

The goblins of the Bilgewater Cartel made their home on the remote island of Kezan. When the Cataclysm ripped Azeroth apart, the goblins sought to flee, only to find themselves betrayed and imprisoned by their leader, Trade Prince Jastor Gallywix. While struggling to survive an attack by the secretive SI:7 branch of King Varian's forces and avoid capture, the goblins struck an accord with the Horde. They rescued the former warchief Thrall, who then helped foil Gallywix's plans and offered the goblins a place in the Horde with Gallywix at the helm— for now. Throwing aside their neutrality, the goblins of the Bilgewater Cartel have fully pledged their loyalty to the Horde in hopes of a mutually beneficial and profitable relationship.

Although small in size, goblins have proven to be ingenious, ruthless, and ultimately valuable allies.

A NEW HOME FOR THE HORDE

The roots of the Horde began on Draenor. There the orc clans were formed into an army for the Burning Legion, and manipulated by the warlock Gul'dan and his Shadow Council. The Old Horde clans that had invaded Azeroth collapsed at the end of the Second War. Those captured were placed in Alliance internment camps until Thrall, son of Durotan and eventual leader of the Frostwolf Clan, broke free of his enslavement and led the orcs to freedom as a new Horde. Thrall's vision of a greater destiny for his people led to their eventual arrival and settlement in Kalimdor. It also helped bring about the acceptance of new races into the Horde's ranks, including the tauren, trolls, Forsaken, blood elves, and goblins.

The new Horde owes its existence to Thrall, who escaped from human captivity and freed the orcs from internment camps.

"HONOR—NO MATTER HOW DIRE THE BATTLE, NEVER FORSAKE IT."

VAROK SAURFANG

The Blackrock clan once made its home deep underground in Blackrock Mountain. Today, many Blackrock orcs have been granted amnesty and joined the new Horde at the behest of Warchief Hellscream.

THE ORCISH CLANS

The orcish race stands as the backbone of the Horde. Originally, the orcs of Draenor were scattered into various clans, some with more notoriety than others. Many of these clans banded together under the banner of the Old Horde and participated in the invasion of Azeroth. When Warchief Thrall rose to power and brought about the new Horde, the clan system was by and large abolished. Although many orcs still proudly carry the name of their clan, the clans themselves are all united under the banner of one Horde. Notable clans in the Horde include the Frostwolf, the Warsong, the Shattered Hand, the Bleeding Hollow, and most recently, the Dragonmaw. There are some clans, however, that did not share Thrall's vision of a new Horde, and choose instead to follow their own, darker paths. Most notable of these is the Blackrock clan, who established their own base in Blackrock Mountain, led by Rend Blackhand.

NEW ALLIES

After being freed by Thrall from their internment, the orcs migrated across the Great Sea to Kalimdor, where they encountered many new races. The trolls and tauren in particular shared similar beliefs with Thrall's vision of the Horde. The Darkspear tribe of trolls, cast out from Stranglethorn Vale, were rescued by Thrall and evacuated from their hazardous island home. They shared many of the same beliefs as their orc rescuers. As for the tauren, they originally had their roots in nomadic tribes. And similar to Thrall's vision of a united Horde, Chieftain Cairne Bloodhoof sought to bring together the nomadic tribes of tauren and unite them in Mulgore.

The unification of these three races under one banner marked the beginning of the new face of the Horde. The Horde would later benefit from other members, including the undead Forsaken, blood elves, goblins, and Huojin pandaren. These alliances have gained the Horde additional territory in the Eastern Kingdoms and abroad as well as powerful arcane and technological advancements. No longer a bloodthirsty tool for the Burning Legion, Thrall's Horde was instead shaped to be a refuge, a safe haven dedicated to survival and prosperity—one that included any race that sought shelter from a harsh, unforgiving world.

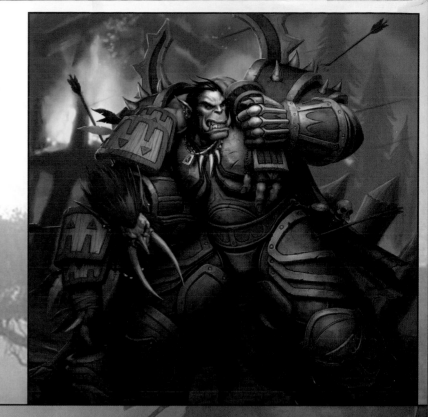

Several ogre clans are friendly with the Horde. These include the Stonemaul ogres of Dustwallow Marsh. In addition, the half-ogre Rexxar was accepted and subsequently became Champion of the Horde (above, right).

THE UNCORRUPTED

Years before Kil'jaeden came to Draenor and began his plans of manipulation, a disease called the red pox spread among the orc clans. Those infected were sent to Nagrand, where an internment village was quickly established and named Garadar. While the rest of the orcish race fell to the manipulation of the Burning Legion, those that were quarantined avoided corruption. Declaring themselves Mag'har, or "uncorrupted," these refugees from disparate orcish clans united under a banner of their own, one of proud tradition that held to the original shamanistic roots of the orc race. When the Dark Portal was reopened, these untainted survivors were discovered, much to Warchief Thrall's surprise. Among Garadar's residents were Thrall's grandmother, Geyah, and Garrosh Hellscream, son of Thrall's old friend, Grom.

Garrosh Hellscream was the first of the Mag'har to set foot in Orgrimmar, the capital of the orcs, after Thrall brought him back to Azeroth to serve as his advisor.

Captured and raised by humans, Thrall escaped and led his people to freedom. From his early days as a gladiator, he rose to embrace the life of a shaman and worked as a diplomat and leader. Thrall has worked tirelessly to safeguard his Horde brothers and sisters, but his sense of responsibility extends beyond his own kind.

THRALL (GO'EL)

"I straddle two worlds. I was raised by humans, but born an orc, and I have gleaned strength from both. I know both."

GUARDIAN OF THE ELEMENTS

Thrall wouldn't have escaped captivity without the intervention of his human friend, Taretha Foxton.

Thrall is the son of Durotan, the former chieftain of the Frostwolf clan of orcs. While he was still a baby, his parents were murdered on the orders of the warlock Gul'dan. Found and taken in by the human Aedelas Blackmoore, Thrall ("slave" in the human tongue) began his life in imprisonment, forced into gladiatorial combat. Thrall escaped with the help of Taretha Foxton—his friend from childhood. She was one of the few humans who taught him the meaning of honor and decency. Thrall then set out to find his true people. Thrall subsequently freed the orcs from slavery, becoming a shaman and then Warchief of the Horde. However, the threat of the Burning Legion remained in the orcs' lives. A prophecy convinced Thrall to bring the Horde across the Great Sea to the continent of Kalimdor. There, he helped to finally free the orcs from the Legion's damnation.

Since the day he became Warchief, Thrall has accomplished many feats: helping defeat the Burning Legion in the Third War, leading the many races of the Horde, reuniting with his ancestors on Outland, and finally, stepping down as Horde leader and joining the shaman of the Earthen Ring. When the great Cataclysm tore Azeroth apart, Thrall appointed Garrosh Hellscream as Warchief in his stead. Thrall worked to heal the wounded world, uniting with the great dragon Aspects and wielding the Dragon Soul to finally end Deathwing's life. In the dawn of the Age of Mortals, Thrall has taken a new role in teaching the young shaman of Azeroth and simply living in peace with his life-mate, Aggra, and his young son. A slave no longer, Thrall has embraced his destiny, and the name his parents intended him to bear: Go'el.

WARCHIEF OF THE HORDE
As Warchief of the Horde, Thrall embraced diplomacy, taking in the world's outcast, wayward races and uniting them under the proud banner of the Horde. In return, Thrall was known as a wise diplomat and an even wiser ruler.

DISCOVERING OLD BONDS
In Outland, Thrall discovered Garrosh Hellscream, one of the uncorrupted Mag'har and son of his old friend, Grom Hellscream (pictured right). Years before, Grom had sacrificed his life taking down the pit lord Mannoroth, freeing the orcs from the blood curse that bound them to the Burning Legion. Thrall returned to Azeroth with Garrosh as a new advisor. Years later, when Thrall stepped down, he appointed Garrosh his successor, which was widely regarded as a controversial decision.

THRALL'S BELOVED
Aggra, Thrall's life-mate, is a shaman of the Mag'har and member of the Earthen Ring. She was Thrall's mentor during his time in Outland and instrumental in his decision to rename (and renew) himself. Aggra and Thrall have a newborn son together.

KEY DATA

NAME Thrall (Go'el)

GENDER AND RACE
Male orc

AFFILIATION Horde, Earthen Ring

STATUS Living

TITLES Leader of the Earthen Ring, Warchief of the Horde (former), World Shaman, Chieftain of the Frostwolf clan (former)

RELATIVES Rhakish (maternal great-grandfather, deceased); Garad (paternal grandfather, deceased); Geyah (paternal grandmother); Kelkar (maternal grandfather, deceased); Zuura (maternal grandmother, deceased); Durotan (father, deceased); Draka (mother, deceased); Ga'nar (uncle, deceased); Aggra (mate); Durak (son)

Thrall's great wea... the Doomhammer, was passed on to him by the former Warchief, Orgrim Doomhammer. The image of a Frostwolf was later added to the weapon to denote Thrall's ties to the Frostwolf clan.

ARMOR OF THE WARCHIEF
Upon Orgrim Doomhammer's demise, Thrall immediately donned his black plate armor as the new Warchief of the Horde. He made sure to restore—but not replace—the back plate pierced by the lance that took Doomhammer's life.

When Thrall stepped down as Warchief in order to study the ways of the shaman, he cast aside his old armor, instead taking up garb more reflective of his new role.

As a shaman, Thrall bears a powerful tie to the elements: Air, Earth, Water, and Fire. He can call on them for assistance at a moment's notice.

Initially reluctant to accept power, Garrosh Hellscream has come to crave it. A Mag'har orc raised on tales of his father's shame, Garrosh lived under the shadow of his father's memory, afraid of his own darker urges. Now, as Warchief of the Horde, his rash behavior and brutality may lead him to repeat the mistakes of the past, especially regarding war with the Alliance.

GARROSH HELLSCREAM

"Live by these words: Lok-tar ogar. Victory… or death."

TEARS, BLOOD, AND WAR

Young Garrosh Hellscream was sent to live in Garadar after he contracted the red pox. While the orcs of Garadar proudly took the name Mag'har, "uncorrupted" in the orcish tongue, Garrosh was tormented by tales of his father, Grom Hellscream. Grom was the first to willingly drink the blood of Mannoroth and bind himself in servitude to the Burning Legion, the rest of the orcs eagerly following his lead.

By drinking the blood of the Pit Lord Mannoroth, the orcs were bound to the Burning Legion. Grom Hellscream initiated this Blood Curse, but he ended it when he killed Mannoroth.

Garrosh feared that he, too, would lead the Mag'har down a dark path. Sullen and withdrawn, it wasn't until Warchief Thrall came to his clan and showed him Grom's later heroic deeds that Garrosh was convinced he could be a leader himself.

When Thrall stepped down as Warchief, he appointed Garrosh in his stead, a position Garrosh was reluctant to take. Not all Horde leaders supported Thrall's decision. When High Chieftain Cairne Bloodhoof challenged Garrosh to a duel, it ended in Cairne's death, an incident that foreshadowed events to come. Garrosh's relentless thirst for power at any cost moves even stalwart Horde figures to second-guess their allegiances, but Garrosh dismisses them as cowards and weaklings. Garrosh's mandate is simple: every man, woman, and child is to aid in the fight against the Alliance, and any found shirking their duties will face his wrath.

RELUCTANT WARRIOR
Although a powerful fighter, Garrosh felt ashamed of his father's failure. But Warchief Thrall showed him the truth in Outland; while Grom was the first of the orcs to drink the pit lord's blood, his heroic effort to kill Mannoroth was the deed that freed them all. Later, after Garrosh took part in the Horde's war against the Lich King, Thrall gave him Grom's legendary axe, Gorehowl.

A FATEFUL DUEL
Cairne Bloodhoof challenged Garrosh to a duel, but Garrosh's weapon was poisoned—without his knowledge. This treachery sealed Cairne's fate. Rival tauren leader Magatha Grimtotem perpetrated the deceit, and she earned Garrosh's hatred for robbing him of an honorable fight.

WARCHIEF OR TYRANT?
Garrosh is now ruler of the Horde, but he is consumed with amassing power and glory. He particularly desires the suffering and eventual death of King Varian Wrynn, complete with a blood-soaked and triumphant war with the Alliance.

KEY DATA

NAME Garrosh Hellscream

GENDER AND RACE
Male orc

AFFILIATION Horde

TITLE Warchief of the Horde, Overlord of the
Warsong Offensive

RELATIVES Grom Hellscream (father, deceased)

Garrosh's shoulder
armor was made from
Mannoroth's tusks.

Grom Hellscream wielded the great
axe, Gorehowl, when he killed
Mannoroth. Thrall salvaged it and
bestowed it on Garrosh.

SYMBOL OF BLOOD AND POWER
Mannoroth's skull hangs over Garrosh's throne. This
honors his father, but Garrosh is also stealing glory for
himself. He is unaware that he is in the shadow of evil.

ORCS

Orcish history is entrenched in the ways of shamanism, but also in ferocity and raw strength. Although coerced into servitude by the Burning Legion, the orcs have since freed themselves. Notable orcish heroes are bastions of strength, those who fought and still relentlessly fight on for honor, glory, and the Horde.

AGGRA

Aggra was one of the Mag'har living in Garadar. An accomplished shaman and Greatmother Geyah's student, Aggra was chosen to teach Thrall the ways of the shaman when he traveled to Nagrand. Although irritated that Thrall still clung to a name that means "slave," she found herself warming to him. Aggra traveled back to Azeroth at his side, joining the Earthen Ring and helping to heal Azeroth. When Thrall's spirit was ripped asunder by Majordomo Fandral Staghelm, Aggra did not abandon him, seeking out the scattered aspects of his spirit and, with help from many heroes, saving him. After his recovery, they were wed. Aggra now has an infant son and continues to offer her support, wisdom, and strength to Thrall—now called Go'el, as his parents intended.

"Go'el, as long as you have this great heart to lead—and to love—then know that I will go with you to the ends of any world and beyond."

KEY DATA

TITLE Shaman of The Earthen Ring
STATUS Living
AFFILIATION Independent
RELATIVES Durotan (father-in-law, deceased); Draka (mother-in-law, deceased); Garad (grandfather-in-law, deceased); Geyah (grandmother-in-law); Sarrak (maternal grandmother, deceased); Ryal (mother); Thrall (Go'el, husband); Durak (son)

DRAKA

KEY DATA

TITLE Warrior of the Frostwolf Clan
STATUS Deceased
AFFILIATION (Old) Horde, Independent
RELATIVES Kelkar (father, deceased); Zuura (mother, deceased); Durotan (mate, deceased); Go'el (Thrall, son); Rhakish (paternal grandfather, deceased); Garad (father-in-law, deceased); Geyah (mother-in-law); Ga'nar (brother-in-law, deceased); Aggra (daughter-in-law); Durak (grandson)

Draka was born small and weak. Ostracized by the Frostwolf clan, she went on a quest to find ingredients for a cure, gaining her warrior skills and self-confidence. These won her the attentions of Durotan, and the two were wed. Draka stood at Durotan's side when he refused to drink the blood of pit lord Mannoroth, and later when he realized that the Horde was being tricked by orc warlock Gul'dan. Durotan, Draka, and their son, Go'el, visited Horde lieutenant Orgrim Doomhammer to reveal Gul'dan's treachery. On their way home, Draka and Durotan were killed by Gul'dan's spies, and their son left for dead.

DUROTAN

Durotan, Chieftain of the Frostwolf clan, was a warrior gifted with great foresight and wisdom. He spoke up against Gul'dan and Warchief Blackhand before the First War started, and he and his friend, Orgrim Doomhammer, refused to drink the tainted blood of Mannoroth, which bound the orcs to the Burning Legion. When the orcs passed through the Dark Portal and invaded Azeroth, Durotan and the Frostwolves were exiled by Gul'dan. Afterward, Durotan learned that Gul'dan was using the Horde as a tool for the Burning Legion, and traveled with his wife and son to warn Orgrim. Gul'dan's agents responded by murdering Durotan and his mate, Draka; their infant son, Go'el, was presumed dead.

KEY DATA

TITLE Chieftain of the Frostwolf Clan
STATUS Deceased
AFFILIATION (Old) Horde, Independent
RELATIVES Ga'nar (brother, deceased); Kelkar (father-in-law, deceased); Zuura (mother-in-law, deceased); Garad (father, deceased); Geyah (mother); Draka (mate, deceased); Go'el (Thrall, son); Durak (grandson)

GARONA HALFORCEN

Garona Halforcen was the product of the warlock Gul'dan's breeding experiments. Half orc, half draenei, Garona was magically aged and tortured, eventually being ensorcelled by Gul'dan and forced to serve his Shadow Council as an assassin. When the Dark Portal opened, Garona was used as a liaison to the human race. While on Azeroth, Garona was surprised to find herself growing close to the human sorcerer Medivh. Also surprising was the reception of King Llane Wrynn of Stormwind, who treated Garona with respect and kindness. Later, Garona was magically compelled to assassinate King Llane, then captured and tortured by Warchief Doomhammer, to whom she revealed the location of the Shadow Council. After escaping, she bore Medivh a son named Med'an. Years after the First War, Garona and Med'an were found by the ogre Cho'gall, Gul'dan's protégé. Cho'gall coerced Garona into trying to assassinate King Varian Wrynn, and kidnapped Garona's son. Garona's efforts were thwarted, and her son rescued. Garona helped to hunt down Cho'gall; her years of servitude ended with his death.

KEY DATA

TITLE None
STATUS Living
AFFILIATION Horde; Independent (neutral)
RELATIVES Maraad (uncle); Medivh (lover, deceased); Med'an (son)

GROM HELLSCREAM

KEY DATA

TITLE Chieftain of the Warsong Clan
STATUS Deceased
AFFILIATION (Old) Horde
RELATIVES Garrosh (son)

Grom Hellscream was the leader of the Warsong clan. He was the first to drink the blood of the pit lord Mannoroth and unwittingly pledge himself to the Burning Legion, leading others to follow his example. After the Dark Portal closed, Grom realized his mistake. When Thrall escaped from the internment camps, he received both shelter and wisdom from Grom. Grom became one of Thrall's most trusted advisors, throwing his support behind the new warchief. Yet Grom's lust for power cost him dearly. In Kalimdor, he once again drank the blood of Mannoroth in order to kill the demigod Cenarius. Freed of the demon's control by orc shaman and elven priests marshaled by Thrall, Grom then sought out Mannoroth. With Thrall at his side, his last act was to kill Mannoroth, but at the cost of his own life. His heroic sacrifice freed the orcs from the Burning Legion for good. Years later, Grom's son, Garrosh, became Horde warchief.

ORGRIM DOOMHAMMER

Warchief Orgrim Doomhammer's legacy is one of strength, pride, and blood. He was close friends with Durotan, and his battle prowess made him Warchief Blackhand's trusted lieutenant. However, Orgrim never drank the tainted blood of Mannoroth that bound the orcs to the Burning Legion. He also never trusted Blackhand's supporter, Gul'dan. When Gul'dan lapsed into a coma, Orgrim took the opportunity to kill Blackhand and claim the title of warchief. He then took Gul'dan prisoner, slaughtering most of Gul'dan's Shadow Council. Yet Orgrim was no friend to humanity, and he led the orcs to victory in the First War.

At the end of the Second War, Orgrim killed Commander Anduin Lothar. Anduin's second-in-command, Turalyon, then defeated Orgrim in single combat and captured him, but he soon escaped and led a resistance movement. During this time, Orgrim met Thrall, Durotan's lost son, long thought dead. Battling together to free the orcs from the Lordaeron internment camps, Orgrim took a mortal wound in the back. He named Thrall his successor as warchief, giving Thrall his weapon, the Doomhammer, and black plate armor. He died knowing that Thrall would defend his people and their ideals.

KEY DATA

TITLE Warchief of the Horde, Chieftain of the Blackrock Clan
STATUS Deceased
AFFILIATION (Old) Horde
RELATIVES Telkar (father, deceased)

ORCS

GREATMOTHER GEYAH

Once the mate of the Frostwolf chieftain Garad, Geyah sought to care for those suffering from the red pox plague, establishing a quarantine village that she named Garadar, after her late husband. Because of their sickness, these orcs were never part of the old Horde, later taking the name Mag'har, or "uncorrupted." After the Mag'har joined the new Horde, Geyah joyfully reunited with her grandson Thrall, finally telling him the name his parents had intended him to have: Go'el. Later, Geyah arranged for her student, Aggra, to help teach Thrall the true ways of the shaman.

KEY DATA

TITLE Spiritual leader of the Mag'har
STATUS Living
AFFILIATION (New) Horde
RELATIVES Garad (mate, deceased); Durotan (son, deceased); Ga'nar (son, deceased); Draka (daughter-in-law, deceased); Thrall (Go'el, grandson); Aggra (granddaughter-in-law); Durak (great-grandson)

EITRIGG

Eitrigg served the Horde during the First and Second Wars. He left his people after learning of Gul'dan's betrayal. Years later, he encountered the human paladin Tirion Fordring. Although the two fought, Eitrigg ended up saving Tirion's life. Eitrigg was later captured by the Alliance and sentenced to death, but he was saved by Tirion and Thrall's forces of the new Horde. Since that time, he has been Thrall's loyal advisor and supporter. Although cautious of the new Warchief Hellscream's motives and actions, he tries to advise the warchief and guide him away from repeating the mistakes of the past.

KEY DATA

TITLE Advisor to Warchief Thrall and Garrosh Hellscream
STATUS Living
AFFILIATION Horde (Old and New)
RELATIVES Ariok (son)

MALKOROK

Once a member of the Blackrock clan, Malkorok has now sworn allegiance to Garrosh Hellscream and the Horde. He believes that anyone who questions Garrosh should be executed and that the entire Horde should be watched for signs of treason. As Garrosh becomes more tyrannical, the only issue that Malkorok has is that Garrosh is not ruthless enough.

KEY DATA

TITLE Leader of the Kor'kron
STATUS Living
AFFILIATION (New) Horde
RELATIVES None known

KILROGG DEADEYE

The cunning leader of the Bleeding Hollow clan, Kilrogg fought in the First and Second Wars, evading capture by the Alliance. He then returned to Draenor and served Ner'zhul, helping the old shaman to recover ancient artifacts on Azeroth in order to further Horde invasions of new worlds. Slowing the Alliance forces to help Ner'zhul escape, Kilrogg was killed by Danath Trollbane. Kilrogg's tenacity survives in his son, Jorin Deadeye.

KEY DATA

TITLE Chieftain of the Bleeding Hollow Clan
STATUS Deceased
AFFILIATION (Old) Horde
RELATIVES Jorin (son)

DREK'THAR

Born blind, Drek'Thar became a great shaman and seer of the Frostwolf clan. As the Burning Legion began to corrupt the orcs, the elements turned away from Drek'Thar, leading the shaman to pursue the dark arts of the warlock. He was responsible for the deaths of countless draenei, something that still haunts him. When the Frostwolf clan was exiled by Gul'dan after invading Azeroth, Drek'Thar saw the error of his ways, renouncing the dark arts and again taking up the path of shamanism. After Durotan's death, Drek'Thar became leader of the Frostwolves. He later trained Durotan's son, Thrall, in the ways of the shaman, and fully supported Thrall's rise to warchief.

KEY DATA

TITLES Frostwolf General, Elder Shaman
STATUS Living
AFFILIATION Horde (Old and New)
RELATIVES None known

VAROK SAURFANG

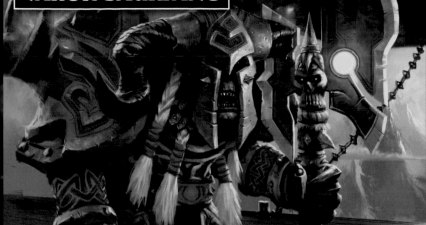

A veteran of the First, Second, and Third Wars, Varok Saurfang regrets the brutal acts he committed as part of the old Horde. Varok served as supreme commander of the united Might of Kalimdor, rallying the army against the forces of the qiraji during their resurgence in Silithus. Years later, Varok lost his beloved son, Dranosh, during the war against the Lich King in Northrend. Varok subsequently remained in Northrend as leader of the Horde forces there.

KEY DATA

TITLES High Overlord of the Kor'kron Guard, Supreme Commander of the Might of Kalimdor
STATUS Living
AFFILIATION Horde (Old and New)
RELATIVES Dranosh (son, deceased); Broxigar (brother, deceased); Thura (niece)

DRANOSH SAURFANG

Dranosh Saurfang (also called Saurfang the Younger) was a strong believer in the ideals of honor espoused by his father Varok. As a youth, he was sent to Garadar to avoid the corruption that tainted the rest of the orcish race. He grew up as one of the Mag'har, later reuniting with his father and returning to Azeroth. Dranosh was the commander of the Kor'kron Vanguard that fought at the Battle of Angrathar the Wrathgate. He was killed there by the Lich King, and his soul was consumed by the Lich King's sword, Frostmourne. His corpse was taken to Icecrown Citadel by the Scourge. There, he was raised as a powerful death knight and tasked with barring the way to the Lich King. After his ultimate defeat, Dranosh's body was sorrowfully claimed by Varok and returned to Nagrand.

KEY DATA

TITLES Commander of the Kor'kron Vanguard, Deathbringer
STATUS Deceased
AFFILIATION (New) Horde, Scourge
RELATIVES Varok (father); Broxigar (uncle, deceased); Thura (cousin)

BLACKHAND

A brutal tyrant, Blackhand the Destroyer was the first warchief of the Horde. He was put into power by Gul'dan, who easily manipulated him to control the Horde. He was finally murdered by his subordinate, Orgrim Doomhammer, who became the next warchief. His sons Rend and Maim created a new Dark Horde but it was defeated; their subsequent deaths marked the end of the Blackhand line.

KEY DATA

TITLES The Destroyer, Warchief of the Horde, Chieftain of the Blackrock Clan
STATUS Deceased
AFFILIATION (Old) Horde
RELATIVES Urukal (mate, deceased); Griselda (daughter, deceased); Rend (son, deceased); Maim (son, deceased)

BROXIGAR

Broxigar was a proud orc veteran of the First, Second, and Third Wars. While investigating a strange temporal disturbance, Broxigar was sent back in time to the War of the Ancients, with the human mage Rhonin, and the mage Krasus (the elven guise of the red dragon Korialstrasz). Broxigar was captured by the night elves, but escaped with the help of Tyrande Whisperwind and Malfurion Stormrage. He joined Tyrande and Malfurion in their fight against the Burning Legion, using a wooden axe crafted by Malfurion and blessed by Cenarius to tear through the demonic armies. In the final moments of the war, Brox leapt through a portal to the Twisting Nether in a heroic attempt to delay Sargeras' arrival on Azeroth. Brox finally came face to face with the leader of the Burning Legion. Broxigar was killed, but he managed what most thought impossible: he wounded Sargeras, slicing him in the leg. Broxigar's heroism lives on. His axe was reclaimed and was later passed on to his niece, Thura.

NAZGREL

Nazgrel was liberated from an orc internment camp in Lordaeron by Thrall after the Second War. Since then, he has become one of Thrall's most trusted advisors. Although he distrusts and dislikes the Alliance, his loyalty compels him to support Thrall's diplomatic efforts. He currently commands the Horde forces of Thrallmar in Hellfire Peninsula.

KEY DATA

TITLES Overseer of Thrallmar, Advisor to Warchief Thrall
STATUS Living
AFFILIATION (New) Horde

KEY DATA

TITLES The Red, The Red Axe
STATUS Deceased
AFFILIATION Horde (Old and New)
RELATIVES Varok Saurfang (brother); Dranosh Saurfang (nephew, deceased); Thura (niece)

ORGRIMMAR

F ounded by the former Warchief Thrall, Orgrimmar is the capital city of the orcs and a central gathering point for the Horde. This vast city was designed to be a welcoming meeting place for every Horde faction, but its defensive location and imposing iron and stone buildings emphasize Orgrimmar's martial focus.

RAGEFIRE CHASM

The Horde overcame subjugation by the Burning Legion many years ago, but issues with corrupting forces continue. Some orcs, such as those who reside within the Ragefire Chasm beneath Orgrimmar, appear to desire a return to those dark times.

FORTRESS OF THE HORDE

Orgrimmar is the central hub and heart of the Horde. Connected to all major Horde cities, it also houses small subdivisions for tauren, troll, and goblin residents. Many parts of Orgrimmar were damaged during the Cataclysm. When Garrosh Hellscream assumed leadership of the Horde, he instituted an enormous redesign intended to fortify the city. New areas were opened to settlement, and existing structures were moved or repurposed. Orgrimmar became a more militant city, with imposing architecture and an increasingly aggressive attitude toward the world.

THE VALLEY OF WISDOM

THE VALLEY OF HONOR

THE DRAG

THE VALLEY OF SPIRITS

THE VALLEY OF STRENGTH

IRON AND STONE

Originally a far more primitive city, the redesign of Orgrimmar was done with protection, safety, and fortification in mind. The new buildings are built from iron and stone, far less susceptible to fire and more easily defended against attack.

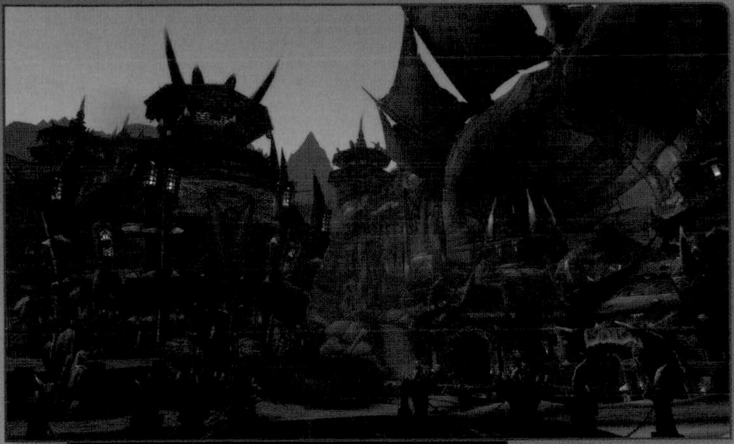

THE VALLEY OF STRENGTH

Orgrimmar's front gates open into the Valley of Strength, the city's main area. In addition to being Orgrimmar's central economic hub, the valley also contains Grommash Hold, a military fortress that also serves as the ruling Warchief's residence.

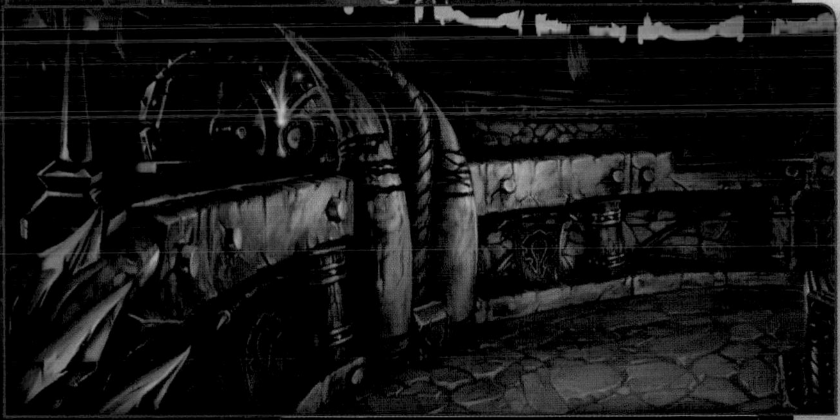

THE RING OF VALOR

The Valley of Honor is dedicated to military pursuits. It contains the Ring of Valor, an arena where gladiators compete for acclaim. A path from the Valley of Honor leads out of the city to the new home of the goblins, Azshara.

Baine Bloodhoof always looked to his father, Cairne, as a role model. Now that Cairne is dead, Baine attempts to follow in his footsteps. While Baine has formidable skill on the battlefield, his true talents lie in the arena of diplomacy. He is a strong force for moderation, calm wisdom, and unity within the Horde, especially in their dealings with the Alliance.

BAINE BLOODHOOF

"Even in the darkest hour, we will bravely hold our heads high, and honor the Earth Mother in all we do."

AS HIS FATHER BEFORE HIM

Vol'jin, leader of the Darkspear trolls, respects Baine. Both prefer talking to fighting. Vol'jin knows that Baine always supports what is best for the Horde, even in difficult circumstances.

Years ago, Baine Bloodhoof was captured by vicious centaurs and rescued by the Horde Champions Rexxar, Rokhan, and Chen Stormstout. When he was returned to his overjoyed father Cairne, Chieftain of the Bloodhoof Tribe, Cairne formally pledged his tribe to the Horde. Baine soon assumed greater responsibilities, assisting Cairne while learning to be a leader himself. He excelled in diplomatic situations and finding nonviolent solutions to disputes. When Cairne was killed in a fateful duel with Garrosh Hellscream, it was discovered that the Grimtotem clan had poisoned Garrosh's weapon. After the Grimtotem took over Thunder Bluff in a coup, Baine led an offensive, exiling their leader, Magatha, and allowing only those who renounced their loyalty to Magatha to stay. The battle against the Grimtotems would not have been successful without the unlikely support of Jaina Proudmoore and Prince Anduin Wrynn of the Alliance. Baine and Anduin had much in common, but renewed tensions between the Horde and Alliance complicated their situation. With Garrosh intent on renewing the conflict between the two factions, Baine is forced to follow the tyrannical new Warchief's orders, lest the rest of the Horde turn against his people.

OLD ENEMIES
Tauren and centaur tribes have long feuded with each other over the lands that the two nomadic races shared. The centaur are known for their brutality and savagery, but support from the Horde has turned the conflict in the tauren's favor, allowing them not only to survive but also to prosper.

THE DEATH OF CAIRNE
Cairne Bloodhoof challenged Garrosh Hellscream to a Mak'Gora, a duel to the death over leadership of the Horde. Unknown to Garrosh, Magatha Grimtotem had poisoned the blade of his axe, Gorehowl. As the poison sank into his veins, Cairne could only watch helplessly while Garrosh raised Gorehowl and struck the final blow, killing him instantly.

WARRIOR AND LEADER
Baine is a powerful warrior in his own right, although he prefers not to rely on fighting. When he does enter a conflict, his goal is to end it as quickly as possible, with minimal bloodshed.

FEARBREAKER
Prince Anduin Wrynn gave Baine the blessed mace known as Fearbreaker during the Grimtotem coup that followed Cairne's untimely death. Before the attack on Theramore, Baine sent a messenger to return it to Jaina Proudmoore with a warning of the impending attack, and a request to return it to Anduin.

Baine prefers diplomatic solutions over brute displays of force, but he will not hesitate to take up arms against any who threaten his people.

Baine, like many tauren, has great respect for nature and reverence toward the Earth Mother.

The totem poles of the tauren people represent a link to their past. The carvings provide a focus for shamanic arts or illustrate stories of famous events or heroic tales.

KEY DATA

NAME Baine Bloodhoof

GENDER AND RACE Male tauren

STATUS Living

AFFILIATION Horde

TITLES High Chieftain of the tauren, Leader of Bloodhoof Village

RELATIVES Elder Bloodhoof (ancestor, deceased); Cairne Bloodhoof (father, deceased); Tamaala (mother, deceased)

TAUREN

The tauren people strive to live honorable, dignified lives filled with respect for nature and the Earth Mother. Although strong and capable warriors when roused in battle, most tauren reserve combat for when all other options are exhausted. They prefer a course of wise discussion and careful rumination before embarking on any great endeavor.

JEVAN GRIMTOTEM

Jevan Grimtotem, also known as Stormsong for his shamanistic affinity with air and water, was a loyal member of the Grimtotem tribe for years. He also admired and respected Cairne Bloodhoof, even if he didn't always agree with Cairne's political decisions. When Cairne died in a duel with Garrosh Hellscream, Jevan was disgusted by the treacherous poisoning of Hellscream's blade by the leader of the Grimtotem, Magatha. Jevan was tasked by Magatha to kill Cairne's son Baine, but instead warned Baine of Magatha's deceit, and the Grimtotem coup. Jevan then helped Baine in his efforts to retake Thunder Bluff from Magatha's forces, proving his loyalty to the new high chieftain. Jevan now resides in Thunder Bluff and acts as advisor to Baine, and leader of those Grimtotem who have also chosen to disassociate with Magatha and her followers.

KEY DATA

TITLE None
STATUS Living
AFFILIATION Horde
RELATIVES None known

XARANTAUR

The druid Xarantaur was taught by Cenarius himself, in the early days of the world.

Where other tauren hunted beasts, he hunted stories, with an endless drive to learn of the past. As the years passed, he left his people and embarked on a world-spanning journey, always seeking greater knowledge. On the eve of his death, Xarantaur was rescued by the bronze dragonflight. He was brought before Nozdormu, Aspect of Time, and gifted with immortality as a Watcher. He is now Xarantaur the Witness, and his task is to bear witness and preserve the history of Azeroth, so that it is always remembered.

KEY DATA

TITLE The Witness
STATUS Living
AFFILIATION Independent (Neutral)
RELATIVES None known

CAIRNE BLOODHOOF

High Chieftain Cairne Bloodhoof was instrumental in changing the face of the tauren race. It was Cairne's vision of a peaceful home for all tauren tribes that led to the unification of the formerly disparate race. Concerned about the rising threat of vicious centaur tribes, Cairne sought to establish a home for all tauren tribes in the land of Mulgore. It was during this journey that Cairne encountered Warchief Thrall, who aided the tauren, defending them against centaur attack. Later, in gratitude for saving his son, Cairne pledged the support of his people to the Horde, quickly becoming Thrall's trusted friend, advisor, and staunch supporter. Yet Cairne was not without his detractors. Although Cairne welcomed all tribes in the newly established capital of Thunder Bluff, Elder Crone Magatha Grimtotem of the Grimtotem tribe often butted heads with the high chieftain, believing she should lead the tauren. When Cairne falsely accused Garrosh Hellscream of the murder of innocents and challenged him to a duel to the death, Magatha took her chance. She poisoned Garrosh's weapon, and when the two fought, the poison seeping into his wounds weakened Cairne, and he was killed. Cairne's death was met with utmost sorrow by the tauren, and his son, Baine, strives to live up to his father's legacy of wise diplomacy and honorable rule.

KEY DATA

TITLE High Chieftain
STATUS Deceased
AFFILIATION Horde
RELATIVES Tamaala (life-mate, deceased); Baine (son)

TAHU SAGEWIND

Tahu Sagewind was once a druid, but his philosophical discussions with Aponi Brightmane began to reveal a new path to him. As a druid, Tahu was well aware that the eyes of the Earth Mother are the sun and moon. Yet the druids followed the teachings of the moon only, as they gained much of their knowledge from the night elves. As such, the influence of the sun was lacking. Many have speculated that this intense pondering led Tahu to create the first priests of the tauren, allowing the tauren to channel the powers of the Light to aid their people.

KEY DATA

TITLE None
STATUS Living
AFFILIATION Horde
RELATIVES None known

ARCHDRUID HAMUUL RUNETOTEM

After the Third War, Hamuul Runetotem sought out the night elf Archdruid Malfurion Stormrage, befriending him and asking to be taught the druidic arts. Malfurion agreed, to the strenuous and xenophobic objections of Archdruid Fandral Staghelm. Hamuul joined the Cenarion Circle, and soon mastered the druidic arts with such proficiency that he rightfully earned the title archdruid for himself. Hamuul strives for diplomacy, having argued for the inclusion of the Forsaken in the Horde, and working side by side with night elf druids in the Cenarion Circle. He was also a founding member of the new Council of Tirisfal. Later, Hamuul was nearly killed in an attack by the Twilight's Hammer cult, resulting in Cairne's false accusation of Garrosh and later, Cairne's death. After the Cataclysm, Hamuul worked side by side with Malfurion to protect Hyjal from the assault of the Firelord, Ragnaros, and the treacherous betrayal of Fandral Staghelm. Currently, Hamuul teaches young druids in Thunder Bluff and stands as a strong supporter, advisor, and friend to Cairne's son, High Chieftain Baine Bloodhoof.

KEY DATA

TITLES Archdruid, member of the New Council of Tirisfal
STATUS Living
AFFILIATION Horde
RELATIVES Bashana Runetotem (daughter); Shakuun Runetotem (grandfather)

MAGATHA GRIMTOTEM

Magatha Grimtotem's advanced age has done nothing to dim her shamanistic gifts or slake her thirst for power. She often argued with High Chieftain Cairne Bloodhoof, believing she deserved leadership of the tauren. When she found she could not remove Cairne politically, Magatha turned to treachery. After Cairne challenged the new Warchief Garrosh Hellscream to a duel to the death, Magatha secretly poisoned Garrosh's weapon. As the combat proceeded, the poison incapacitated Cairne, and he was subsequently killed by Garrosh. Magatha then sought Garrosh's support, pledging the Grimtotem to his cause, and quickly ordered the Grimtotem tribe to take Thunder Bluff and kill Cairne's heir, Baine. Yet Jevan Grimtotem betrayed his tribe and warned Baine. To her fury, Garrosh sent a missive to Thunder Bluff, denying the Grimtotem any Horde support. Eventually, Baine returned in force to reclaim Thunder Bluff, and Magatha and her followers were defeated and exiled.

After the Cataclysm, Magatha was captured by the Twilight's Hammer cult. However, they underestimated Magatha. She soon convinced others to assist her and gather powerful magical artifacts, including the Doomstone, which absorbs and amplifies elemental power. Magatha's whereabouts, as well as what she intends to do with the Doomstone, are currently unknown.

KEY DATA

TITLE Elder Crone of the Grimtotem Tribe
STATUS Living
AFFILIATION Adversarial
RELATIVES Helka Grimtotem (niece); Arnak Grimtotem (nephew, disowned)

APONI BRIGHTMANE

A promising warrior, Aponi Brightmane joined the war against the Lich King in Northrend, where she sustained a grave injury. Forced to return home to Thunder Bluff, Aponi and her close friend, Tahu Sagewind, soon began to have philosophical discussions regarding Mu'sha and An'she, the eyes of the Earth Mother. These discussions eventually led to the re-discovery of the Light (An'she) and the founding of the first order of tauren paladins, the Sunwalkers.

KEY DATA

TITLE Leader of the Sunwalkers
STATUS Living
AFFILIATION Horde
RELATIVES None known

THUNDER BLUFF

Lying in the heart of Kalimdor, the tauren capital city of Thunder Bluff is perched high above the verdant plains of Mulgore, the home of the tauren race. It is an exceptionally defensive location, accessible only by elevators from the land below. The city was established by the late High Chieftain Cairne Bloodhoof, whose son, Baine, now watches over the tauren.

ELEVATED CITY

Four large mesas, or "rises" host Thunder Bluff's various sections. The central mesa is the largest, with three separate levels accessed by an enormous, enclosed staircase. The other three mesas link to the central mesa via rope bridges. The top of the central mesa, also called the High Rise, contains the High Chieftain's home, currently occupied by Baine Bloodhoof. Outside the High Chieftain's quarters, Thunder Bluff's populace can witness important decisions and fateful events in an open-air auditorium.

ELDER RISE

The Tauren have great respect for the wise, spiritual, and elderly among their people. Thus, Elder Rise holds the governing Council of Elders. It is a spiritual center, also housing members of the druidic Cenarion Circle.

MULGORE

The tauren race was originally nomadic in origin, wandering the hills and plains of Kalimdor for millennia. High Chieftain Cairne Bloodhoof sought to unite the wandering tribes of tauren in their home of Mulgore. With the help of the Horde, the tauren were able to successfully drive back their enemies, the centaur, and establish their new home.

HUNTER RISE

The Hunter Rise honors the Tauren people's fighting spirit. Tauren hunters, warriors, and paladins are based here, and also travel here, to receive military training for the ongoing struggle against the Alliance. The trainers reside within the Hunter's Hall and the Sunwalker Lodge.

SPIRIT RISE

Spirit Rise is the center of shamanistic studies within the city. It also has a zeppelin dock, allowing speedy travel to Orgrimmar.

Vol'jin is one of Thrall's closest friends and a loyal supporter of the Horde. He is a Darkspear troll, and his people were nearly destroyed by a naga sea witch and her murlocs. Thrall offered the Darkspear a place of safety within the Horde, which they accepted. With his wisdom scorned by new Warchief Garrosh, Vol'jin proudly commands his people from their newly reclaimed home in the Echo Isles, in opposition to Garrosh's new direction of the Horde.

VOL'JIN

"De Darkspear will have a proper home again. Be ready!"

MASTER OF THE SHADOWS

Thousands of years ago, the trolls ruled much of ancient Kalimdor. The empires fell after years of conflict combined with environmental devastation.

The Darkspear tribe was once part of a vast troll empire, cast out and settling on the Darkspear Islands. They faced near extinction by attacks from a sea witch and her minions, as well as from the encroaching Alliance. When Thrall arrived, Sen'jin recognized the orc from a vision and agreed to let him help. However, the sea witch captured both of them and Sen'jin was mortally wounded. Although the Darkspear won the battle, they were left with nowhere to turn, and Thrall offered the Darkspear a place in the Horde. This began a lasting union of mutual benefit and respect between Vol'jin and Thrall. In recent years, Vol'jin has focused his efforts against the Zandalar tribe's creation of a new troll empire. When Garrosh Hellscream became Horde Warchief, Vol'jin had deep misgivings, but he still tried to counsel his hot-tempered commander. Nevertheless, Vol'jin's open disagreements with the Warchief prompted an assassination attempt by one of Garrosh's agents; Vol'jin narrowly survived. Now he waits and watches from the shadows, carefully considering how to safeguard the Horde from dangers within while keeping his allies safe.

LIFELONG FRIENDSHIP
Thrall and Vol'jin have a mutual respect for each other that has grown into a strong friendship. Though Vol'jin is grateful for the aid Thrall and the Horde provided his people, it is his personal admiration for the one-time Horde leader that strengthens their bond.

KILLING COUSINS
The Zandalar was the earliest known troll tribe from which all other tribes arose. King Rastakhan currently rules the Zandalari. Under the prophet Zul, some have branched off to unite the scattered troll tribes and reclaim their past dominion over the world.

SURVIVOR AND REBEL
Vol'jin's attempts to moderate Warchief Garrosh's aggressive tendencies almost brought his assassination. The Darkspear leader is committed to overthrowing Garrosh, but Vol'jin wants to do so with popular support and minimal bloodshed… or by a swift, personal strike on Garrosh from the dark.

Vol'jin is proficient with the traditional shadow hunter weapon, a long double-bladed sword.

KEY DATA

NAME Vol'jin

GENDER AND RACE Male jungle troll

AFFILIATION Horde

TITLE Chieftain of the Darkspears

RELATIVES Sen'jin (father, deceased)

MAGICAL TALENT
The skulls and materials incorporated into Vol'jin's attire show his status as a powerful shadow hunter, adept at healing magics and voodoo curses.

The raptor mounts that trolls ride into battle are fierce, dangerous, and intelligent creatures. Many foes have underestimated raptors, much to their dismay.

TROLLS

The trolls have a proud history of civilization, and shamanistic worship of the "loa," or spirits. Their individual loyalties generally lie with their tribes—the exceptions are the Darkspear, Shatterspear, and Revantusk tribes, who are allies or friends of the Horde. These tribes loyally uphold their union with the Horde and may engage in open warfare with other trolls, particularly some of their more aggressive cousins.

SEN'JIN

KEY DATA

TITLE Chieftain of the Darkspear Tribe
STATUS Deceased
AFFILIATION Independent
RELATIVES Vol'jin (son)

Chieftain of the Darkspear tribe, Sen'jin led his people in peace on a remote island in the Great Sea. A powerful witch doctor, Sen'jin was a spiritual leader for his people as well. When murlocs began to attack the Darkspears, and humans forces encroached on the islands as well, Sen'jin experienced a powerful vision. In the vision, he saw a young champion who would save the Darkspears, leading them from the islands. The vision came true when Warchief Thrall came to the island. Thrall fought alongside the Darkspears and pushed back the human invaders, but an ambush resulted in Thrall and Sen'jin's capture. Thrall managed to escape, but Sen'jin was mortally wounded by a murloc sorcerer. With his last breath, Sen'jin asked Thrall to save his people and lead the Darkspears to their destiny. Thrall asked the Darkspears to join the Horde, and they willingly agreed. Today, Sen'jin's son, Vol'jin, now leads the Darkspear tribe from the Echo Isles and the small village named for his father.

ZUL'JIN

By the time of the First War, the ancient Amani empire of the forest trolls had been crushed by high elves of Quel'Thalas and humans of Arathor. But there were those that remembered its greatness and yearned for vengeance. Zul'jin watched as the orc Horde butchered its way across the Eastern Kingdoms, and saw a chance for revenge. He united his Amani brethren to the Horde cause, and under Warchief Orgrim Doomhammer, Zul'jin's forces cut a bloody path through the forests of Quel'Thalas. But in the Second War, Orgrim saw Lordaeron as the greater prize and withdrew the majority of his forces from Quel'Thalas. After the Second War was lost, the fragile union of the Amani and the Horde fractured. Zul'jin was captured by his high elf enemies and brutally tortured, losing his right eye and eventually cutting off his own arm to escape. Still burning with hatred, Zul'jin turned to dark sorcery in the Amani capital of Zul'Aman. After learning that the high elves—now called blood elves—had been accepted by the Horde, Zul'jin furiously declared war on both Alliance and Horde. Yet despite the vast powers he had gained and the army he had amassed, Zul'jin was finally slain in Zul'Aman.

KEY DATA

TITLES Warlord of Zul'Aman, Chieftain of the Amani
STATUS Deceased
AFFILIATION Adversarial (formerly Old Horde)
RELATIVES None known

ZEN'TABRA

After the Darkspears settled on the Echo Isles, their island home was taken over by the traitor Zalazane, who cut off Zen'tabra and other witch doctors from the loa. Ashamed, Zen'tabra and the witch doctors remained behind when Vol'jin ordered the retreat from the Echo Isles. That night, a vision led her and the witch doctors to the path of druidism. When Vol'jin returned to reclaim the Echo Isles, Zen'tabra and her fellow druids joined him and helped defeat Zalazane. She now teaches trolls the druidic arts. Zen'tabra helped to convince the night elves of the Cenarion Circle to accept Darkspear druids into their ranks.

KEY DATA

TITLE Member of the Cenarion Circle
STATUS Living
AFFILIATION Horde
RELATIVES None known

GARA'JAL

Gara'jal was one of many Zandalari trolls who came to Pandaria seeking the help and alliance of the ancient mogu race. As part of the alliance, the Zandalari resurrected Lei Shen, the Thunder King, the most powerful warlord in mogu history. Gara'jal sought to possess the arcane power of the mogu by delving into the Mogu'shan Vaults. Gara'jal was killed there by a group of heroes, but his spirit lived on, waiting to bind itself with a new body. As a loyal supporter of the mogu, Gara'jal sought to empower the Council of Elders, powerful representatives from other troll tribes—the Drakkari, Amani, Farraki, and Gurubashi. Although defeated, it is unknown if Gara'jal's spirit lingers on.

KEY DATA

TITLE The Spiritbinder
STATUS Deceased
AFFILIATION Adversarial
RELATIVES None known

ZUL

A member of the Zanchuli Council, the mysterious prophet Zul began having terrible visions when he was just a child, foreseeing great tragedies before they came to pass. Years ago, Zul saw visions of the horrific Cataclysm that ripped Azeroth asunder. Yet upon warning King Rastakhan of these terrible visions, the king did nothing. Twice more Zul tried to warn the king, to no avail; many thought Zul was merely seeking to increase his own status and power. In the end, Rastakhan gave ships to Zul so that he and his followers could seek a new land for their people if the visions came to pass. And Zul's visions did come to pass—as Zandalar Isle began to sink into the sea, many followed Zul on his vision to unite the scattered troll tribes of Azeroth into one mighty troll empire. Although few have seen Zul in person, the dark prophet still orchestrates the assault on Pandaria from behind the scenes.

KEY DATA

TITLE Dark Prophet of the Zanchuli Council
STATUS Living
AFFILIATION Adversarial
RELATIVES None known

ZANZIL

Outcast by his own kind, the witch doctor Zanzil was infamous for his experiments in mind-altering and behavior-altering concoctions, resulting in the creation of zombie-like slaves. Although cast out by the Gurubashi, Zanzil was recently approached and brought back into the tribe, his unique skills used to resurrect the bodies of important high priests and priestesses of the empire. Yet Zanzil's mad experiments would not last for long. He was killed in the Gurubashi capital of Zul'Gurub, failing in his attempts to redeem himself to the empire.

KEY DATA

TITLE The Outcast
STATUS Deceased
AFFILIATION Adversarial
RELATIVES None known

ZALAZANE

As a child, Zalazane was the best friend of Vol'jin, son of the Chieftain of the Darkspear tribe. As a youth, Vol'jin convinced Zalazane to join him and be tested by the loa in the forests of First Home. Neither expected the powerful visions they witnessed. While Vol'jin saw visions of his future, Zalazane saw himself become the new leader of the Darkspears, and the tribe split in half. Years later, Zalazane fulfilled the forgotten visions. Driven mad by his power as a witch doctor, Zalazane began to use dark voodoo to rob the Darkspear trolls of their free will, taking control of the Echo Isles and betraying Vol'jin's trust. After years of biding his time, Vol'jin finally struck back, allying with the powerful loa Bwonsamdi, guardian of the dead, and bringing Zalazane's life to an end.

KEY DATA

TITLE Traitor of the Darkspears
STATUS Deceased
AFFILIATION Adversarial
RELATIVES None known

MAR'LI

Once a champion of the primal gods, Mar'li was the high priestess of the spider loa, Elortha no Shadra, in the ancient city of Zul'Gurub. High Priestess Mar'li later acted as the representative of the Gurubashi tribe in the Council of Elders, joined by representatives from the Drakkari, Amani, and Farraki tribes. Although empowered by the Spiritbinder Gara'jal, the Council was defeated and Mar'li was killed.

KEY DATA

TITLE High Priestess
STATUS Deceased
AFFILIATION Adversarial
RELATIVES None known

ECHO ISLES

The Darkspear tribe of trolls joined the Horde and traveled to Durotar, establishing a new home on the Echo Isles. Located off the coast of Durotar, this group of islands would not be home for long. The islands were taken over by the witch doctor Zalazane, who used his dark powers to enslave some of the Darkspears. Years later, Zalazane was killed and the islands reclaimed thanks to the Darkspears' leader, Vol'jin, and the help of the Horde.

THE LOA
The trolls are guided by the loa, spirits that grant blessings and curses. One loa is Bwonsamdi, loa of the dead, who guards the spirits of deceased Darkspear. His help was instrumental in reclaiming Echo Isles for the Darkspear.

THE ISLANDS OF THE TROLLS
Originally part of the Gurubashi empire in Stranglethorn Vale, warring within the empire forced the Darkspear tribe to relocate to an island in the Great Sea. Years later, during a conflict between the Darkspears and a naga sea witch, the Darkspears were offered assistance by Warchief Thrall, who offered them a new home in the Horde. Eventually the trolls joined up with Thrall in Kalimdor.

DUROTAR

SPITESCALE COVE

DARKSPEAR ISLE

DARKSPEAR TRAINING GROUNDS

ZALAZANE'S FALL

DARKSPEAR HOLD

BLOODTALON SHORE

SEN'JIN VILLAGE
Sen'jin Village is a small settlement on the Durotar coast. It was founded by Darkspear leader Vol'jin after the Darkspear were forced to evacuate the Echo Isles.

ZALAZANE'S FALL

Witch doctor Zalazane was once the best friend of Vol'jin (right), but the friendship ended in betrayal. Zalazane wanted power, and when the Darkspear settled on the islands, he went mad. Using dark voodoo, Zalazane enslaved many of the Darkspear, forcing Vol'jin to flee. Eventually, Vol'jin was able to reclaim the island and put an end to Zalazane.

NATIVE FAUNA

In addition to the Darkspear trolls, the Echo Isles are home to abundant wildlife. Tigers and other dangerous predators abound, and the troll inhabitants have tamed feral raptors to serve as their mounts.

In life, the high elf Sylvanas Windrunner was the renowned ranger-general of Silvermoon, leader of the Farstrider rangers. During the Third War, she was slain by the death knight Arthas Menethil, who tore her soul from her body and converted it into a banshee. In time Sylvanas reclaimed her free will, gathering rogue undead into her Forsaken army. With Arthas finally destroyed, Sylvanas will do whatever is necessary to maintain her position, extend her existence, and perpetuate the Forsaken.

SYLVANAS WINDRUNNER

"I've walked the realms of the dead. I have seen the infinite dark. Nothing you say. Or do. Could possibly frighten me."

THE DARK LADY

In life, Sylvanas was known for her tactical skills and obstinacy. She even appointed a human, Nathanos Marris, as a ranger lord, despite the protests of others.

As ranger-general of Silvermoon, the high elf capital, Sylvanas Windrunner led her forces against the death knight Arthas Menethil, champion of the Lich King, during the Third War. Despite her strong resistance, the Scourge ripped through Quel'Thalas and she met defeat at the hands of Arthas. He denied her a clean death and instead transformed her soul into a banshee, forced to serve the Scourge.

When the Lich King's grasp wavered, Sylvanas regained her free will. She reclaimed her body, gathered those similarly free of the Lich King's sway into her personal army, renaming them "Forsaken", and established her base in the Undercity, beneath the Lordaeron ruins. Though she joined the Horde to help secure her kingdom, she wanted her vengeance: the death of Arthas, now the Lich King, for what he did to her and her people.

When Tirion Fordring and heroes of Azeroth killed Arthas, Sylvanas struggled with a lack of purpose now that her revenge was complete. She sought to end her undead state by destroying herself. However, she learned that her afterlife would be a ceaseless torment and, without her leadership, the Forsaken would be obliterated. Thus, she accepted a pact with the Val'kyr, the Lich King's former undead agents. This bonded their souls to hers, bolstering Forsaken ranks through the Val'kyrs' powers of undeath. The pact has kept Sylvanas in the realm of the living, but she is terrified of what awaits her in eternity. She considers her existence and her people to be entwined—she and the Forsaken will survive at any cost.

THE DARK RITUAL
The ritual that Arthas used to turn Sylvanas into a banshee involved tearing her soul out of her still-living body. It infinitely prolonged her existence as a creature filled with hate toward all life.

QUEEN OF THE FORSAKEN
While the Alliance and Horde fought the Lich King in Northrend, Grand Apothecary Putress and the dreadlord Varimathras attempted a coup against Sylvanas. They occupied the Undercity, but Sylvanas escape She returned at the head of a Horde army, recaptured the city, and slew Varimathras.

MAIDENS OF NIGHTMARE
Arthas created the Val'kyr from the female vrykul of Valkyrion to serve as his agents. After Arthas was destroyed, the nine remaining Val'kyr elders entered into a pact with Sylvanas. This bound their souls to Sylvanas, granting them freedom from the Lich King, and in return spared Sylvanas from the terrors of the afterlife that awaited her.

KEY DATA

NAME Sylvanas Windrunner

GENDER AND RACE Female Forsaken (former high elf)

AFFILIATION Horde

STATUS Undead

TITLES The Dark Lady, Queen of the Forsaken, the Banshee Queen, Ranger-General of Silvermoon

RELATIVES Alleria (sister); Arator (nephew); Vereesa (sister); Rhonin (brother-in-law, deceased); Giramar (nephew); Galadin (nephew); Lirath (brother, deceased); Zendarin (cousin, deceased)

The Banshee Queen is aptly named. Her screams have the power to silence and weaken her enemies, or bolster the power of her allies.

Sylvanas was raised as a banshee, an incorporeal spirit. It wasn't until the Lich King's grasp wavered and she regained her free will that she was able to recover and reclaim her body.

In life, Sylvanas Windrunner was a formidable archer as the ranger-general of Silvermoon. Even after her death, she retained her deadly proficiency with the bow.

THE WINDRUNNER FAMILY
The Windrunner family has a long and tragic history. While the fates of some are lost to the ages, those of three sisters—Alleria, Sylvanas, and Vereesa (pictured above)—continue to shape Azeroth's destiny.

FORSAKEN

The undead Forsaken are a faction of former Scourge who have regained their free will. Led by the Banshee Queen Sylvanas Windrunner, many Forsaken bear a bitter view of the living, as most living creatures look upon them with fear, derision, and hatred. Notable members of the Forsaken have embraced their state of undeath and moved beyond it, whether for altruistic purposes, or far darker intent.

GRAND APOTHECARY PUTRESS

Grand Apothecary Putress rose to prominence during the second Scourge invasion, when his research on the Scourge and undead plague led to the development of a cure. As the war against the Lich King moved forward, Putress represented the Forsaken and, ostensibly, Banshee Queen Sylvanas' interests in Northrend. He focused on the development of the blight, a new plague developed as a weapon against the Lich King. But Putress betrayed both Alliance and Horde when he unleashed the blight during the Battle of Angrathar the Wrathgate, resulting in the deaths of countless soldiers. In the battle's aftermath, Putress revealed his true intentions: a coup attempt against Sylvanas. In reality, Putress had been working with the Burning Legion along with the dreadlord Varimathras, and they had taken control of the Undercity. Putress did not foresee that the Alliance would join the Horde to reclaim the Undercity. He was killed by King Varian Wrynn, and the Undercity was retaken for the Forsaken.

KEY DATA

TITLE Grand Apothecary
STATUS Deceased
AFFILIATION Horde/Adversarial
RELATIVES None known

LORD GODFREY

Possessing a fierce hatred of the worgen, Gilnean nobleman Vincent Godfrey turned on King Genn Greymane after discovering Genn had succumbed to the worgen curse. Rather than accept a worgen for a king, Godfrey leapt to his death. Found and raised into undeath by the Forsaken, he joined the forces attacking Gilneas. After kidnapping Lorna Crowley, Godfrey was enraged when Sylvanas Windrunner let both Lorna and her worgen father, Darius Crowley, go free in exchange for the Gilnean forces' surrender. In a surprise move, he killed Sylvanas, who was later brought back by her Val'kyr. Godfrey fled to Shadowfang Keep, where he met his final end.

KEY DATA

TITLE Lord of Gilneas
STATUS Deceased
AFFILIATION Adversarial
RELATIVES None known

MASTER APOTHECARY FARANELL

Faranell was a respected alchemist who spent his life studying medicine in Dalaran. After his death and undeath as a Forsaken, Faranell became one of the foremost experts on the undead plague, loyal to the Banshee Queen. At Sylvanas' order, Faranell now leads the Royal Apothecary Society, creating alchemical monstrosities and designing virulent plagues and toxins.

KEY DATA

TITLE Master Apothecary
STATUS Undead
AFFILIATION Horde
RELATIVES None known

ALEXI BAROV

Before the Third War, the wealthy Barov family made a deal with necromancer Kel'Thuzad. In return for a promise of immortality, the Barovs turned their home into a school of necromancy called Scholomance. The Barovs were turned into servants of the Scourge, yet Alexi Barov, one of two Barov sons, broke free of the Scourge and became a Forsaken. Initially at odds with his living brother, Weldon, over the ownership of Barov lands, Alexi later reunited with his brother and both turned their attention to Scholomance itself, attempting to rid their former home of the Scourge. Both Alexi and Weldon have since disappeared, their current whereabouts unknown.

KEY DATA

TITLE Heir of the Barov family
STATUS Undead
AFFILIATION Horde
RELATIVES Alexei Barov (father, deceased); Illucia Barov (mother, deceased); Jandice (sister, deceased); Weldon (brother)

VARIMATHRAS

During the Third War, Lordaeron was under the Burning Legion's control, with dreadlord brothers Balnazzar, Detheroc, and Varimathras in charge. After the demon lord Archimonde's defeat, Arthas returned to Lordaeron to regain his kingdom. The dreadlords escaped and overthrew Arthas in a simultaneous coup with Banshee Queen Sylvanas Windrunner, taking over Lordaeron. Sylvanas then attacked Varimathras. To save himself, he told her the locations of his brothers and swore to serve her. Sylvanas then killed Detheroc, and Varimathras seemingly proved his loyalty by killing his brother Balnazzar. The Forsaken claimed Lordaeron, and Varimathras continued to outwardly support Sylvanas. Varimathras secretly remained loyal to the Burning Legion. He plotted with Grand Apothecary Putress, staging a coup of the Undercity during the war with the Lich King. Sylvanas, the Alliance, and the Horde reclaimed the Undercity and defeated Varimathras. He lives on in the Twisting Nether, presumably plotting revenge with his demon brothers.

KEY DATA

TITLE Arch Lord of the Undercity (former)
STATUS Defeated
AFFILIATION Horde/Adversarial
RELATIVES Balnazzar (defeated); Detheroc (defeated)

GALEN TROLLBANE

The son of King Thoras Trollbane, Prince Galen Trollbane was the only apparent leader of the kingdom following his father's untimely demise. He and his forces fought within the ruins of Stromgarde's walls, attempting to defend the city from sieges by both Boulderfist ogres, and a human criminal organization called the Syndicate. Although Trollbane desperately sought to reclaim his kingdom and restore it to its former glory, he fell in combat and was raised as a Forsaken. Now, Trollbane seems to have forgotten the desperate goals of his former life, committing himself wholly to serving the Banshee Queen.

KEY DATA

TITLE Prince of Stromgarde
STATUS Undead
AFFILIATION Horde
RELATIVES Ignaeus Trollbane (ancestor, deceased); Thoras Trollbane (father, deceased); Danath Trollbane (cousin)

LILIAN VOSS

Lilian Voss was the daughter of High Priest Benedictus Voss, a high-ranking member of the Scarlet Crusade. He raised his daughter within the Scarlet Crusade, training her to fight against the Scourge. Lilian was later killed in combat and raised as a Forsaken, to her utter horror. She fled to find her father, hoping for his aid, but was cruelly informed that her father had disowned and denounced her, ordering her execution upon learning of her fate. Enraged, Lilian killed her father and many members of the Scarlet Crusade before turning her wrath on the Scourge necromancers of Scholomance. Forced to fight by Darkmaster Gandling, Lilian was gravely wounded in Scholomance, and left alone to die.

KEY DATA

TITLE None
STATUS Deceased
AFFILIATION Independent
RELATIVES Archbishop Benedictus Voss (father, deceased)

NATHANOS BLIGHTCALLER

In the years before the Third War, Nathanos Marris was trained as a ranger by the high elf ranger-general Sylvanas Windrunner of Quel'Thalas. He was the first and only human to become a ranger lord, though many high elves protested his inclusion. Nathanos went on to earn great acclaim for his tactical and strategic skills, yet perhaps because of high elven prejudices, Nathanos chose to live in his family home, the Marris Stead, instead of Quel'Thalas. He was murdered in his home by a horrific abomination called Ramstein the Gorger during the Third War. Raised as an undead Scourge, Nathanos was one of many to break free of the Lich King's grasp and become a Forsaken, joining his former mentor and her followers. Yet the Alliance discovered his new identity as Nathanos Blightcaller and his new position as Champion of the Banshee Queen, and attempted to have him slain. Nathanos retreated to the Undercity, where he now trains Forsaken rangers.

KEY DATA

TITLES Champion of the Banshee Queen, Ranger Lord (former)
STATUS Undead
AFFILIATION Horde
RELATIVES None known

THE UNDERCITY

Built under the foundations of Lordaeron's ruined capital, the Undercity is a twisted warren of catacombs and dungeons inhabited by the undead Forsaken. More than anything else, the Undercity is a place of secrets, and the inhabitants do not easily reveal their intentions.

CAPITAL CITY
A majestic city of soaring spires, Lordaeron's capital served as the headquarters of the Alliance of Lordaeron during the Second War, but was later destroyed by Prince Arthas and his Scourge army.

REFUGE OF THE LOST
Lordaeron's capital was once a thriving city, but the Undercity was never a prosperous place. It was built under the royal palace to serve as its crypts and dungeon. However, the poor and destitute, those who had nowhere else, came to inhabit the Undercity. Its roughly symmetrical quarters surround a circular center. The Rogues' Quarter is home to the more underhanded Forsaken, including poison venders and the Rogues' Guild. The Magic Quarter is the center of Forsaken arcane research and training. It also features a Temple of the Damned—an unholy structure used to channel necromantic energies. The War Quarter houses the powerful Forsaken military.

LORDAERON THRONE ROOM
The throne room of Lordaeron still stands today. Those who examine the floor closely will notice a small trail of blood staining the floor near the throne, marking the spot where King Terenas' bloody crown fell from his head.

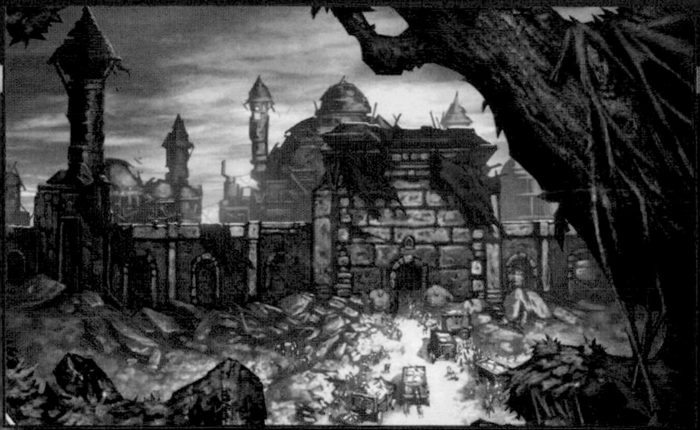

A MONUMENT TO TRAGEDY

During the Third War, Prince Arthas Menethil, now a death knight, returned to Lordaeron and murdered his father, King Terenas Menethil II. Scourge forces sacked the city and Arthas claimed it as his own. When Sylvanas broke free of the Lich King's will, she launched a successful rebellion, taking Lordaeron (which she renamed the Undercity). She then named her people the Forsaken.

THE APOTHECARIUM

The Apothecarium is the home to the Royal Apothecary Society, an organization of undead working to create virulent plagues to use against their enemies. Master Apothecary Faranell and his alchemist minions work to brew their newest toxins, as well as creating more powerful abominations to serve the Forsaken.

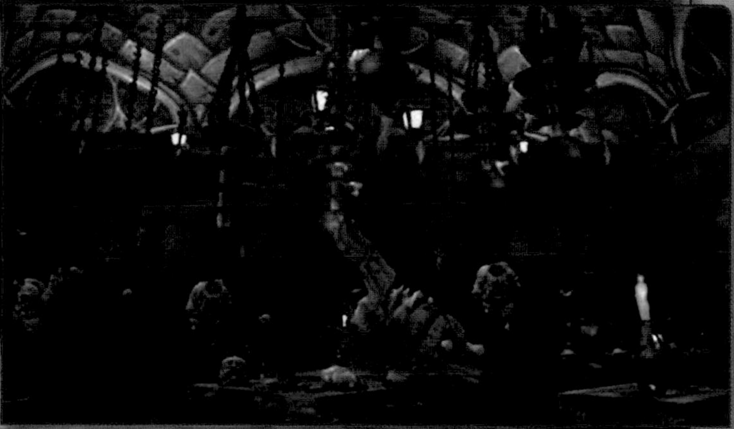

As Regent and then Regent Lord of Quel'Thalas, Lor'themar Theron has an enormous task ahead of him. The Scourge invasion of the Third War heavily damaged Quel'Thalas. The involvement of blood elven forces in Outland with Illidan's army and the Burning Legion severely hampered relations abroad. Lor'themar works to repair connections with the other races while he restores Quel'Thalas and governs his people.

LOR'THEMAR THERON

"All we can do is walk the road we are given with such dignity as we can muster, each to our own glory or demise…"

TOWARD THE SUN

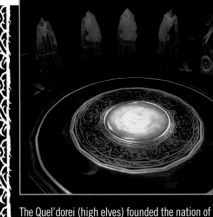

The Quel'dorei (high elves) founded the nation of Quel'Thalas after being exiled from the night elf lands. These magically gifted people drew their arcane powers from the Sunwell. After the decimation of Quel'Thalas' population, the survivors became known as the Sin'dorei (blood elves), in honor of the sacrifices of their brethren.

Before he was chosen to lead his people, Lor'themar Theron had a distinguished career as a high elf Ranger. He was second-in-command to Sylvanas Windrunner, Ranger-General of Silvermoon, and later charged with protecting the Sunwell, a mystical fount of arcane power that sustained his homeland and people.

After the Second War, King Anasterian Sunstrider removed the kingdom from the Alliance of Lordaeron, claiming that poor leadership by the humans had caused unnecessary hardships for his people.

Later, during the Third War, the undead Scourge, led by the death knight Arthas Menethil, sacked Silvermoon. The populace was butchered, including Anasterian and Sylvanas, who was turned into a banshee. Lor'themar was out on patrol at the time of the attack, and raced back to Silvermoon, but was seriously wounded and arrived too late to prevent the Sunwell from being defiled by Arthas. Anasterian's son, Prince Kael'thas Sunstrider, left for the shattered world of Outland to seek a cure for the magical addiction that ravaged what remained of his people. He appointed Lor'themar as Regent of Quel'Thalas in his stead. Kael'thas later betrayed the blood elves to the Burning Legion, but Lor'themar rose to his people's defense. Ever since, he has opposed anything he views as tyranny or injustice. He believes that Quel'Thalas is best served by being in the Horde, but the needs of his people come first.

THE FALL OF QUEL'THALAS
Under the guise of friendship, blood elf Magister Dar'Khan Drathir gained vital information from Lor'themar, which he then relayed to Scourge commander Arthas Menethil. Arthas used this knowledge to nearly raze Silvermoon City and defile the Sunwell. Now, both Dar'Khan and Arthas are finally dead, giving Lor'themar a measure of peace.

RANGER-GENERAL OF SILVERMOON
Halduron Brightwing, Lor'themar's old friend and confidant, serves as the Farstriders' leader and Silvermoon's Ranger-General. He provides level-headed counsel to the Regent Lord, with few of the haughty prejudices for which the blood elves are known.

GRAND MAGISTER OF SILVERMOON
Grand Magister Rommath, Prince Kael'thas Sunstrider's close companion, was sent to Silvermoon to rebuild it and teach the blood elves how to sate their addiction to magic. When Kael'thas' betrayed the blood elves, Rommath smoothly transferred his allegiance to Lor'themar. Rommath's true loyalty is to his people.

KEY DATA

NAME Lor'themar Theron

GENDER AND RACE
Male blood elf

AFFILIATION Horde

STATUS Living

TITLES Ranger Lord, Regent Lord of Quel'Thalas

RELATIVES None known

Lor'themar would lose his left eye during the Third War, after discovering the treachery of Dar'Khan and fighting his way past the reanimated corpses of high elf guardians. He made it to the Sunwell, but he was too late; Arthas had already defiled the magical fount, threatening the lives of the survivors.

Being regent lord has afforded Lor'themar little time for combat. However, recent events have allowed him to showcase his deadly prowess with both bow and blade.

Lor'themar remains uncrowned. He has not married and has no children. In many ways, he finds ruling Quel'Thalas to be a difficult balancing act between practical necessities and higher ideals for his people. In light of this, Lor'themar has no plans to begin his own dynasty.

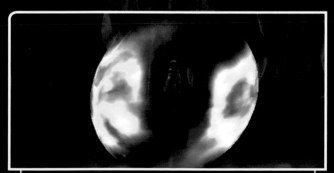

ANVEENA TEAGUE: THE SUNWELL REBORN
Anveena Teague had the appearance of a human girl, but in reality she was the energy of the Sunwell in corporeal form, created by the red dragon Korialstrasz. After defeating Dar'Khan Drathir, she went into hiding with the blue dragon Kalecgos. Later, Prince Kael'thas abducted her, hoping to use her latent energy to bring his master, the demon lord Kil'jaeden, into the world through the Sunwell. Anveena sacrificed herself to weaken Kil'jaeden and bring about his downfall.

BLOOD ELVES

Nearly driven to extinction in the Third War, the blood elves, or sin'dorei, are a proud and resilient race. Although their numbers may have dwindled due to tragedy, notable members of blood elf society stand as beacons of tenacity, courage, and the strength to fight on, regardless of what foes stand in their way.

KAEL'THAS SUNSTRIDER

Prince Kael'thas Sunstrider was a master mage, one of the Council of Six, the high council of the Kirin Tor, in the mage capital of Dalaran. Although heir to Quel'Thalas, it wasn't until his father's death during Scourge attacks in the Third War that Kael'thas returned to Silvermoon, the high elven capital. Renaming the remnants of his beleaguered people blood elves, in honor of those fallen, Kael'thas was dismayed to discover that the blood elves suffered from an addiction to magic. The destruction of the Sunwell during the Third War had cut them off from the source of their magic and they were literally wasting away. Meanwhile, Grand Marshal Garithos, the human leader of the Alliance forces revealed his scorn for the blood elves by sending them on impossible missions against the Scourge. During one of them, Kael'thas accepted help from the naga Lady Vashj—and was promptly imprisoned for treason by Garithos. Lady Vashj helped him to escape, and intimated that her master, Illidan Stormrage, could help find a cure for the blood elves' addiction. So Kael'thas left Silvermoon in the hands of Lor'themar Theron and set out for the shattered world of Outland, where Illidan was based.

Time passed, and Kael'thas sent Grand Magister Rommath to teach the blood elves how to siphon magic and sate their addiction. The blood elves allied with the Horde and awaited the day they could make the pilgrimage to Outland and unite with their Prince. But Kael'thas had turned to darker forces, allying with the Burning Legion. He claimed the naaru citadel Tempest Keep, capturing its guardian, M'uru, and sending the naaru back to Silvermoon to be siphoned of his magical energy. Mad with power, Kael'thas continued to work for the Burning Legion, removing the energies of the Twisting Nether with great manaforges, until a group of adventurers confronted him. Although defeated, he managed to escape and returned to Silvermoon. He was a shadow of his former self, corrupted by fel magic and intent on harnessing the latent powers of the Sunwell to summon his dark master Kil'jaeden to Azeroth. Kael'thas assaulted Silvermoon itself, stealing M'uru and taking over the Isle of Quel'Danas, home of the Sunwell. Prince Kael'thas' efforts were finally thwarted by the Shattered Sun Offensive. He was killed and buried on the Isle of Quel'Danas, bringing an unhappy end to the Sunstrider dynasty that cast a bitter pall over the blood elves left behind.

KEY DATA

TITLES Lord of the Blood Elves
STATUS Deceased
AFFILIATION Adversarial
RELATIVES Anasterian Sunstrider (deceased)

VALEERA SANGUINAR

Valeera Sanguinar was distantly descended from a member of the Council of Tirisfal, a powerful group of magi. In her youth, her family was killed by bandits. Orphaned, Valeera managed to survive by becoming a thief, but she was eventually caught, imprisoned, and sold as a gladiator slave. During this time, she befriended the night elf Broll Bearmantle and Lo'Gosh, a human warrior. When Lo'Gosh was revealed to be part of King Varian Wrynn, she helped Varian reclaim his true identity and his throne. Valeera suffered from the same magical addiction that ravaged her people, and she often struggled to control the pangs and withdrawals. She later helped to recruit members for the new Council of Tirisfal, and saved the new Guardian, Med'an. She cares little for either the Horde or Alliance, but is fiercely loyal to Varian and his son. She was last seen in Stormwind; however, Valeera's current whereabouts are unknown.

KEY DATA

TITLE None
STATUS Living
AFFILIATION Independent
RELATIVES Relfthra (distant ancestor, deceased)

VOREN'THAL THE SEER

Voren'thal was a potent magister who followed Prince Kael'thas to Outland. Under the orders of Kael'thas and Illidan Stormrage, Voren'thal led a contingent of blood elves against Shattrath City. Yet when he arrived, he and his forces laid their weapons aside, seeking audience with the naaru leader, A'dal. He spoke to A'dal of a vision he had received, in which the naaru were the blood elves' only hope for survival, and then pledged the service of his forces to the naaru. Among Voren'thal's followers were some of the brightest and most gifted scholars and magic users in Kael'thas' army, and their defection was a serious blow. After taking their place in Shattrath City, the blood elves named their organization the Scryers, and appointed Voren'thal as their leader.

KEY DATA

TITLES The Seer, Leader of the Scryers
STATUS Living
AFFILIATION Independent
RELATIVES None known

LADY LIADRIN

Once a priestess of the Light, Lady Liadrin renounced her vows after the Scourge razed Quel'Thalas, feeling, as many did, that the Light had abandoned the blood elves in their greatest hour of need. Yet when offered the chance to siphon the Light from the captured naaru, M'uru, Liadrin readily agreed. She was the first to siphon the naaru's power, twisting the Light to serve her needs and becoming what would be the first of the Blood Knights, an organization of paladins. Under her leadership, the Blood Knights thrived. Fiercely loyal to Kael'thas, his betrayal affected Liadrin deeply. After witnessing Kael'thas' return and the abduction of M'uru, Liadrin traveled to Outland to seek an audience with the leader of the naaru, A'dal, where she was revealed to be the subject of a naaru prophecy. Ashamed of her actions, she renounced the House of Sunstrider and pledged herself and the Blood Knights to the Shattered Sun Offensive. M'uru was killed during the assault on Sunwell Plateau, but his heart was used by the Prophet Velen to restore the Sunwell, an act that Liadrin witnessed firsthand. The surge of Light through the Sunwell served to reignite Liadrin's faith in the Light. Today, Liadrin continues to train and teach new paladins to embrace the Light, rather than twisting it to serve their own needs.

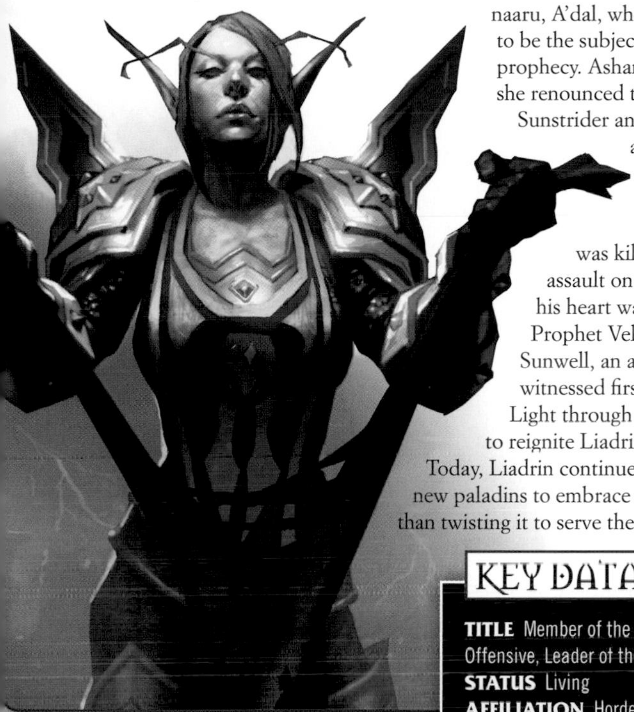

KEY DATA

TITLE Member of the Shattered Sun Offensive, Leader of the Blood Knights
STATUS Living
AFFILIATION Horde
RELATIVES None known

HALDURON BRIGHTWING

Halduron Brightwing is the leader of the Farstriders and the Ranger-General of Silvermoon. A longtime friend to Lor'themar Theron, Halduron is also confidant and advisor to the Regent Lord. Originally serving under Ranger-general Sylvanas Windrunner, Halduron eventually inherited Sylvanas' title and the forces she commanded following her death in the Third War. Halduron was opposed to the creation of the Blood Knights, and deeply concerned with the treatment of M'uru. After the betrayal of Kael'thas, Halduron continued his support of Lor'themar, although he was willing to cross boundaries when necessary. With the resurgence of the trolls of Zul'Aman after the Cataclysm, Halduron invited the high elf Vereesa Windrunner and her forces to combat the menace, over Lor'themar's objections. As of late, Halduron and his Farstrider rangers have been seen in Pandaria, assisting Lor'themar and the Sunreaver Onslaught against Zandalari and mogu forces.

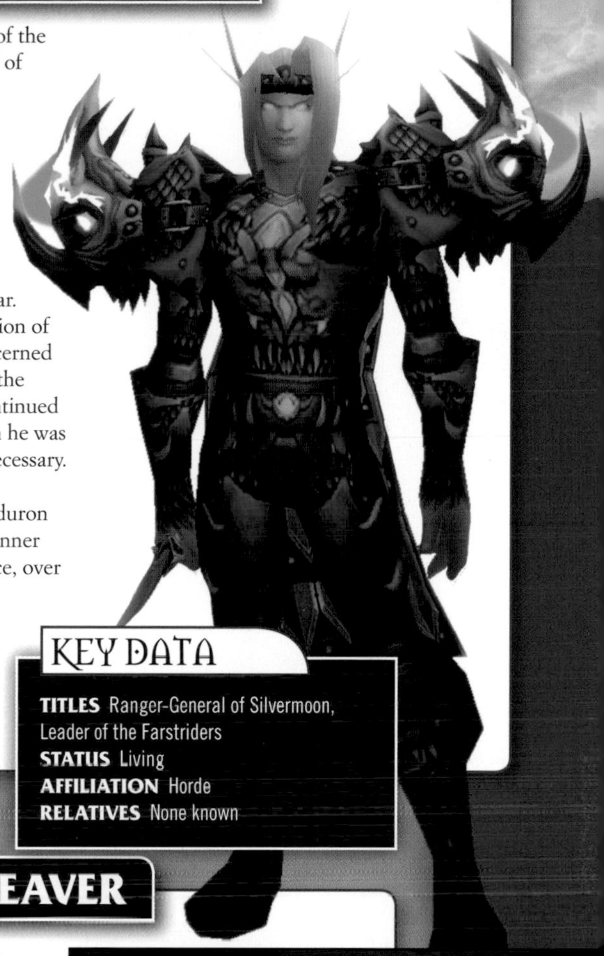

KEY DATA

TITLES Ranger-General of Silvermoon, Leader of the Farstriders
STATUS Living
AFFILIATION Horde
RELATIVES None known

GRAND MAGISTER ROMMATH

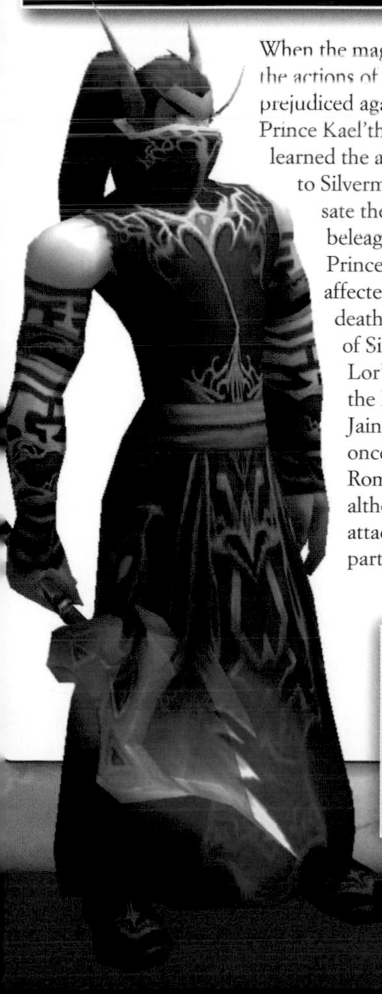

When the magi of Dalaran's Kirin Tor turned a blind eye to the actions of the human Grand Marshal Garithos, who was prejudiced against the blood elves, Rommath gladly followed Prince Kael'thas Sunstrider to Outland. There, Garithos learned the arts of siphoning magic. He was later sent back to Silvermoon to teach the remaining blood elves how to sate their addiction to magic, and to help rebuild the beleaguered city. Fiercely devoted to Kael'thas, the Prince's subsequent betrayal of the blood elves affected Rommath deeply. Shattered by the Prince's death, Rommath continued his unwavering support of Silvermoon, earning the respect of both Lor'themar and Halduron. He holds no love for the Kirin Tor, showing little surprise when Lady Jaina Proudmoore threw the support of the once-neutral organization behind the Alliance. Rommath still acts as advisor to Lor'themar, although his role is a more active one, overseeing attacks on mogu forces on the Isle of Thunder as part of the Sunreaver Onslaught.

KEY DATA

TITLES Grand Magister of Quel'Thalas, Herald of Prince Kael'thas Sunstrider (former)
STATUS Living
AFFILIATION Horde
RELATIVES None known

AETHAS SUNREAVER

Although young, Aethas Sunreaver quickly made his way up the ranks of the Kirin Tor, eventually taking a seat on the Council of Six in Dalaran. A heavy proponent of neutrality, Aethas and Grand Magister Rommath often butted heads regarding the blood elves and their place in the Kirin Tor. Yet Aethas worked hard as a champion of the Horde's cause, eventually earning the Horde a place in Dalaran during the war in Northrend. Outgoing and enthusiastic, Aethas' eternal optimism, as well as his neutral stance, were tested when the Horde began to openly declare war on the Alliance after the Cataclysm. When events in Pandaria resulted in the expulsion of the Sunreavers from Dalaran, Aethas pledged the service of the Sunreavers to Silvermoon, although in his eyes, Warchief Hellscream was just as much to blame for the purge of Dalaran as Lady Jaina Proudmoore. The Sunreaver Onslaught later began an assault on the Isle of Thunder in Pandaria—both to combat the combined forces of mogu and Zandalari, and to try to discover and harness the powers the mogu had mastered.

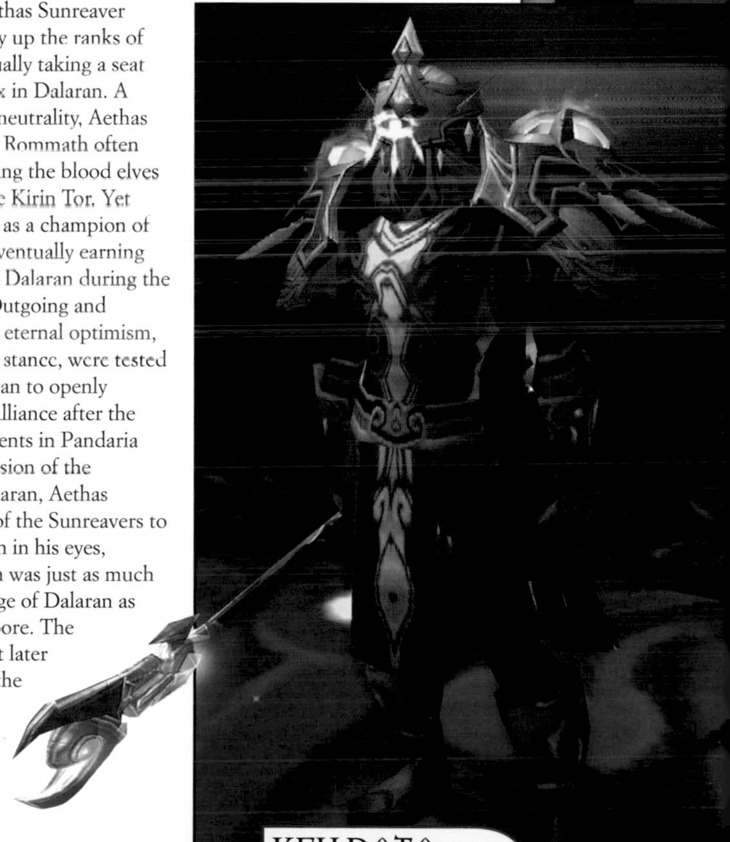

KEY DATA

TITLE Archmage
STATUS Living
AFFILIATION Independent/Horde
RELATIVES None known

SILVERMOON CITY

The capital of Quel'Thalas, home of the blood elves, Silvermoon City is a beacon of magic and power. Located in the northernmost reaches of the Eastern Kingdoms, Quel'Thalas and Silvermoon City were established on what was originally sacred troll lands. Nearly destroyed during the Third War, Silvermoon City has now, with the judicious use of magic, been mostly restored.

THE RESTORATION OF QUEL'THALAS

The blood elves had a difficult time reclaiming their treasured capital. Success was only obtained when Prince Kael'thas Sunstrider first destroyed the defiled Sunwell and then allied with the demon Illidan Stormrage to cure the majority of blood elves' withdrawal symptoms from an addiction to magic. Much of Silvermoon was magically restored almost overnight.

THE FALL OF SILVERMOON

During the Third War, the death knight Arthas Menethil led an army of Scourge against Quel'Thalas. Arthas slew High King Anasterian Sunstrider and reanimated the sorcerer Kel'Thuzad, defiling the Sunwell, a fount of mystical power. The Scourge's path through the countryside can still be seen today—a swath of destruction called the Dead Scar—and the city's western portion remains in partial ruins.

CITY OF MAGIC

Silvermoon City is filled with magical power; floating flowerpots and ensorcelled brooms beautify the town. The city has no rival in beauty or grandeur—at least according to its blood elf inhabitants.

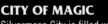

SUNFURY SPIRE

COURT OF THE SUN · FARSTRIDERS' SQUARE

MURDER ROW

THE DEAD SCAR

THE ROYAL EXCHANGE

THE BAZAAR

WALK OF ELDERS

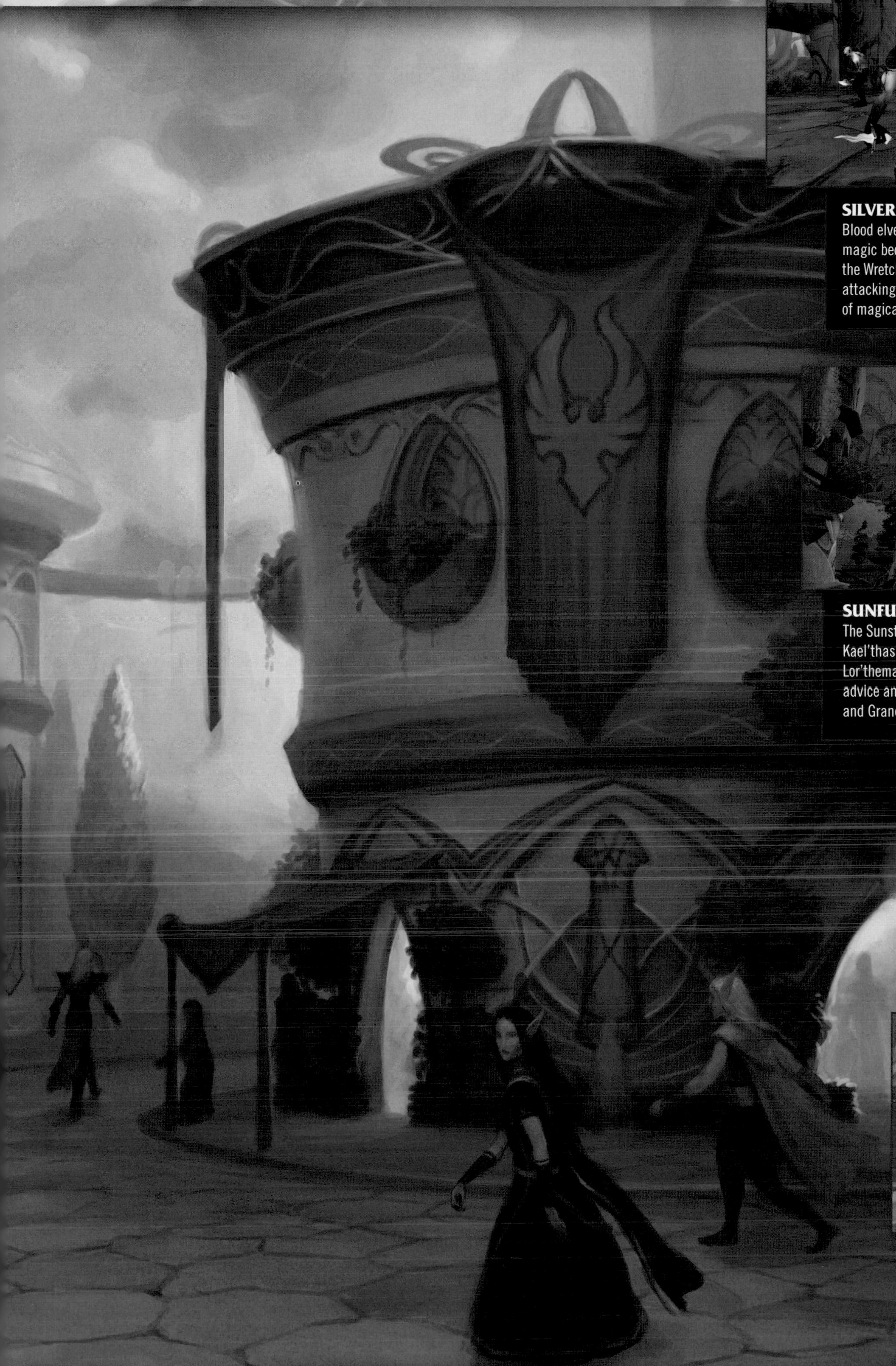

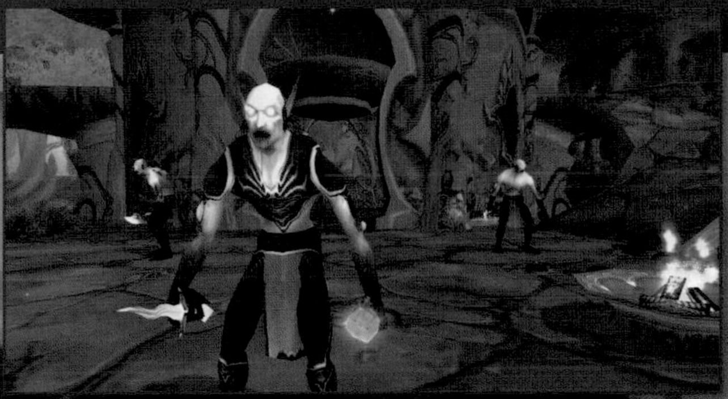

SILVERMOON WRETCHED
Blood elves who fail to control their addiction to magic become pale, thin, and warped. Known as the Wretched, they prowl the Ruins of Silvermoon, attacking travelers and searching for remnants of magical power on which to feed.

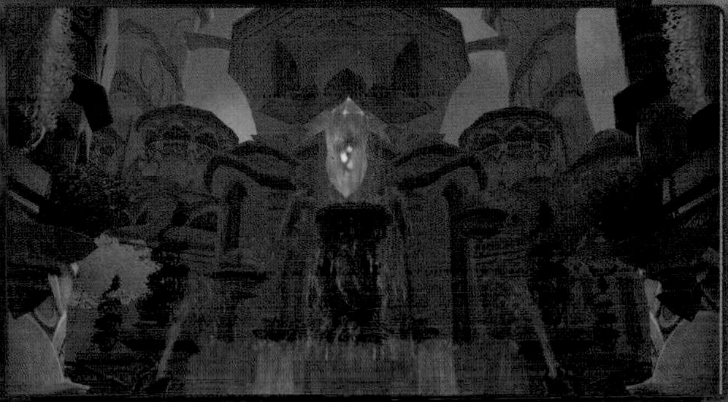

SUNFURY SPIRE AND COURT OF THE SUN
The Sunstrider dynasty came to an end when Prince Kael'thas betrayed his people. Today, Regent Lord Lor'themar Theron governs from the Sunfury Spire with the advice and council of Ranger-general Halduron Brightwing and Grand Magister Rommath.

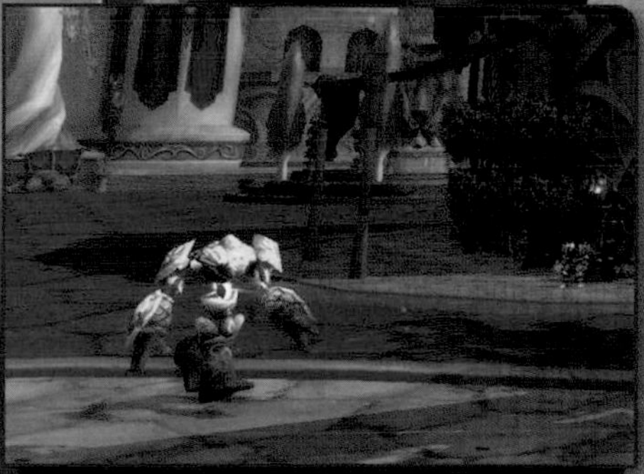

ARCANE GUARDIAN
Although beautiful, Silvermoon City is far from defenseless. Few can ignore the ever-present Arcane Guardians—magical golem-like sentries that patrol the city—who keep the peace, but are quick to defend against any would-be attackers.

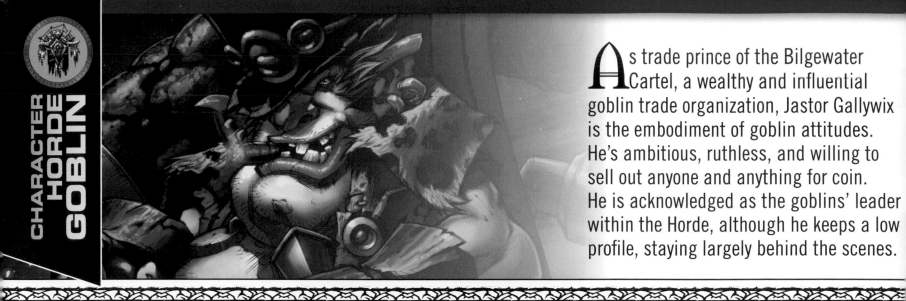

As trade prince of the Bilgewater Cartel, a wealthy and influential goblin trade organization, Jastor Gallywix is the embodiment of goblin attitudes. He's ambitious, ruthless, and willing to sell out anyone and anything for coin. He is acknowledged as the goblins' leader within the Horde, although he keeps a low profile, staying largely behind the scenes.

JASTOR GALLYWIX

"There ain't a goblin alive more powerful and dangerous than me. I can give you everything you need to succeed."

MERCHANT PRINCE

The goblins Candy Cane and Chip Endale have become notable supporters of Jastor Gallywix, at the expense of previous love interests. They will come to regret their disloyalty.

Jastor was born on the island of Kezan, the poor son of a tinker, Luzik—his mother had left them to pursue a life of piracy. Even at a young age, Jastor displayed the ruthlessness that would later define him. At age ten, when a street gang not only assaulted his father for money, but stole a cookie that he had obtained for Jastor, Jastor struck back. He blew up the gang by booby-trapping their payment with explosives, took over their territory, and set about expanding his empire.

Jastor soon amassed enough money and influence to become the trade prince of the Bilgewater Cartel. When Azeroth was torn asunder by the event known as the Cataclysm, nearby Mount Kajaro erupted, leaving the goblin homeland of Kezan facing destruction. Jastor, not wasting an opportunity for profit, offered citizens passage on his ship… at the price of their life savings. When an Alliance warship engaging a Horde craft near the Lost Isles destroyed Jastor's ship, he recovered quickly. He forced some of the survivors into slavery, compelling them to mine kaja'mite at the Gallywix Labor Mine. Unfortunately for Jastor, the surviving orcs from the earlier naval battle allied with the enslaved goblins and foiled his plans. Jastor was defeated, but Thrall, the former Horde Warchief, allowed Jastor to continue to lead… for now. The Bilgewater Cartel would have a new home in Azshara, and it would set aside its neutrality to join the Horde.

LIFE OF A TRADE PRINCE
Despite Jastor's ruthlessness, his position as Trade Prince was coming under threat from his competitors before the Cataclysm. Nonetheless, he was quick to exploit the chaos and secure his place.

ACCEPTANCE INTO THE HORDE
Despite inauspicious beginnings, the goblins of the Bilgewater Cartel are members of the Horde in good standing. Their employment of guile, arcane arts, and engineering prowess has earned them distinction among their allies.

MONUMENT TO GREED
Jastor's residence, Gallywix's Pleasure Palace, is in western Azshara. It boasts beautiful ocean views, a pool, a private grenade-based golf course, sauna, and secret booze cellar. All of these luxuries are surveyed by a giant sculpted head of Jastor.

Jastor absolutely loves his top hat; it's a symbol of his status and position.

Quick-witted and ruthless, Jastor can take advantage of any situation to turn a quick profit.

KEY DATA

NAME Jastor Gallywix

GENDER AND RACE Male goblin

AFFILIATION Horde

STATUS Living

TITLES Trade Prince of the Bilgewater Cartel, Big G

RELATIVES Luzik Gallywix (father, unknown fate)

Even the disastrous Cataclysm turned in Jastor's favor. He used the opportunity to try to enslave goblin survivors, stealing their life's savings in the process.

LOVE-HATE RELATIONSHIP
Jastor fell in love with Nessa, daughter of the previous Trade Prince Maldy. To prove both his ruthlessness and worth to Nessa, Jastor bought the majority of Maldy's holdings, ruining him and claiming his position. Maldy and Nessa were exiled, with Maldy later dying "accidentally." Each year, Jastor sends Nessa a painting of himself enjoying his riches, and in return she sends him boxes wired with explosives.

GOBLINS

§hrewd, greedy, and ruthless, goblins have a long-standing reputation for being neutral in the rest of the world. Although one goblin cartel did in fact side with the Horde during the Second War, currently the only goblins to abandon their neutrality are those of the Bilgewater Cartel, formerly of the isle of Kezan. Heroes of goblin society are not bastions of honor or integrity. Instead, goblins tend to admire the ruthless acquisition of profit, by any means necessary.

BARON REVILGAZ

Baron Revilgaz is the leader of the Blackwater Raiders, a group of privateers and pirates closely affiliated with the Steamwheedle Cartel. Revilgaz controls the neutral town of Booty Bay in the Cape of Stranglethorn, and he is significantly invested in maintaining Booty Bay's independent affiliation. Overseeing the port town's operation from atop the Salty Sailor Tavern, Revilgaz keeps a watchful eye on what transpires in his town and the docks, as well as the movements of visitors and tourists. His advisor, the tauren Fleet Master Seahorn, assists in managing Revilgaz's navy and defending the town from the Bloodsail Buccaneers, another pirate organization that vies for control of the region.

KEY DATA

TITLE Baron, Head of the Blackwater Raiders
STATUS Living
AFFILIATION Independent (Neutral)
RELATIVES None known

GAZLOWE

Gazlowe is the acknowledged leader of the port town of Ratchet in the Northern Barrens of Kalimdor. Now affiliated with the Steamwheedle Cartel, Gazlowe was once contracted by Warchief Thrall as Chief Engineer for the Horde. He aided significantly in the reconstruction of Orgrimmar following the Cataclysm. A clever engineer, Gazlowe's devices and explosives helped tauren High Chieftain Baine Bloodhoof reclaim Thunder Bluff from the treacherous grasp of Magatha Grimtotem—and in an unexpected show of respect for Baine and his recently deceased father, Cairne, Gazlowe offered his aid at a discount. Yet although Gazlowe has shown much support for the Horde and little love for the Alliance, he still maintains a neutral stance, and is just as happy to take Alliance coin as Horde.

KEY DATA

TITLE Chief Engineer and leader of Ratchet
STATUS Living
AFFILIATION Independent (Neutral)
RELATIVES None known

TRADE PRINCE DONAIS

It has never been clear exactly what cartel Trade Prince Donais leads. Currently, he appears to be working with Trade Prince Jastor Gallywix and the Bilgewater Cartel in some capacity. Those searching for Donais can find him in Gallywix's Pleasure Palace in Azshara, taking advantage of the many delights found there; however, he doesn't like to be disturbed.

KEY DATA

TITLE Trade Prince
STATUS Living
AFFILIATION Independent
RELATIVES None known

BOSS MIDA

Boss Mida of the Bilgewater Cartel, known as Her Tallness, oversees the Goblin Slums of Orgrimmar. Her companions are her personal assistant Kazit, Bruiser Janx, and Engineer Niff. Cunning, ruthless, and efficient, Mida makes sure that the goblins are well represented in Horde political and economic affairs. She uses her large mechanical Shredder to move around the city, and her shrewd eye for business has managed to make quite a reputation, as well as profit, for herself.

KEY DATA

TITLE Her Tallness
STATUS Living
AFFILIATION Horde
RELATIVES None known

POZZIK

Pozzik, a goblin affiliated with the Bilgewater Cartel, is a rocket car enthusiast. He has a long-standing rivalry with gnome engineer Fizzle Brassbolts over which is superior: goblin or gnomish engineering. In an attempt to prove the superiority of their respective race, Pozzik and Fizzle built the Mirage Raceway on the Shimmering Flats in Thousand Needles, and both built rocket cars and enlisted teams to drive them.

KEY DATA

TITLE None
STATUS Living
AFFILIATION Horde
RELATIVES None known

KEZAN/AZSHARA

Kezan boasted a number of natural resources. An unusual mineral ore known as kaja'mite was mined from under Mount Kajaro.

The goblin city of Bilgewater Port was located on the tropical island of Kezan. This large port linked to the underground goblin metropolis of Undermine. Although it was once a profitable port city, Bilgewater Port was destroyed when Kezan's volcano, Mount Kajaro, erupted during the Cataclysm, forcing its residents to flee to safety.

The Bilgewater Cartel, run by Trade Prince Gallywix, controlled Bilgewater Port. It bestowed enormous wealth upon Gallywix, who oversaw its—and his own—interests in Undermine.

During the Cataclysm, the upheaval that the great black dragon Deathwing caused set Mount Kajaro ablaze. The volcano erupted, and molten lava threatened to incinerate the island. The goblins of Bilgewater Port escaped, but the ultimate fate of Kezan and the goblin capital of Undermine remains unknown.

AZSHARA

Now members of the Horde, the goblins of the Bilgewater Cartel have chosen to settle in Azshara, just to the north of Orgrimmar. As a unique token of their gratitude, they have terraformed the region into a giant Horde symbol, and established the town of Bilgewater Harbor on an island in the Bay of Storms. The Harbor acts as both home to the goblins, and as a naval port for the entire Orgrimmar fleet.

THE REVENGE OF SYLVANAS

Defeated by Arthas Menethil in the Third War, Sylvanas
Windrunner was not allowed to rest. Arthas brutally transformed
her into a banshee, bound to serve the Scourge. Although
Sylvanas eventually regained her body, her free will, and an
army of Forsaken followers, one thing eluded her: Vengeance.
For years, Sylvanas dedicated herself and her people to seeking
vengeance on Arthas. When at last he made his move, Sylvanas
was among the first to leap at the opportunity to lay siege to
Northrend and put an end to him once and for all.

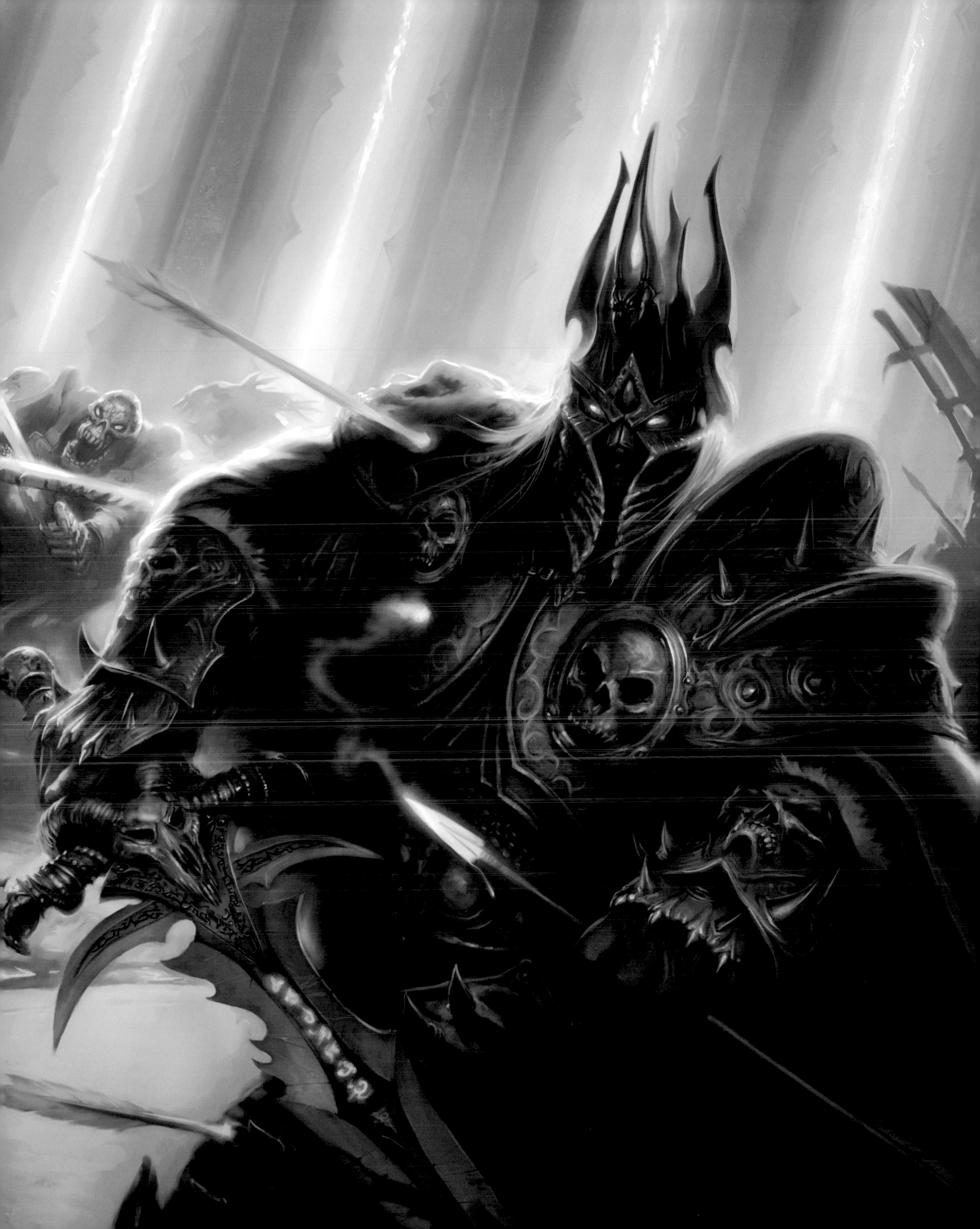

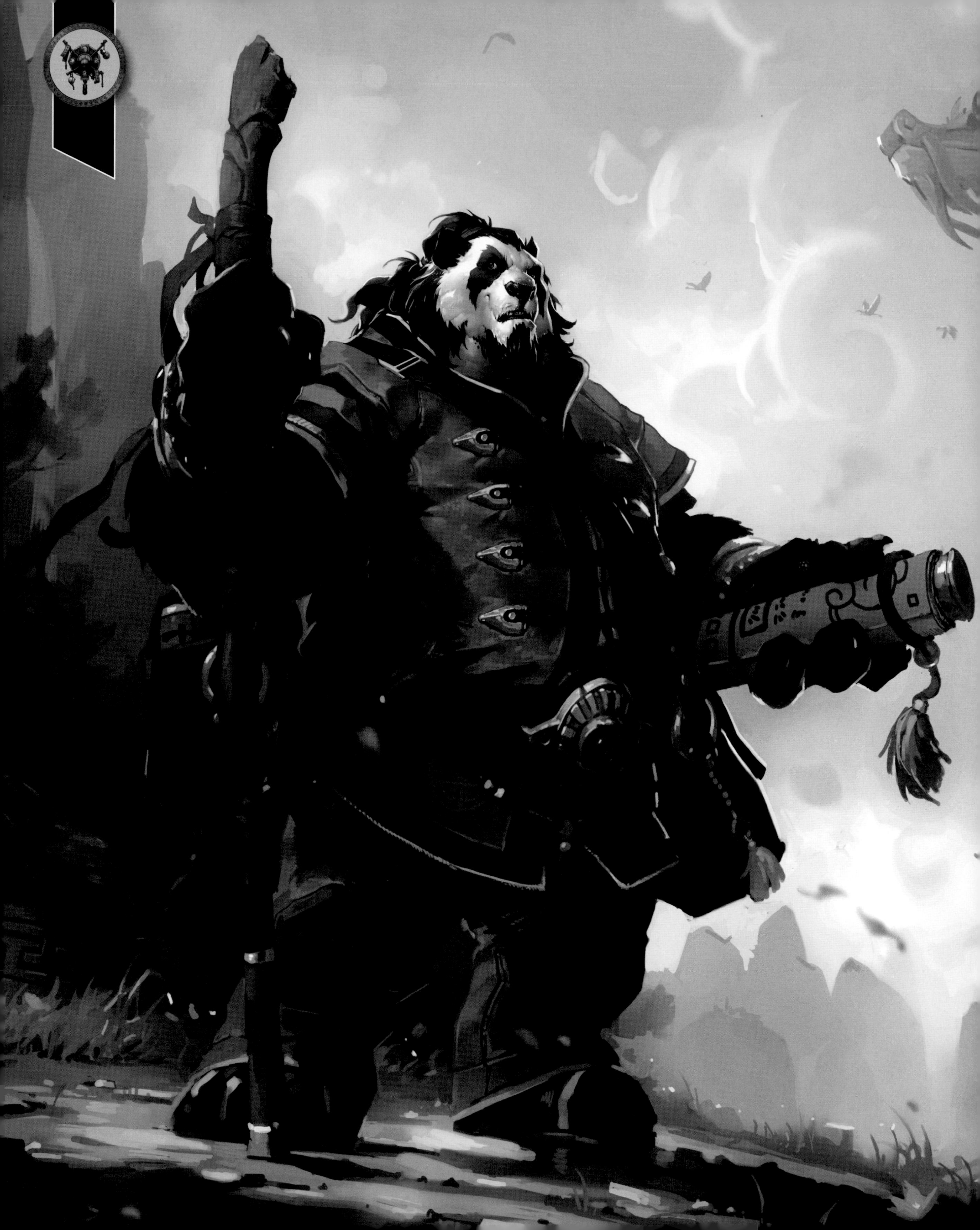

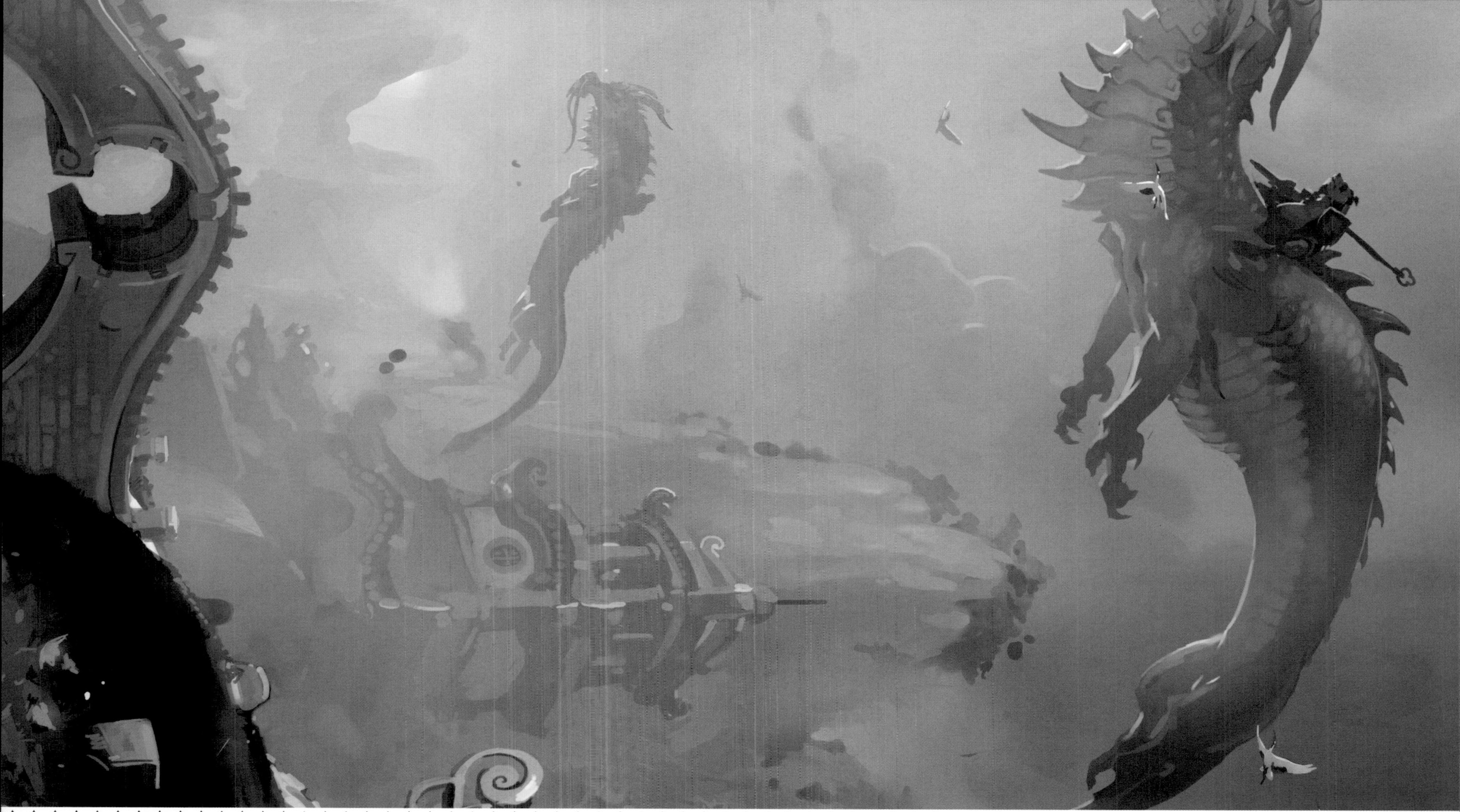

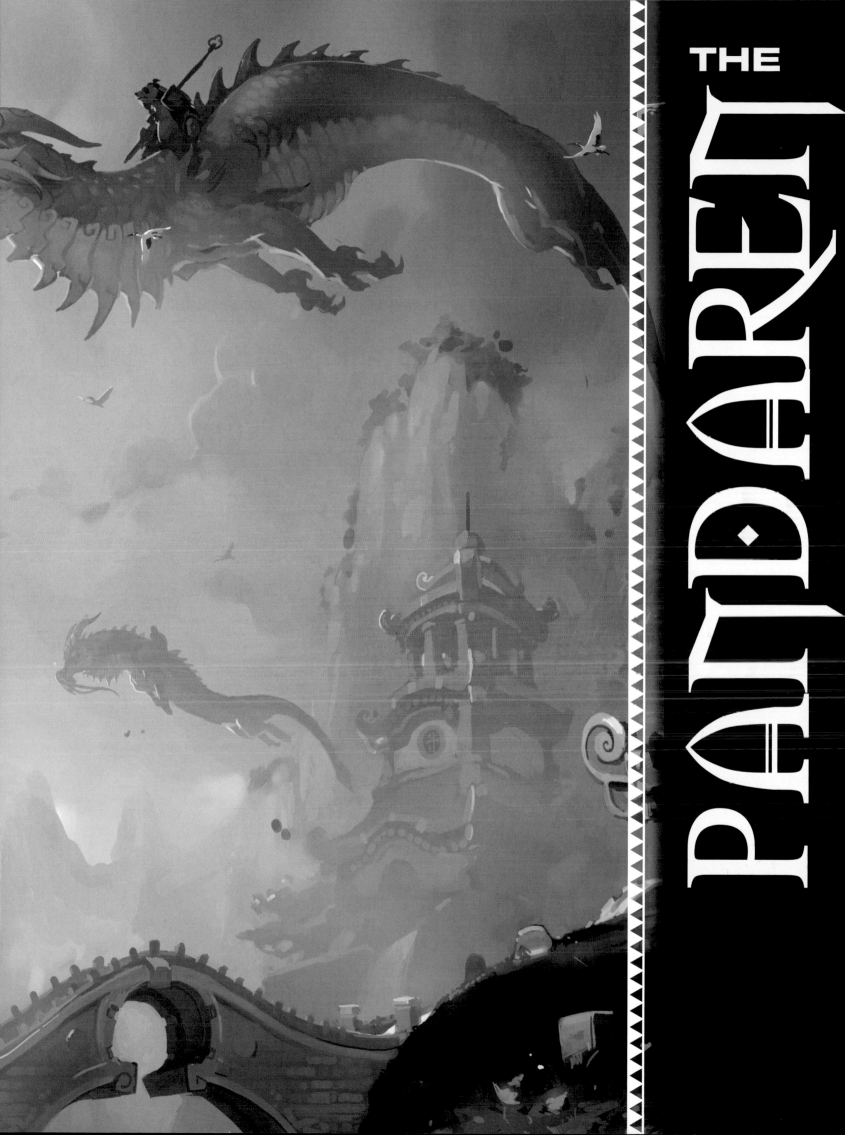

THE PANDAREN

Wanderer and explorer Chen spent years roaming the lands of Azeroth, making friends and sampling brews. Although he fought when he felt he must, he spent most of his time in jovial contemplation and searching for exotic ingredients to enhance his alcoholic refreshments. Chen exemplifies many pandaren ideals, such as the importance of a good heart and loyalty to friends and family.

CHEN STORMSTOUT

"Every one you meet is a story. Every place you go is an adventure. Every drink you have is the best you've ever tasted. This is not such a bad life, is it?"

THE WANDERER'S WAY

Chen's niece Li Li wanted to be an adventurer like her uncle. Chen saved her from a fel orc Blademaster and a naga sea witch.

Chen Stormstout was born and raised on the Wandering Isle, a traveling island outside Pandaria that Chen's ancestors inhabited long ago in their quest to explore Azeroth. Chen spent his youth studying martial arts with his brother, Chon Po, and best friend, Strongbo. But Chen always dreamed of traveling, and he soon left for lands unknown. Obsessed with brewing, his search for ingredients led him across Azeroth, meeting many prominent figures along the way—including Warchief Thrall, Vol'jin, and Rexxar.

Eventually Chen resolved to find Pandaria, and he embarked on a journey with his niece, Li Li. Once they found Pandaria, Chen and Li Li met their long-lost relations and discovered a link among their family: the Stormstout Brewery. After clearing the Brewery of the hozen and virmen that had infiltrated it, Chen set out to the Dread Wastes to locate the rest of his relatives and help with the mantid threat.

He stayed with his relatives until events beyond his control unfolded, when he discovered Vol'jin, leader of the troll Darkspear Tribe, wounded alongside a river. Tending to Vol'jin's wounds, he took him to Shado-Pan Monastery to recover. This deed would test Chen's—and Pandaria's—old friendships and long-valued neutrality.

CHEN'S FAMILY

Leaving the Wandering Isle meant leaving family behind. Both Chen's best friend, Strongbo (on left), and Chen's brother, Chon Po, weren't happy about Chen's abrupt departure from the Wandering Isle. Chon Po went so far as to forbid his daughter Li Li from following in Chen's footsteps.

THE WANDERING ISLE

Chen's birthplace, the Wandering Isle, is actually the back of a giant sea turtle named Shen-zin Su. Shen-zin Su travels the oceans of Azeroth, never staying in one place for long.

STORMSTOUT BREWERY

Chen's remarkable skill with brewing ale turned out to be a family trait. His ancestors on Pandaria were renowned for their brewing and founded the Stormstout Brewery, famous for its many varieties of delicious ale.

Chen is a powerful martial arts specialist. He chose to leave rather than fight his best friend, Bo, for leadership of his school.

Brewing is an ancient art among the pandaren, and throughout his travels Chen has left behind potent kegs of his renowned brew.

SHADOWS OF THE HORDE
Agents of Warchief Garrosh Hellscream nearly killed the troll leader in an assassination attempt. Chen helped the badly hurt Vol'jin recover. Time will tell if Vol'jin can learn Chen's wisdom and survive in the land of Pandaria.

The pandaren philosophy, according to Chen: "Why do we fight? To protect Home and Family... to preserve Balance and bring Harmony. For my kind, the true question is: What is worth fighting for?"

KEY DATA

NAME Chen Stormstout

GENDER AND RACE Male pandaren

AFFILIATION Independent (Neutral)

STATUS Living

TITLE Brewmaster

RELATIVES Chon Po (brother); Xiu Li (sister-in-law, deceased); Li Li (niece); Shisai (nephew); Big Dan (distant relation); Mama (distant relation); Gao (distant relation); Han (distant relation); Evie (distant relation, deceased)

PANDAREN

The pandaren culture stretches back for thousands of years. In ancient times, they were enslaved by the mogu, a tyrannical, brutal race. Thousands of years before the Great Sundering, the pandaren race began a rebellion that ended the mogu tyranny and began a time of peace. Notable pandaren are typically explorers, storytellers, and masters of combat.

JI FIREPAW

Ji Firepaw is a native of the Wandering Isle, and a follower of the Huojin philosophy. His belief is that a person must act to defend what he or she believes in and what he or she cares about, and that inaction is the greatest injustice. When an Alliance ship crashed on the Wandering Isle, carrying Horde prisoners, Ji met with representatives of the Horde and found a strong resonance between Horde values and his own. Thus, he moved to Orgrimmar to act as the pandaren representative within the Horde, where he helps to explain the way of monks to anyone within the Horde that is willing to learn. He has been known to both watch and engage others in the arena, showing them the graceful martial skills of the monks.

KEY DATA

TITLE Leader of Huojin Pandaren
STATUS Living
AFFILIATION Horde
RELATIVES None known

EMPEROR SHAOHAO

The Last Emperor of Pandaria, Shaohao came into power and received news of a vision from a jinyu waterspeaker, foretelling the Burning Legion entering into Azeroth and the Great Sundering. Wanting to protect his kingdom, Shaohao sought out the wisdom of the Jade Serpent, who told him to divest himself of negative emotion and become one with the land. Shaohao traveled the world to combat the physical manifestations of his own inner demons, also known as the sha.

After defeating the sha, Shaohao established the Shado-Pan to continue to watch and protect against the sha menace. Having become one with himself, Shaohao fulfilled his destiny and became one with the land, enshrouding Pandaria in dense mists. It remained hidden from the rest of Azeroth for thousands of years.

KEY DATA

TITLE Emperor of Pandaria
STATUS Unknown
AFFILIATION Independent (Neutral)
RELATIVES None known

AYSA CLOUDSINGER

Aysa Cloudsinger is a master of the Tushui philosophy, which holds that life is meant to be lived through training, meditation, and moral conviction. She believes that the ends do not justify the means and that dishonor must be avoided. As Master Feng once said, "Discipline is not a war that is won. It is a battle, constantly fought." This concept is at the core of Tushui philosophy. When an Alliance ship crash-landed on the Wandering Isle, Aysa was immediately drawn to the Alliance, finding their ideals similar to her own. She then traveled to Stormwind City, where she acts as a representative for the pandaren people and provides training to interested individuals.

KEY DATA

TITLE Master of the Tushui
STATUS Living
AFFILIATION Alliance
RELATIVES None known

LI LI STORMSTOUT

Precocious and mischievous, Li Li Stormstout is the niece of Chen Stormstout, and shares his thirst for exploration. Raised by her father Chon Po, Li Li always yearned to follow in her uncle's footsteps and explore the world, much to her father's dismay. She ran away from the Wandering Isle in order to search for her wayward uncle, and after many adventures eventually located Chen, returning to the Isle in triumph. Later, Chen and Li Li departed the Wandering Isle once more—this time, to successfully find and explore the lost continent of Pandaria. Li Li is quick to make friends, but a fierce fighter as well, and enjoys keeping records of all of her travels in journals.

KEY DATA

TITLE None
STATUS Living
AFFILIATION Independent (Neutral)
RELATIVES Chon Po (father); Xiu Li (mother, deceased); Shisai (brother); Chen (uncle); Mei (grandmother)

LIU LANG

Thousands of years ago, Liu Lang longed to see the world beyond Pandaria's mists. He set out on his journey on the back of a great sea turtle, surmising that sea turtles would always return to the beach where they were born, and therefore he could always find his way back home. Liu Lang named the turtle Shen-zin Su. Few pandarens expected to see Liu Lang again, and they were astonished when he returned to Pandaria with his tales of the world abroad. He asked if any wanted to travel with him, and initially only one replied—a pandaren named Shinizi, who later became his wife. As the years passed, the turtle Shen-zin Su grew larger, and more and more like-minded pandaren joined Liu Lang on his journeys. At the age of 122, Liu Lang passed away. After Liu Lang died, Shen-zin Su never returned to Pandaria, but Liu Lang's followers continue to live on Shen-zin Su, now known as the Wandering Isle, to this day.

KEY DATA

TITLE None
STATUS Deceased
AFFILIATION Independent (Neutral)
RELATIVES Shinizi (wife, deceased)

LOREWALKER CHO

Cho is a Lorewalker, one of many historians dedicated to uncovering and preserving Pandaria's rich history. Enchanted with the tales of both Alliance and Horde, Cho is quick to make friends with both factions. Cho traveled Pandaria in search of the secrets of its past, uncovering the history of the mogu, the Zandalari, and their resurrection of the Thunder King. Inquisitive and wise, Cho continues to catalogue the history of Pandaria in the Vale of Eternal Blossoms—and entertain travelers with tales of the continent.

KEY DATA

TITLE Lorewalker
STATUS Living
AFFILIATION Independent (Neutral)
RELATIVES None known

MASTER SHANG XI

Master Shang Xi was a skilled teacher of martial arts and philosophy. Both Aysa Cloudsinger and Ji Firepaw were his students, as were other pandaren heroes in their youth. Rather than telling his students what to believe, he introduced them to ideas and let them find their own way. Compassionate and wise, Shang Xi sensed Shen-zin Su's illness, which led to the discovery of the Alliance and Horde forces on the Wandering Isle. Shang Xi passed on before he could meet the strangers himself, but his students remain true to his legacy.

KEY DATA

TITLE Master
STATUS Deceased
AFFILIATION Independent (Neutral)
RELATIVES None known

TARAN ZHU

Taran Zhu is the leader of the Shado-Pan, an order of monks that was established to protect Pandaria from the sha—malevolent entities born of negative emotion. When he discovered the arrival of Alliance and Horde forces on Pandaria, he warned each of the sha and the consequences of their actions. Angered by the actions of each faction, Taran Zhu eventually became possessed by the Sha of Hatred, later freed by adventurers. Although still rightfully wary of both factions, Taran Zhu is willing to put this reticence aside and accept the help of the strangers, as the threat of the sha, mogu, and mantid is far larger than perhaps even the Shado-Pan can handle. Taran Zhu's gruff nature can be off-putting to some, but this gruffness is born of dedication to protecting Pandaria. Devoted to this task, Taran Zhu will stop at nothing to keep Pandaria safe—and when Alliance and Horde tensions rise to a fever pitch on the Isle of Thunder, he is quick to demand a stop to the fighting, pointing out that tensions always lead to a deadly circle of violence.

KEY DATA

TITLE Lord of the Shado-Pan
STATUS Living
AFFILIATION Independent (Neutral)
RELATIVES None Known

PANDARIA

Ten thousand years ago, the pandaren Emperor Shaohao became one with the land of Pandaria in order to protect the country from the Great Sundering, and enshrouded Pandaria with dense mists. Hidden away, many thought the homeland of the pandaren race was merely a legend, until the island was revealed to the world after the Cataclysm.

STORMSTOUT BREWERY

The Stormstout family is renowned for its many varieties of delicious brew. The Stormstout Brewery, located in the Valley of the Four Winds, has been a presence on Pandaria for generations. In recent years, the Brewery has fallen to the watch of Uncle Gao Stormstout. While well-meaning, Uncle Gao has been unable to prevent an invasion by hozen and virmen pests.

ANCIENT HERITAGE

Thousands of years ago, the races of Pandaria were enslaved by the brutal mogu. Much of the architecture in Pandaria was carved by slaves. The pandaren eventually learned to fight without weapons and rebelled against their mogu masters, crushing the mogu empire for good. Yet most of the architecture built during that time still stands, a reminder of that dark and important period in Pandaria's history.

KUN-LAI SUMMIT

THE JADE FOREST

TOWNLONG STEPPES

VALE OF ETERNAL BLOSSOMS

DREAD WASTES

VALLEY OF THE FOUR WINDS

KRASARANG WILDS

MOGU ARCHITECTURE

Remnants of mogu architecture are still scattered throughout Pandaria. The opulent structures, mighty palaces, and massive statues are a testament to the might of the mogu empire, and a reminder of the slaves that created them. In recent years, the mogu have begun to resurge, seeking to reclaim these ancient places that hide secrets of mogu power.

THE SERPENT'S SPINE

The Serpent's Spine is a great wall that separates the Townlong Steppes and the Dread Wastes from the rest of Pandaria. Thousands of years ago, the first mogu emperor, Lei Shen, realized the mantid race could never be enslaved, remaining a constant threat. Thus, Lei Shen ordered the construction of the Serpent's Spine in order to seal the mantid away. Built by slaves, the Serpent's Spine still stands, now protecting the citizens of Pandaria from mantid invasion.

SHADO-PAN MONASTERY

Ten thousand years ago, the pandaren Emperor Shaohao bested his own negative emotions while on the journey to protect Pandaria from the imminent sundering of the world. Realizing that the sha—malevolent entities spawned from negative emotion—would forever be a threat, he founded the Shado-Pan. This organization of Pandaria's finest warriors continues to restrain the sha to this day. Their home and training ground, the Shado-Pan Monastery, stands on the very location that Emperor Shaohao founded the organization.

TEMPLE OF THE WHITE TIGER

High atop the peaks of Kun-Lai Summit, the Temple of the White Tiger is a training ground for any who seek to improve their strength and martial prowess. The Temple is also home to Xuen the White Tiger, one of the four great spirits known as August Celestials who watch over and protect Pandaria. Xuen is the spirit of strength, and often offers challenges of physical prowess and skill to willing travelers.

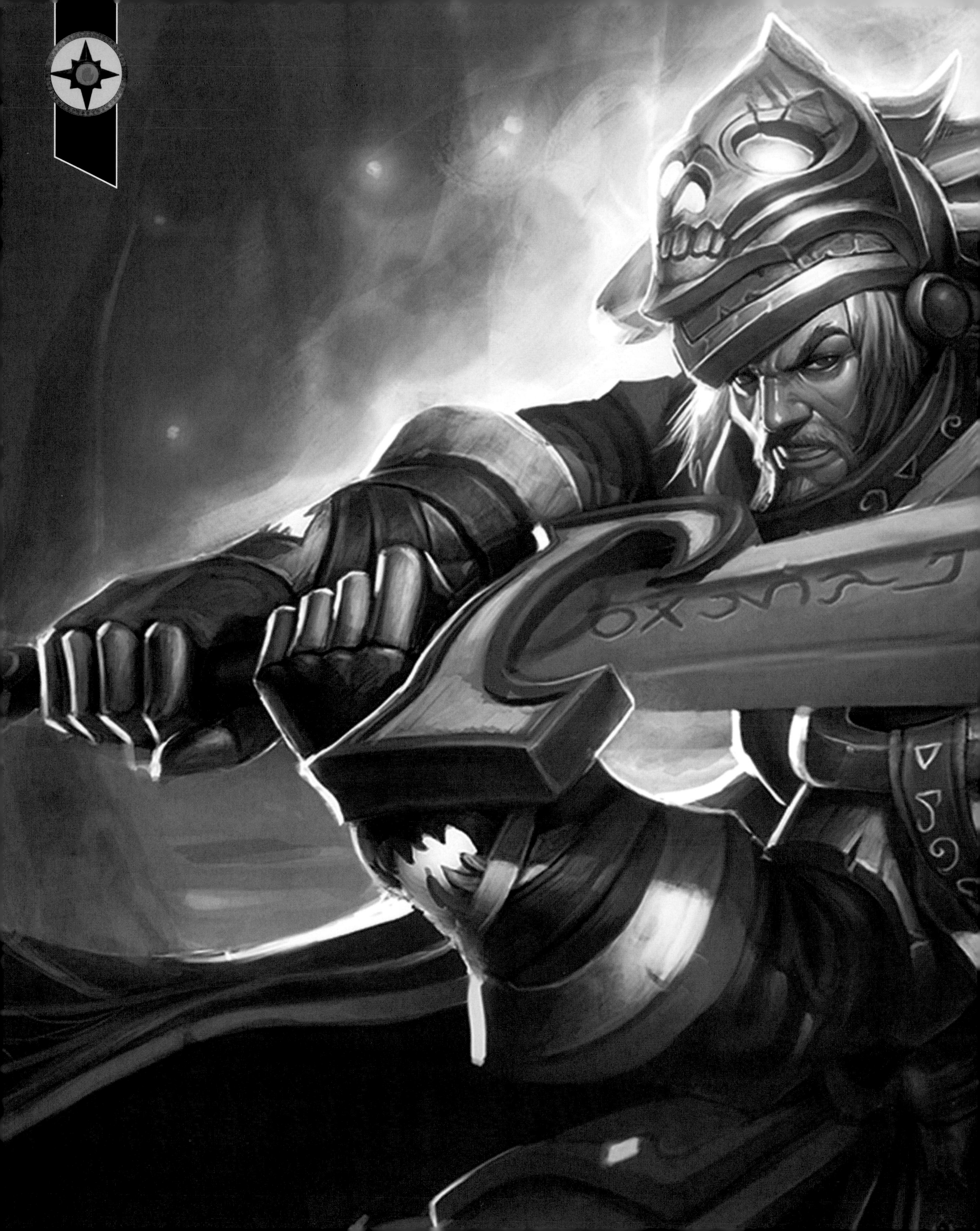

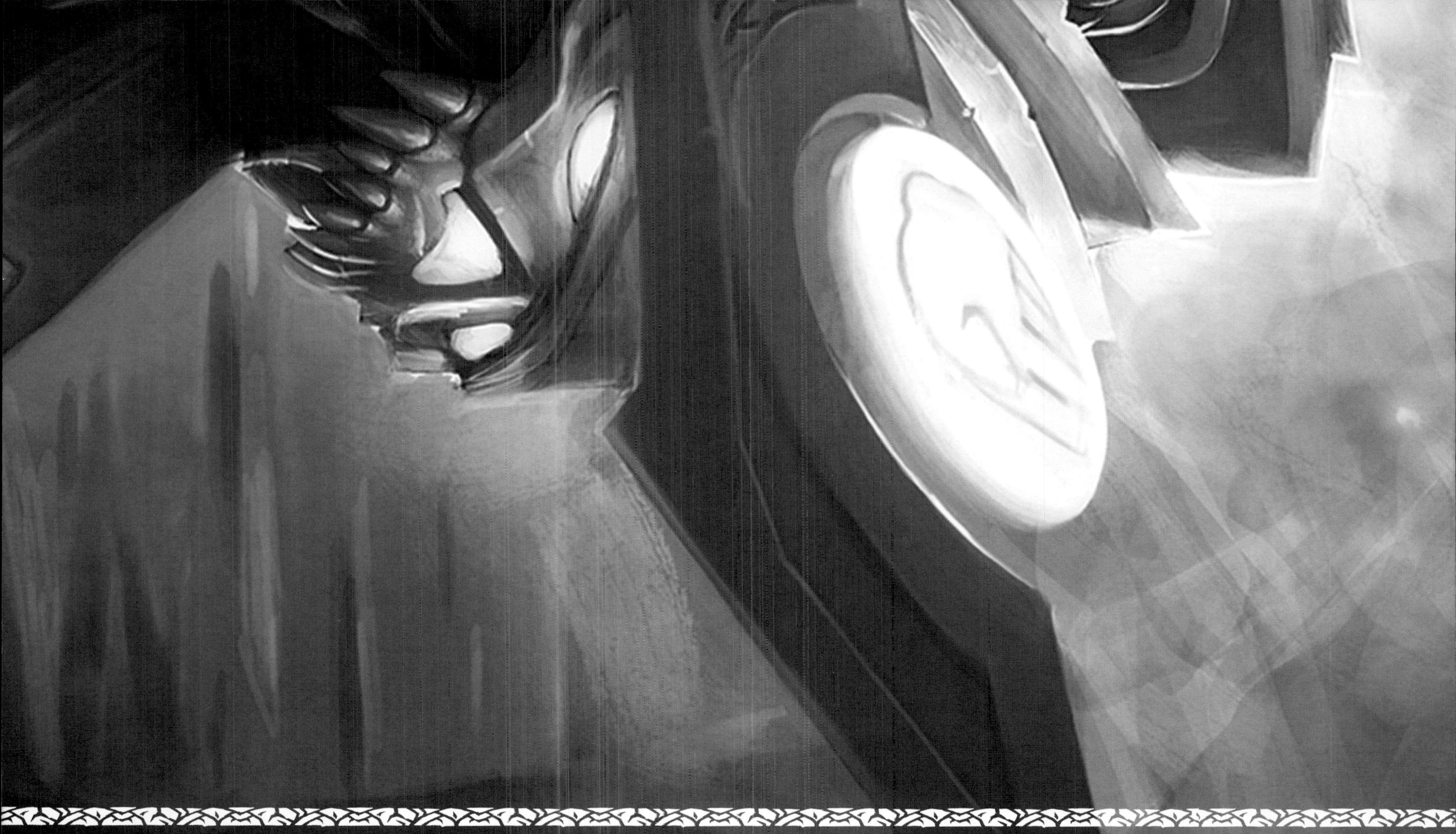

HEROES AND VILLAINS

INDEPENDENT FACTIONS

Throughout Azeroth's history, there have been significant groups that have transcended racial, cultural, and factional borders. They were formed to represent specific ideals or accomplish a specific purpose. Although some do not accept members from outside their ranks, most welcome assistance by interested parties, and reward those who demonstrate an appreciation for their values or further their cause.

THE ARGENT CRUSADE

The Argent Crusade is comprised of members of the Argent Dawn—an organization dedicated to protecting Azeroth from outside threats—and paladins from the Order of the Silver Hand. Created during the recent Scourge invasion, the Argent Crusade was formed as a direct result of a Scourge attack on the Light's Hope Chapel in the Eastern Kingdoms. After a confrontation with the Lich King himself, Highlord Tirion Fordring assumed leadership over the Argent Dawn and united the two organizations. The Argent Crusade's purpose was simple—to travel to the peaks of Icecrown, confront the Lich King for his crimes, and put an end to him once and for all. While the mission was a success, the cost of the war was staggering. Currently, the Argent Crusade maintains bases in both the Eastern and Western Plaguelands, seeking to root out and destroy the last remnants of the Scourge in both regions and restore the corrupted land, while also keeping a close eye on Sylvanas Windrunner and her Forsaken.

THE KNIGHTS OF THE SILVER HAND

Saddened by the casualties suffered by priests during the First War, Archbishop Alonsus Faol sought a solution. He began to train knights in the way of the Light, and priests in the arts of martial combat. The first of these holy warriors, dubbed paladins—Uther the Lightbringer, Turalyon, Tirion Fordring, Gavinrad the Dire, and Saidan Dathrohan—were anointed in Alonsus Chapel in Stratholme. Thus was created the Knights of the Silver Hand. After the order's resounding success in the Second War, more members were recruited. The Knights of the Silver Hand was effectively disbanded by Prince Arthas Menethil during the Third War. However, Tirion Fordring later emerged from his exile and took his place as Highlord of the Silver Hand. Fordring subsequently merged the Knights of the Silver Hand with the Argent Dawn, creating the Argent Crusade.

THE KNIGHTS OF THE EBON BLADE

The death knight Darion Mograine was given command of an army and ordered by the Lich King to crush the Scarlet Crusade and Argent Dawn. After butchering the Scarlet Crusade, Darion's forces met the Argent Dawn at Light's Hope Chapel. However, the arrival of Tirion Fordring allowed the Argent Dawn to overcome the death knights, and Darion's army surrendered. The surrender was interrupted by the arrival of the Lich King. Darion's efforts were revealed to be merely a suicide mission designed to draw Tirion out of hiding. Inspired by a vision of his father, Darion turned against the Lich King and gave Tirion the corrupted blade, Ashbringer. Tirion cleansed the blade, and used it to attack the Lich King, who was forced to retreat. Darion pledged the death knights to destroying the Lich King, and named them the Knights of the Ebon Blade.

THE CENARION CIRCLE

Thousands of years ago, during a conflict known as the War of the Satyr, many young night elf druids used a pack form that shapeshifted them into vicious wolves. To prevent future druids from making the same mistake, combat the threat posed by the wolves, and to establish a tradition of druidism, Malfurion Stormrage, the first of the mortal druids on Azeroth, formed the Cenarion Circle, named after his mentor, the demigod Cenarius. After the threat was resolved, the Cenarion Circle remained as an organization of druids dedicated to protecting and preserving nature. It also provided young druids with guidance, preventing any further misuse of druidic power. Today, the Cenarion Circle embraces members of many different races, and strives to maintain the natural balance of the world.

THE EARTHEN RING

The shamanistic organization of the Earthen Ring is dedicated to preserving and studying the elemental balance of the world. An obscure organization, the group only recently made its presence known to the entire world. Originally led by the shaman Muln Earthfury and the Elder Council—a group of the most powerful shaman on Azeroth—the Earthen Ring was instrumental in preventing further damage wrought by Deathwing's abrupt emergence from the elemental plane into Azeroth. After Deathwing's demise, Muln stepped down as leader, and Thrall succeeded him. Today, the Earthen Ring still works to restore the elements to harmony and repair the damage caused by Deathwing's emergence.

THE TWILIGHT'S HAMMER

The Twilight's Hammer was originally an orc clan on Draenor, prior to being put under the control of the ogre mage Cho'gall, a member of the Shadow Council. Under Cho'gall's rule, the clan reveled in destruction and chaos, eventually seeking the end of the world itself. Thought destroyed in the Second War, the Twilight's Hammer survived, as did Cho'gall. Sometimes called the Twilight's Hammer cult, the organization fell under the sway of the Old God C'Thun, with Cho'gall still at the helm. During the Cataclysm, the cult grew substantially in numbers, working in tandem with the black dragon Deathwing and the Old Gods to bring about the Hour of Twilight, the end of all life on Azeroth. Cho'gall and Deathwing were both killed for their efforts. Today, the remaining members of the Twilight's Hammer have largely scattered.

THE SCARLET CRUSADE

After the Knights of the Silver Hand broke up around the time of the Third War, many of the knights desired to continue their assault against the undead Scourge. Some founded the Scarlet Crusade, with their goal the complete destruction of the Scourge. Unfortunately, they pursued this aim with unquestioning zealotry, killing not only Scourge, but any who were remotely suspected to be undead as well. They became fanatically driven to destroy evil wherever they thought they had found it, without mercy or compassion. Their intolerant attitudes led them to despise all non-human races. Contributing to this was the fact that their Lord Commander, Saidan Dathrohan, was actually the dreadlord Balnazzar of the Burning Legion, who had infiltrated the organization at its inception. Today, few members of the Scarlet Crusade remain alive. Many who perished at the hands of Balnazzar were later raised into undeath using the dreadlord's necromantic powers, becoming The Risen, and forced to live on as the very creatures they had once zealously sought to destroy.

THE SCOURGE

The Scourge was created by the Burning Legion as a monstrous army of undead under the command of the Lich King. The legions of the Scourge devastated the kingdom of Lordaeron and the elven kingdom of Quel'Thalas during the Third War. Although many Scourge are mindless slaves, other recruits to the Lich King's army have proved formidable enemies in their own right.

BLOOD QUEEN LANA'THEL

Lana'thel was the leader of the San'layn, a group of Kael'thas' greatest followers, raised into undeath by the Lich King and transformed into vampiric beings. In life, Lana'thel wielded the enchanted blade Quel'Delar and served in Prince Kael'thas' army when it marched on Northrend. Arthas Menethil defeated the blood elves and routed their surviving forces. Lana'thel was cornered by the Lich King who turned her into the Blood Queen, leader of the San'layn. Yet a small portion of Lana'thel remembered her life as a mortal. She was constantly distracted by Quel'Delar and its remembrances of her former life. In time, these memories drove Lana'thel into a fury, and she shattered the sword. Its pieces were scattered throughout Northrend, awaiting the day it could be forged anew. As for Lana'thel, she met her ultimate demise in the halls of Icecrown Citadel.

KEY DATA

TITLE Blood Queen
STATUS Deceased
AFFILIATION Scourge
RELATIVES None Known

KEL'THUZAD

Once a powerful sorcerer who sat on the Council of Six, Kel'Thuzad grew obsessed with the dark arts of necromancy. As this obsession grew, he was threatened with banishment from the Kirin Tor. Kel'Thuzad traveled to Northrend, answering the call of the Lich King. Upon his return to Lordaeron in the floating dread citadel Naxxramas, Kel'Thuzad established the Cult of the Damned, a group of living servants to the Lich King, and began to distribute the Plague of Undeath across Lordaeron via grain shipments. His efforts were halted by Prince Arthas Menethil, and he was slain. After Arthas' decent into darkness, the former Prince of Lordaeron sought to raise Kel'Thuzad into undeath at the behest of the dreadlord Tichondrius. Arthas plunged Kel'Thuzad's remains into the Sunwell, defiling the magical fount and bringing Kel'Thuzad back as a monstrous, skeletal lich. Kel'Thuzad remained a loyal servant of Arthas and the Lich King, helping Arthas reach Northrend. He served the Lich King from the necropolis of Naxxramas for many years, eventually returning the citadel to Northrend. Although he has suffered a number of defeats within Naxxramas, Kel'Thuzad cannot be killed until his phylactery, the container that holds his spiritual essence, is destroyed.

KEY DATA

TITLES Lord of Naxxramas, leader of the Cult of the Damned (former)
STATUS Undead
AFFILIATION Scourge
RELATIVES None known

PRINCE VALANAR

Prince Valanar was the Scourge overlord of the Borean Tundra. He knew that the Alliance was a serious threat to the Scourge in his area, but instead of fighting them head on, he devised a plan to erode the Alliance's power from within. He disguised himself as Counselor Talbot, an advisor to the Alliance leaders in the Borean Tundra. This treachery was eventually revealed, and Valanar was defeated. Afterward, Valanar, with Princes Keleseth and Taldaram, were raised into undeath yet again by the Lich King to form the Blood Prince Council. Their duty was to avenge themselves on the heroes that slew them and to protect Blood Queen Lana'thel. They were unsuccessful once again, and Valanar was defeated in Icecrown Citadel.

KEY DATA

TITLES Prince
STATUS Deceased
AFFILIATION Scourge
RELATIVES Prince Keleseth (brother, deceased)

PRINCE KELESETH

Prince Keleseth was the Scourge overlord of Howling Fjord and also served as a representative to the Lich King's allies, the vrykul. His primary residence was Utgarde Keep, where he assisted Ingvar the Plunderer in organizing raids on the surrounding territory. During the assault on Utgarde Keep, Keleseth was slain by invading heroes. Yet the Lich King raised Keleseth into undeath once again, assigning him, as well as his brother, Prince Valanar, and Prince Taldaram, to the Blood Prince Council. This new position proved to have the same outcome as his previous one, and he was defeated in Icecrown Citadel.

KEY DATA

TITLES Prince
STATUS Deceased
AFFILIATION Scourge
RELATIVES Prince Valanar (brother, deceased)

DEATHBRINGER SAURFANG

Dranosh Saurfang, son of Horde hero Varok Saurfang, was a Mag'har orc from Draenor with a promising future ahead of him. As a youth, Dranosh fought the enemies of his people in Outland, leading an ill-fated attack against Sunspring Post in Nagrand. Dranosh survived and, following in his father's footsteps, traveled to the world of Azeroth. When the Horde moved to combat the Lich King in Northrend, Dranosh joined the Warsong Offensive and was placed in charge of the Kor'kron Vanguard. He kept a truce with the Alliance and waited for the siege on Icecrown Citadel. Like many others, he fought and fell at the Battle of Angrathar the Wrathgate, when Alliance and Horde forces attacked the Lich King. Dranosh was slain at an entrance to Icecrown Citadel by the Lich King himself—but his body was taken by the Scourge and his soul snatched by the dread blade Frostmourne. Dranosh was raised into undeath by the Lich King. As Deathbringer Saurfang, his new task was to prevent enemies from attacking the Lich King's fortress. He was killed during the assault on Icecrown Citadel, and his body was finally claimed by his father to be laid to rest in Nagrand, next to the pyres of his mother and his ancestors.

KEY DATA

TITLES Deathbringer, Commander of the Kor'kron Vanguard (former)
STATUS Deceased
AFFILIATION Scourge
RELATIVES Varok Saurfang (father), Broxigar (uncle, deceased), Thura (cousin)

AMNENNAR THE COLDBRINGER

Amnennar the Coldbringer fought alongside the Lich King's army during the assault on Mount Hyjal in the Third War. After the war, the Lich King ordered Amnennar to look for ways to expand the Lord of the Scourge's domain. Amnennar saw potential in the quilboar of Kalimdor and fought to turn them toward undeath. His base, Razorfen Downs, is one of the Scourge's few strongholds in Kalimdor. Amnennar controls a group known as Death's Head, officially led by Charlga Razorflank. Most of the members are undead quilboar that have given their allegiance in death to the Scourge. Although Amnennar has been slain many times, he can never truly die until the phylactery containing his spiritual essence, is destroyed. Until then, Amnennar will return to perpetuate his evil.

KEY DATA

TITLE Ruler of Razorfen Downs
STATUS Undead
AFFILIATION Scourge
RELATIVES None Known

KING YMIRON

King Ymiron was the head of the Dragonflayer clan and leader of the vrykul. Thousands of years ago, King Ymiron decreed to his people that the titans had abandoned them, pledging to protect them himself. He sought to destroy the small, aberrant children born to the vrykul, but these children were hidden away from him, eventually becoming the human race. For thousands of years, King Ymiron slept within the vrykul fortress Gjalerbron, but was awakened and pledged his allegiance and that of his people to the Lich King. Raised into undeath, Ymiron was given control of Utgarde Pinnacle. He was killed by adventurers when this vrykul stronghold was taken.

KEY DATA

TITLES King of the Vrykul, Leader of the Dragonflayer Clan
STATUS Deceased
AFFILIATION Scourge
RELATIVES Queen Angerboda (wife, deceased)

BARON RIVENDARE

In life, Baron Rivendare was a rich landowner in Stratholme. He was friends with Kel'Thuzad, and the latter convinced him to join the Cult of the Damned. Rivendare eventually became a death knight, and was placed in control of the burning remains of Stratholme. He held the city against the Scarlet Crusade and a number of heroes before he was eventually defeated. Rivendare then joined Kel'Thuzad in the latter's stronghold Naxxramas, where he became one of Kel'Thuzad's Four Horsemen. His existence remains a mystery, but it is likely that he will never fully be destroyed until Kel'Thuzad meets his end.

KEY DATA

TITLES Member of the Four Horsemen, Master of Stratholme, Baron
STATUS Undead
AFFILIATION Scourge
RELATIVES Aurius Rivendare (son)

ANUB'ARAK

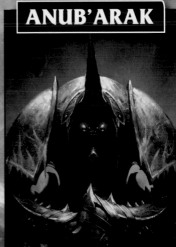

The last king of the nerubian empire of Azjol-Nerub, Anub'arak was slain by the armies of the Lich King during the War of the Spider, years before Arthas Menethil's ascent of Icecrown Glacier. Forcibly turned against his own people by the Lich King, Anub'arak became a crypt lord, assisting Arthas in traveling to the Frozen Throne. Although a servant of the Lich King, Anub'arak was not a willing one. Viewed as a traitor by his people, Anub'arak nonetheless continued to carry out the Lich King's command within the ruins of Azjol-Nerub for years until he was defeated by adventurers. Risen once more, the crypt lord was then moved beneath the Crusaders' Coliseum in Icecrown, sent to plague the Argent Tournament. This, too, proved unsuccessful, as Anub'arak met his end a final time at the hands of those participating in the Trials of the Crusader at the Argent Tournament.

KEY DATA

TITLES The Traitor King, King of Azjol-Nerub
STATUS Deceased
AFFILIATION Scourge
RELATIVES None Known

ICECROWN CITADEL

LOCATION NON-ALIGNED SCOURGE

The massive fortress of the undead Scourge, Icecrown Citadel dominates the frozen wastes of Icecrown Glacier in Northrend. Most of the glacier has been split, and the citadel was constructed within and around the fissure. Some of the most terrifying and horrible of the Scourge forces patrol the area, and the chill of the grave surrounds the stronghold. The Frozen Throne—the tangible embodiment of Scourge power—rests atop the tallest spire in the Citadel.

KOR'KRON VANGUARD AND FORDRAGON HOLD

Kor'kron Vanguard and Fordragon Hold flank Icecrown Citadel. These redoubts represent Horde and Alliance staging grounds, respectively, against the Scourge.

BASTION OF THE LICH KING

Icecrown Citadel is an enormous and fearsome fortress. The southern entrance is Angrathar the Wrathgate, formerly the scene of ferocious fighting between the Alliance and Horde on one side, and the armies of the Scourge on the other. The northern entrance is heavily fortified and surrounded by the Court of Bones. The interior of the citadel is known as the Frozen Halls. Icecrown Citadel was constructed from saronite, a mineral formed from the Old God Yogg-Saron's blood. Saronite is mined by both Alliance and Horde prisoners of the Scourge from the Pit of Saron.

THE FROZEN THRONE

The Frozen Throne was formed when the demon lord Kil'jaeden hurled the icy casket containing the orc shaman Ner'zhul's consciousness into Azeroth. The shard of crystalline ice, warped and scarred by its descent, came to resemble a throne. When Arthas Menethil placed the Lich King's helm upon his head, he merged with and became the Lich King himself. Icecrown Citadel was later constructed around the Frozen Throne.

THE FORGE OF SOULS

The Forge of Souls, part of the Frozen Halls, is a massive production facility that houses machines called soul grinders. These twisted engines grind down spirits of the damned to fuel the many engines of the Scourge.

JAILER OF THE DAMNED

Bolvar Fordragon was taken to Icecrown Citadel and tortured by the Lich King (right), but Bolvar refused to submit. Upon the Lich King's death, Bolvar took the helm and placed it on his head, for the Scourge could not be without a ruler—there must always be a Lich King. Bolvar's body was encased in ice on the Frozen Throne, and his will holds the Scourge's evil at bay.

THE DRAGONFLIGHTS

Long ago, the titans imbued five proto-dragons with special powers, and charged them with the task of safeguarding the world of Azeroth. These later became the dragon Aspects, and their dragonflights—red, green, blue, bronze, and black—worked tirelessly to fulfill their ancient purpose. Some were corrupted, but the remaining Aspects expended their power to prevent the destruction of the world and now look to the mortal races to protect Azeroth.

ALEXSTRASZA

The titans gave Alexstrasza, Aspect of the red dragonflight, stewardship over all life. During the War of the Ancients, Deathwing manipulated the Aspects into giving him their power, consolidating it within the Dragon Soul artifact. He then attacked the dragonflights, controlling them with the Dragon Soul, but was defeated. The artifact was altered so that no dragon could ever use it again and sent to a secret location by the druid Malfurion. During the Second War, the Dragon Soul was found by the orc shaman Zuluhed, and given to the Horde warlord Nekros, who used it to enslave Alexstrasza. She was freed during the Battle of Grim Batol, where Deathwing was defeated once again and the Dragon Soul destroyed. After participating in the defeat of Deathwing, Alexstrasza expended the last of her power. Compassionate and wise, Alexstrasza treasures life in all its forms. Now mortal, she has passed on her legacy to the mortals of the world.

KEY DATA

TITLES Dragonqueen, Life-Binder, Aspect of Life (former), Queen of Life (former) Aspect of the red dragonflight (former)
STATUS Living
AFFILIATION Independent (Neutral)
RELATIVES Ysera (sister); Dralad (brother, deceased); Tyranastrasz (consort, deceased); Korialstrasz (consort, deceased); Caelestrasz (son, deceased); Vaelastrasz (son, deceased)

KALECGOS

The blue dragon Kalecgos was instrumental in the preservation and ultimate restoration of the Sunwell, as well as the defeat of the black dragon Sinestra. After the death of the blue Aspect Malygos, Kalecgos was chosen by his fellow blue dragons to lead as the new Aspect of the blue dragonflight. His leadership was short-lived, his powers as Aspect expended during the final battle to defeat Deathwing. Kalecgos assisted the sorceress Jaina Proudmoore defend against a Horde assault on Theramore, and later joined her in Dalaran as a member of the Kirin Tor. With the disbanding of the blue dragonflight, Kalecgos has taken it upon himself to continue the task of studying and preserving artifacts of magical significance.

KEY DATA

TITLES Aspect of Magic (former), Spell-Weaver (former) Aspect of the blue dragonflight (former)
STATUS Living
AFFILIATION Alliance
RELATIVES Tarecgosa (adopted sister, deceased); Jaina Proudmoore (lover)

YSERA

The titans charged Ysera, Aspect of the green dragonflight, with guardianship and preservation of nature. She immediately fell into an eternal trance, joining with the Emerald Dream and raising the demigod Cenarius as her adopted son. She emerged during the War of the Ancients and Battle of Grim Batol, to fight against Deathwing. Years later, Ysera became trapped in the Emerald Dream, as it became corrupted by the Nightmare. She was saved by her allies, the Dream was cleansed, and Ysera was fully awakened. After the Cataclysm, Ysera joined her sister, Alexstrasza, and the other Aspects to destroy Deathwing. Though Ysera is now mortal, she continues to provide guidance and wisdom to all who revere nature, acting as mentor to the druids of Azeroth.

KEY DATA

TITLES The Dreamer (former), The Awakened, Aspect of Dreams (former), Aspect of the green dragonflight (former)
STATUS Living
AFFILIATION Independent (Neutral)
RELATIVES Alexstrasza (sister); Dralad (brother, deceased); Eranikus (consort, deceased); Merithra (daughter); Cenarius (adopted son)

NOZDORMU

The bronze dragon Nozdormu was given the power to safeguard the streams of time by the titans, who then showed Nozdormu the moment of his demise in order to demonstrate that his power was not without its limits. Nozdormu rarely intervened in the events of the world, becoming lost in the timeways, but emerged to battle against Deathwing. In his absence, his flight was left to battle the Infinite dragonflight, who sought to undo the certain events of time. It was later discovered that the Infinite dragonflight was spawned by Nozdormu himself in one potential future, where he had turned into the maddened dragon Murozond. After Deathwing's defeat, Nozdormu became mortal with the other Aspects.

KEY DATA
TITLES The Timeless One, Aspect of the bronze dragonflight (former)
STATUS Living
AFFILIATION Independent (Neutral)
RELATIVES Soridormi (consort); Anachronos (son); Murozond (future self, deceased)

KORIALSTRASZ

Korialstrasz was a consort of the Dragonqueen Alexstrasza. Korialstrasz often interacted with mortals, taking on many guises to do so. In the guise of Krasus, an archmage of the Kirin Tor, Korialstrasz worked to free Alexstrasza from her enslavement, succeeding in the Battle of Grim Batol. Later, he was sent back in time to participate in the War of the Ancients. He also preserved the remnants of the Sunwell's energy after its destruction in the Third War, giving them the guise of a human woman named Anveena Teague. After the Cataclysm, Korialstrasz heroically sacrificed his life, destroying the lower sanctums of Wyrmrest Temple to eradicate dragon eggs corrupted by the Twilight's Hammer Cult.

KEY DATA
TITLES Consort of Alexstrasza, Archmage of the Kirin Tor
STATUS Deceased
AFFILIATION Independent (Neutral)
RELATIVES Alexstrasza (consort)

SINDRAGOSA

During an attack by Deathwing in the War of the Ancients, Sindragosa, prime consort of the Aspect Malygos, was mortally wounded. She flew to Northrend, desperately attempting to reach the Dragonblight, the ancestral graveyard of dragonkind. Weakened, Sindragosa fell in the peaks of Icecrown and perished with the knowledge that her spirit would never find rest. Years later, the Lich King found her corpse and raised her into enslavement as a terrifying skeletal frost wyrm, Queen of the Frostbrood. She was finally defeated in Icecrown Citadel.

KEY DATA
TITLES Queen of the Frostbrood, Prime Consort of Malygos (former)
STATUS Deceased
AFFILIATION Scourge
RELATIVES Malygos (consort)

ONYXIA

The daughter of Deathwing, Onyxia assisted her brother Nefarian to follow in their father's footsteps and replenish the black dragonflight. While Nefarian worked to secure the servitude of the Blackrock orcs, Onyxia took on the guise of Katrana Prestor and infiltrated Stormwind's House of Nobles. She had King Varian Wrynn of Stormwind captured, and separated him into two personalities: one that she could control, and the second, a warrior who would later be called Lo'Gosh, who subsequently escaped her grasp. When Lo'Gosh returned to Stormwind, he revealed Lady Prestor as Onyxia. She fled, kidnapping Varian's young son Prince Anduin. Varian's two personalities merged during the rescue attempt, and he beheaded the black dragon. She was later raised into undeath by her brother, Nefarian, but died once more inside Blackwing Descent.

KEY DATA
TITLE Broodmother of the black dragonflight
STATUS Deceased
AFFILIATION Adversarial
RELATIVES Neltharion (Deathwing, father, deceased), Sintharia (mother, deceased); Nefarian (brother, deceased), Sabellian (half-brother); Wrathion (half-brother)

NEFARIAN

While Deathwing recuperated following his defeat at Grim Batol, his son, Nefarian, gained the servitude of the Blackrock orcs. He ruled from the peaks of Blackrock Spire for many years, attempting to create a new chromatic dragonflight before meeting his demise. After the Cataclysm, Deathwing raised his son into undeath and charged him to continue his experiments. Nefarian in turn reanimated his sister, Onyxia, and worked to create new monstrosities for Deathwing until he was defeated once more by heroes of Azeroth.

KEY DATA
TITLES Creator of chromatic dragonflight, Lord of Blackrock Spire
STATUS Deceased
AFFILIATION Adversarial
RELATIVES Neltharion (Deathwing, father, deceased); Sintharia (mother, deceased); Onyxia (sister, deceased); Sabellian (half-brother); Wrathion (half-brother)

NAGA

The serpentine naga are some of the most formidable villains of Azeroth. Masters of sorcery, the naga were formerly night elves, members of Queen Azshara's court in the War of the Ancients. They were transformed into naga by the Old Gods, and now haunt the seas of Azeroth, building a great civilization on the ocean floor.

LADY VASHJ

Lady Vashj was the daughter of Lestharia Vashj, leader of the city Vashj'ir. As a Highborne, Vashj served as a favored handmaiden to Queen Azshara, fiercely devoted to her queen. After the Great Sundering, Vashj was transformed into a naga with many other members of Azshara's court. Thousands of years later, Illidan Stormrage, seeking allies for his plans to destroy the Lich King, cast a powerful spell that reached the depths of the ocean. This spell was felt by a group of naga led by Lady Vashj. Remembering Illidan from the War of the Ancients and respecting his power as a demon, Vashj agreed to help him obtain the Eye of Sargeras, a powerful artefact. She later recruited the blood elf Prince Kael'thas Sunstrider to Illidan's cause as well. Loyal to Illidan, Vashj saved his life and returned him to Outland after he was gravely wounded in battle with Arthas Menethil in Northrend. As time passed, Vashj worked in Outland to strengthen her power and that of her master by draining the waters of Zangarmarsh into Coilfang Reservoir. She oversaw operations from the depths of Serpentshrine Cavern, where she was killed by a party of adventurers.

KEY DATA

TITLES Lady, Coilfang Matron, Handmaiden of Queen Azshara (former)
STATUS Deceased
AFFILIATION Adversarial
RELATIVES Lestharia Vashj (mother, deceased)

QUEEN AZSHARA

Queen Azshara's golden eyes marked her out for greatness. The leader of the night elves, she was adored and worshipped by her people for her beauty, leadership, and skill with magic. She ruled from the palace of Zin-Azshari, renamed in her honor. Obsessed with the arcane arts, Azshara selected night elves with unusual intelligence, strength, skills, or wealth. These privileged elves controlled access to the mystical Well of Eternity and came to call themselves Highborne. The Highborne's reckless use of magic and Azshara's own manipulation of the magical waters of the Well eventually drew the attention of Sargeras, leader of the Burning Legion. Sensing Sargeras' immeasurable power, Azshara agreed to craft a portal to bring the demons of the Burning Legion to Azeroth. In return, Sargeras promised her a world suited to her perfection. Thus began the War of the Ancients, which pitted the Highborne and the Burning Legion against the rest of night elf society. The war was eventually lost, and Zin-Azshari began to sink beneath the sea. As Queen Azshara prepared to drown, voices whispered to her, promising her unimaginable power in exchange for her loyalty. As soon as she agreed, Azshara expanded with hate and rage, becoming the first of the naga, her followers transforming with her. Azshara rules the naga from the ocean depths, a loyal servant of the Old Gods that transformed her. Filled with hatred for those that condemned her in the War of the Ancients, she still seeks revenge on the night elves.

KEY DATA

TITLES Queen of the Naga, Empress of Nazjatar, Queen of the Kaldorei Empire (former)
STATUS Living
AFFILIATION Adversarial
RELATIVES None known

HIGH WARLORD NAJ'ENTUS

Male naga are usually large and powerful in combat, but few matched the strength of High Warlord Naj'entus. A servant of Lady Vashj and Illidan Stormrage, Naj'entus was entrusted with protecting Illidan's stronghold in Outland, the Black Temple. His superior abilities allowed him to surround himself with deadly cold, and his spines and needles could inflict horrific wounds. He was killed during the assault on the Black Temple by Akama, Maiev Shadowsong, and a group of heroes.

KEY DATA

TITLE High Warlord
STATUS Deceased
AFFILIATION Adversarial
RELATIVES None known

WARLORD KALITHRESH

Kalithresh was the overseer of the Steamvault, in Lady Vashj's domain of the Coilfang Reservoir. The Steamvault was put in place to help drain the water out of Zangarmarsh, so that Lady Vashj could expand her underground lair, and control the limited supplies of water left on Outland. Ultimately the naga planned to drain all the water from Zangarmarsh. To help defend the Steamvault, Kalithresh relied on a number of potent mixtures. His seat of power was lined by a series of tubes containing rare liquids, which could be used to augment his already significant strength. Yet all of Kalithresh's power was of no avail; he was killed by adventurers associated with the Cenarion Expedition.

KEY DATA

TITLE Warlord
STATUS Deceased
AFFILIATION Adversarial
RELATIVES None known

LADY NAZ'JAR

Lady Naz'jar, a sea witch in the service of Queen Azshara, played an important part in the retaking of Vashj'ir after the Cataclysm. Together with allies sent by the Old Gods, Lady Naz'jar pushed back the forces of the kvaldir and reclaimed the ancient city. Lady Naz'jar's plan was later revealed: at the behest of the Old Gods, she sought to capture the Elemental Lord Neptulon, formerly their slave. Although successful in breaching the Abyssal Maw, the water region of the elemental plane, and cornering Neptulon, Naz'jar was slain in the Throne of Tides.

KEY DATA

TITLE Lady
STATUS Deceased
AFFILIATION Adversarial
RELATIVES None known

RAJAH HAGHAZED

Rajah Haghazed was the leader of the Darkcrest naga, one of the tribes that controlled sections of Zangarmarsh. The Darkcrest patrolled the lands near one of the marsh's many lakes, leading many attacks against the Cenarion Expedition. A fearless warrior, Rajah Haghazed was one of the Cenarion Expedition's most feared adversaries, and a bounty was placed on his head. He was killed at their behest, the bounty collected by adventurers.

KEY DATA

TITLE Leader of the Darkcrest naga
STATUS Deceased
AFFILIATION Adversarial
RELATIVES None known

RAJIS FYASHE

Rajis Fyashe was the powerful sorceress leader of the Bloodscale naga, who controlled sections of Zangarmarsh. Both the Darkcrest and Bloodscale clans were charged with keeping outsiders away from the pumps that fed Coilfang Reservoir. Unfortunately for Rajis Fyashe, all of her magical skills proved ineffective against agents of the Cenarion Expedition, and she was killed to collect the bounty placed on her head.

KEY DATA

TITLE Leader of the Bloodscale naga
STATUS Deceased
AFFILIATION Adversarial
RELATIVES None known

ELEMENTALS

Elementals are manifestations of volatile energy. Their exact origins are unknown. These innately chaotic entities once raged freely on primordial Azeroth until the Old Gods arrived and enslaved them. As servants of the Old Gods, the elementals were later defeated by titanic forces and banished to a specially crafted prison known as the Elemental Plane. Although most elementals remain in the Elemental Plane, they can be summoned to Azeroth by those who seek to use their power.

RAGNAROS

Ragnaros the Firelord was one of the four Elemental Lords, banished in ancient times to the region of the Elemental Plane known as the Firelands. Thousands of years later, he was recklessly summoned to Azeroth by Sorcerer-Thane Thaurissan of the Dark Iron dwarves during the War of the Three Hammers. Ragnaros seethed beneath Blackrock Mountain for many years, unable to return to the Firelands or stray far from Blackrock's Molten Core, until he was banished to the Firelands by adventurers. Still in servitude to the Old Gods, Ragnaros allied with Deathwing after the Cataclysm and renewed his efforts to set Azeroth ablaze, sending his minions to launch an assault on the peaks of Mount Hyjal. To assist him in his efforts, he corrupted the night elf Arch Druid Fandral Staghelm, offering the druid unimaginable power and creating the Druids of the Flame. The Cenarion Circle established an army in response, to combat Ragnaros' efforts and launch an assault into the Firelands. Ragnaros' fortress, Sulfuron Keep, was breached, and Ragnaros was slain with the assistance of the demigod Cenarius, Malfurion Stormrage, Hamuul Runetotem and other heroes. Although killed, the primal power Ragnaros represents can never be truly vanquished. The druids of the Cenarion Circle keep a close watch on the Firelands.

KEY DATA

TITLES Elemental Lord, Firelord, Ruler of the Firelands
STATUS Deceased
AFFILIATION Adversarial
RELATIVES None known

AL'AKIR

In Azeroth's earliest days, the Windlord Al'Akir served as one of four lieutenants in the army of the Old Gods. After the war between the Old Gods and the forces of the titans, Al'Akir was banished to the Skywall region of the Elemental Plane. Al'Akir remained bound to the Elemental Plane until the Cataclysm shattered the world and Deathwing returned to Azeroth. Al'Akir readily agreed to serve the Old Gods once more, assisting Deathwing as he attempted to obtain a re-origination device hidden in the desert sands of Uldum. Al'Akir unleashed his wrath on any tol'vir—stone constructs created by the titans to safeguard the secrets of Uldum—who did not agree to serve Deathwing. From his seat in Skywall, Al'Akir gathered the Conclave of Wind, a group of four wind elementals nearly as powerful as Al'Akir himself to scour Uldum of life and seize control of the mysterious titan-forged Halls of Origination. His efforts were thwarted when heroes of Azeroth stormed Skywall and put an end to him for good.

KEY DATA

TITLES Elemental Lord, Windlord, Ruler of Skywall
STATUS Deceased
AFFILIATION Adversarial
RELATIVES None known

THERAZANE

Therazane the Stonemother was the third of the Elemental Lords that led the armies of the Old Gods in ancient times. She was banished by titanic forces to Deepholm, the earthen region of the Elemental Plane. Her realm was the hiding place of the dragon Deathwing for many years, attracting the attention of members of the Twilight Cult. Angered by this incursion into her domain, Therazane wanted no part in the plans of the Old Gods. Neither did she want any part in the plans of the mortals who traveled to Deepholm, as mortals had been responsible for the death of her daughter, Princess Theradras. Yet as the mortals of Azeroth proved their worth, Therazane allowed them to complete the re-construction of the World Pillar, a great pillar of stone that bore the weight of Deepholm and prevented its collapse. With the help of Therazane, the mortals were successful in their mission—and promptly asked to leave. For all her great power, it appears that Therazane prefers to be left alone, although she allows the Earthen Ring, Azeroth's most influential shamanistic organization, to stay and continue its work.

KEY DATA

TITLES Elemental Lord, Stonemother
STATUS Living
AFFILIATION Independent (Neutral)
RELATIVES Princess Theradras
(daughter, deceased)

NEPTULON

Master of Azeroth's oceans, Neptulon the Tidehunter was banished to the Abyssal Maw, the water region of the Elemental Plane, by the forces of the titans. Little is known of the ages that followed, but Neptulon seemingly wanted no place in the plans of the Old Gods following the Cataclysm. It was perhaps because of this reticence that the naga, led by Lady Naz'jar, sought to attack the Abyssal Maw and draw Neptulon out. With the help of the monstrous kraken, Ozumat, Naz'jar was able to force Neptulon to flee into his chambers within the Throne of Tides. Although Neptulon fought valiantly against the naga forces, he was ultimately captured by Ozumat and carried away. Neptulon's current fate is unknown.

KEY DATA

TITLES Elemental Lord, The Tidehunter
STATUS Unknown
AFFILIATION Independent (Neutral)
RELATIVES None known

DENIZENS OF AZEROTH

Although both Alliance and Horde have taken in a variety of races under their respective banners, there are many other sentient races that remain, by and large, neutral—or, to the constant frustration of others, unnaturally aggressive to all. These denizens of Azeroth and beyond each have their own unique histories, customs, and social structures.

OGRE

Originally from Draenor, these imposing, brutish humanoids occupy many locations on Azeroth and beyond. Ogres are known for their considerable strength and endurance and are formidable opponents. Their society is based on a clan structure, each clan acting independently of the others. Within the clan, besting a rival is usually the only way to advance. Ogres greatly respect strength in combat. Although they are usually indifferent or hostile to other races, some ogre clans became staunch allies of the Horde. Generally, ogres are not known for their intelligence, but ogre magic users were not totally unheard of on Draenor, and through the orc warlock Gul'dan's mystical intervention, many more ogres gained enhanced intellect and an ability to cast spells. These ogre magi often enjoy an elevated position among the ogre clans.

GNOLL

Brutish and belligerent, gnolls value strength over everything else. Although fierce and formidable in battle, gnolls are not the most intelligent of races. The gnoll race seems to spend just as much time fighting with each other as they do with the other races of the world. Gnolls have been employed as mercenaries, but their penchant for vicious fighting and their limited intelligence requires constant supervision. One particularly fierce individual, known as Hogger, used to terrorize the Redridge Mountains and Elwynn Forest, but is now incarcerated in the Stockade in Stormwind City.

QUILBOAR

Quilboar are aggressive, boar-like humanoids, known for their fearlessness and savagery. Believed to be the mortal descendants of the demigod Ancient Agamaggan, they have long clashed with other races, such as the centaur and tauren, over land and food. Quilboar build their homes among the colossal, thorn-covered vines, believed to have been grown from the blood of Agamaggan, that make up their colonies. The most prominent of these are Razorfen Downs and Razorfen Kraul in Kalimdor, home to the Razorfen and Death's Head tribes. Quilboar are fiercely loyal to their tribe, and defend their territory with reckless ferocity. Though warriors are highly prized in quilboar society, a powerful shaman often rules quilboar tribes.

SATYR

Satyr are cunning, manipulative creatures, foul servants of the Burning Legion who delight in inflicting physical and emotional pain on their enemies. The first satyr was Xavius, high councilor of the former night elf Queen Azshara. Xavius was killed by Malfurion Stormrage, and his failure and death angered Sargeras, Lord of the Burning Legion. After torturing Xavius' disembodied spirit, he re-shaped and disfigured the night elf into the first satyr, granting him the power to transform others into satyr as well. Although satyr are currently divided into many different sects, each with its own goals, these cruel, corrupted beings always answer the call of the Burning Legion.

NAARU

The enigmatic naaru are a race of sentient energy beings that possess a deep affinity for the Light. The altruistic naaru were saviors of the draenei, those eredar that sought to flee the world of Argus and escape Sargeras' grasp. Masters of unfathomable technological and magical power, the naaru seek to spread the message of the Light and put an end to the Burning Legion. They also act as teachers in the methods of wielding the Light's power. While they appear to be immortal, in very rare circumstances naaru can enter into a darkened state, leaving them susceptible to corruption.

TROGG

Corrupted versions of the original earthen race, troggs are misshapen, brutish, and dangerous creatures. Buried deep within the earth by the titans, the troggs lay undisturbed for thousands of years until the dwarves excavated titan strongholds, such as Uldaman. Once disturbed, the troggs poured out of the ground, eager to take out their aggression on their distant dwarven cousins. Though they are cunning in battle, troggs do not usually possess high intelligence. Instead, they depend on their ferocity and tough hides to see them through. Most are vicious fighters, though some slightly more intelligent troggs have become spell casters as well.

MURLOC

Murlocs remain a legendary encounter for adventurers on Azeroth. Known for their gurgling battle cry (actually Nerglish, their native language) murlocs have a penchant for overwhelming the unprepared with an assault of crude spears, slimy limbs, fishy breath, and elemental magic. They dwell along coastlines, rivers, and lakes, and always appear in numbers. They are social creatures and, when attacked, tend to retreat from battle toward the security of an even larger group of their fellows. Murlocs are rumored to be descended from a great frog Ancient, sharing an ancestry with the gorloc race of the arctic Borean Tundra. Instances exist of murlocs interacting peacefully with outsiders, but they are rare.

DENIZENS OF AZEROTH

MAGNATAUR

Magnataur are huge, with the upper body of a giant and the lower body of a mammoth. Although they have a lengthy life span, magnataur lack patience. Consequently, larger magnataur societies are uncommon and rarely exist for long. Magnataur are rumored to engage in cannibalism when food is scarce, although this has never been proven. Despite a deep hatred for most races, some magnataur have become tolerant of the arctic kobolds in the northern reaches of Northrend.

CENTAUR

Centaur share many things: a lust for battle, hatred for both their progenitors and the tauren, and an all-consuming abhorrence of centaur from other tribes. Legend states that the centaur race was born of the union of Zaetar, son of the Ancient Cenarius, and Theradras, daughter of the Stonemother, Therazane. Vicious, brutal, and cruel, the centaur killed their father, Zaetar. Despite early attempts to keep centaur aggression focused on other centaur tribes, efforts by the Alliance and Horde to unite the tribes, in order to deal with the threat posed by the Burning Blade clan of orcs in Desolace, western Kalimdor, have met with some success.

SHA

Indigenous to Pandaria, the terrifying sha are physical manifestations of negative emotions such as anger, hatred, or fear. The sha present a persistent threat to the native races of Pandaria, and possess an intriguing history. At the dawn of time, the mantid race worshipped the seven-headed Old God Y'Shaarj. The Old God was killed by the forces of the titans, and his last terrible breath forever haunted the land, becoming the sha. Thousands of years ago, the last pandaren Emperor Shaohao defeated his own inner demons, which were manifested as sha. However they have recently enjoyed a resurgence, owing to new conflicts on Pandaria's soil. More than one hero has fallen under their control, as intangible hatred and fear can be difficult enemies to fight.

MANTID

Mantid are an intelligent and highly evolved race of insect-like creatures. They live in the Dread Wastes region in Pandaria, but share their history with the qiraji and silithid. These insect-like humanoids have emerged to menace the inhabitants of Pandaria at regular, predictable intervals since prehistoric times. However, an internal upheaval recently stirred them to action sooner than expected. This change concerned the Klaxxi, a mantid order dedicated to the history and culture of their species, who work with adventurers to restore their massive civilization's delicate balance.

NERUBIAN

Centered in the once great subterranean kingdom of Azjol-Nerub, the nerubians are an ancient race of highly intelligent arachnoids. By nature they are cruel, and usually attack other races on sight—unless they see an advantage in working with them. Each of the several nerubian types possesses unique physical traits and occupies a different place in nerubian society. Though the nerubians' evil empire once spanned much of Northrend, a long war of attrition against the Scourge has reduced these former conquerors to a fraction of their previous power. Even so, pockets of nerubian warriors remain a danger.

QIRAJI

The qiraji once ruled an empire spanning all of Silithus, the southwestern corner of Kalimdor. Hundreds of years ago, these aggressive and intelligent insectoids, along with their silithid minions, waged a brutal war against the night elves. Finally, with the bronze dragonflight's help, the qiraji were driven back into their ancient city of Ahn'Qiraj. Sealed inside, their threat was contained for centuries. Years later, the qiraji stirred behind the walls of Ahn'Qiraj a second time, under the influence of the Old God C'Thun. To combat the threat, a joint assault by the Alliance and Horde was launched on the city. Contained for now, the qiraji remain a threat to the peace of Azeroth.

SILITHID

The silithid are an insectoid race found primarily in Kalimdor. Unlike the qiraji, the silithid are non-sentient, though they remain dangerous foes. Silithid society consists of several castes. Each caste has a unique physical type, ranging in size from fairly small wasps to huge silithid colossi. Every caste has its function within the hive. Their massive underground hives consist primarily of circuitous tunnels providing living space, as well as protection for their vulnerable eggs and larvae. Though not all silithid are innately hostile, all fiercely defend their hives when threatened.

DENIZENS OF AZEROTH

TAUNKA

Long thought to be lost, the taunka were rediscovered by Horde forces upon their arrival in Northrend. The taunka are a proud, stoic race, widely believed to be ancestral cousins to the tauren. They have carved a home from their northern continent's harsh lands. Like the tauren, the taunka have a close relationship with nature. However, their grim existence in the rough Northrend environment has shaped their views; they interact with nature not as supplicants, but seek to bend it to their will. Led by High Chieftain Roanauk Icemist, the taunka occupy several settlements across the inhospitable continent. Their deep resolve and grim perseverance make them steadfast allies—and dangerous foes.

VRYKUL

Vrykul are large, brutal warriors native to Northrend. Discovered to be the progenitors of humanity, the exact origins of the vrykul race remain a mystery. Having disappeared without explanation long ago, the vrykul have recently reappeared to reclaim their settlements and even the great fortress, Utgarde Keep. Led by King Ymiron, they have accepted the Lich King's rule, believing him to be their god of death. Among the several vrykul factions, many are hostile to Horde and Alliance alike, not only defending their settlements but striking out against these new enemies whenever they encounter them.

TUSKARR

The tuskarr are a peaceful, humanoid, walrus-like people indigenous to the cold shores of Northrend. Their society centers around fishing and whaling. This is of such vital importance that a tuskarr's ability to fish affects its social standing within the community. While tuskarr do hunt land animals in lean times, their primary sustenance comes from the sea, and most of their settlements line Northrend's coastlines. Though they prefer peace, the tuskarr fiercely defend their settlements when necessary, and they are no strangers to the conflicts erupting across their home continent.

ETHEREAL

Ethereals were once a mortal race that inhabited a world called K'aresh. An invasion by the armies of the void lord Dimensius started a chain of events that resulted in the loss of their bodies, but allowed their souls to subsist without them. With enhanced magical abilities, the ethereals briefly halted the invaders, yet were ultimately driven into the Twisting Nether. They have since become collectors and traders of arcane items, and when they eventually discovered Outland and its treasures, they created settlements where factions known as "companies"—notably the Consortium, Ethereum, and Protectorate—often work against each other. A few ethereals now also reside on Azeroth, offering a dazzling array of technological marvels to its inhabitants.

KEEPER OF THE GROVE/DRYAD

Keepers of the grove and dryads both descend from the demigod Cenarius. Dryads are daughters of Cenarius, while keepers of the grove are thought to be descendants of Cenarius' sons, Remulos and Zaetar. Dryads have the torso of a female night elf and the lower body of a fawn. Keepers of the grove appear to be a combination of a powerful stag and a night elf male with one branch-like arm. Both prefer peace, but neither shies from employing violence when necessary. Dryads are curious, but few leave the forests. Keepers of the grove are revered for their healing ability, but feared for their nature-based magic.

FURBOLG

According to furbolg oral tradition, their race has ancient origins. They reluctantly took part in the War of the Ancients against the Burning Legion, after which they formed positive relations with the night elves and tauren. They lived in peaceful isolation until the Third War and the Burning Legion's corruption of the forests the furbolg call home. Some of the tribes were corrupted as well, becoming more violent and opting for warlike leaders who called for raids on nearby settlements. The uncorrupted tribes grew more insular, fearing that contact with the outside world might bring corruption into their now-safe homes.

WILDKIN

The wildkin are serene, powerful creatures, thought by the night elves to have been created by the moon goddess Elune. They resemble a cross between a bear and a horned owl, which explains both their wisdom and ferocity. Wildkin have long been allies of the night elves, helping to protect their sacred sites. Though they are thoughtful creatures, wildkin harbor a particular hatred for the Burning Legion and the Scourge, recognizing the danger they pose. While wildkin are not naturally hostile to the other denizens of Azeroth, some who have been corrupted or otherwise manipulated have become aggressive, lashing out at travelers—and even their night elf allies.

WOLVAR

This primitive race of fur-covered humanoids resembles wolverines, with their sharp claws posing a deadly threat in a fight. They are fierce fighters that do not hesitate to defend their territory. Generally eschewing the arcane arts, wolvar often follow the path of the warrior, hunter, or shaman. Among the several prominent wolvar tribes, such as the Frenzyheart, each has its own leader and goals. Although often hostile, the wolvar are capable of diplomatic relations with other races. However, it is advised to approach the wolvar with caution.

HARPY

While some stories claimed harpies were the offspring of a group of night elves cursed by Queen Azshara, they are now known to be descendants of the demigoddess Ancient, Aviana. Despite physical similarities with the night elves, these ferocious beings have little in common with that race. Harpies employ nature-based magic like night elves, but they destroy the environments in which they settle, killing every creature they encounter and despoiling the land to build nests noted for their noxious odor. Harpies were found originally in Stonetalon Mountains, but have now spread as far as the Storm Peaks in Northrend.

JINYU

The fish-like jinyu are descendants of the murloc race, evolving after prolonged exposure to the magical waters in the Vale of Eternal Blossoms in Pandaria. Legend states that the jinyu learned to commune with water itself, leading to the many revered jinyu waterspeakers that can see visions in the waters of the continent. Jinyu society is built upon a rigid caste system, with workers, warriors, and priests chosen at a young age. Once numerous, the jinyu engaged in a centuries-long war with the hozen, and now have a greatly diminished population. Most jinyu now reside in Pearlfin Village, in the Jade Forest.

MOGU

The mogu were once ancient creations of the titans, and guardians of the land now known as Pandaria. However, the titans fell silent, and the mogu became afflicted with the curse of flesh. As their stone bodies turned to flesh, they succumbed to pride and greed, and felt fear and anger. One mogu, Lei Shen, sought to unite the fractured mogu race and give it purpose. Becoming emperor, Lei Shen named himself the Thunder King and successfully brought about the rise of the mogu empire, enslaving the pandaren race and conquering what would later become Pandaria. Although eventually overthrown by the pandaren, the mogu have recently resurged on Pandaria, renewing an alliance with the Zandalari trolls and resurrecting Lei Shen in an effort to restore their once-great empire.

HOZEN

Hozen are a simian race with an average lifespan of less than twenty years. Despite quick tempers, individual hozen manage to work together and live in tribes found throughout Pandaria. Hozen are driven by their passions, and display a love of hunting and fishing. The tribes of Kun-Lai Summit are regarded as unusually ferocious, even by hozen standards. As if to balance things, some hozen possess more even temperaments, and have been seen working peacefully alongside the pandaren.

KOBOLD

The rat-like, subterranean kobolds are rumored to be descendants of the troggs. Despite living underground, kobolds do not have keen nocturnal sight, and rely on candles to traverse the mines they call home. Fearful of other races, kobolds are usually found inside a mine, or on the surface near one. Incredibly, kobold clans have successfully forged ties with two races not known for their peaceful relations with others: the vicious harpies, and the magnataurs found in Northrend.

ARAKKOA

Native to Draenor, this bipedal, keenly intelligent avian race has an affinity for arcane magic and secrecy. An advanced arakkoan civilization, the Apexis, rose and fell centuries prior to the Horde's formation. Due to their secretive nature, little is known of what transpired between that time and the rise of the godlike Terokk, who built the city of Skettis. In recent times, small factions departed Skettis to settle in new homes. Exiles found refuge among the naaru in Shattrath's Lower City. Others followed Talon King Ikiss to Sethekk Halls in ruined Auchindoun, convinced he is Terokk reborn.

MAKRURA

Makrura, sometimes known as lobstrok, are primarily an aquatic race, though they can survive in air for short periods of time. These crustaceans live in colonies along the shores of Azeroth and in the deeper oceans. The naga that settled in Zangarmarsh in Outland breed creatures called bogstroks that closely resemble makrura, although the bogstrok are thought to be native to Outland.
Unusually powerful makrura began appearing on the rediscovered continent of Pandaria, creating a great deal of concern among the pandaren population.

SAUROK

The saurok are fierce, lizard-like humanoids who make their home primarily in Pandaria. Wishing to expand their empire, the ruling mogu used their magical prowess to twist several types of indigenous reptiles into fearsome warriors, bolstering their army. The saurok's innate ferocity and brute strength made them fierce opponents, but they soon turned on their mogu masters, waging a costly revolt. Though the mogu tried to hunt them into extinction, they failed. Today, the saurok are divided into tribes that reside in Pandaria's wilds, pillaging what they can from the land's more peaceful inhabitants.

THE FIRELANDS

The Firelands were created to imprison the Elemental
Lord Ragnaros, servant of the Old Gods, and his raging
minions. It is the least hospitable region of the Elemental
Plane, laden with noxious fumes, oceans of magma, and
terrifying fire elementals.

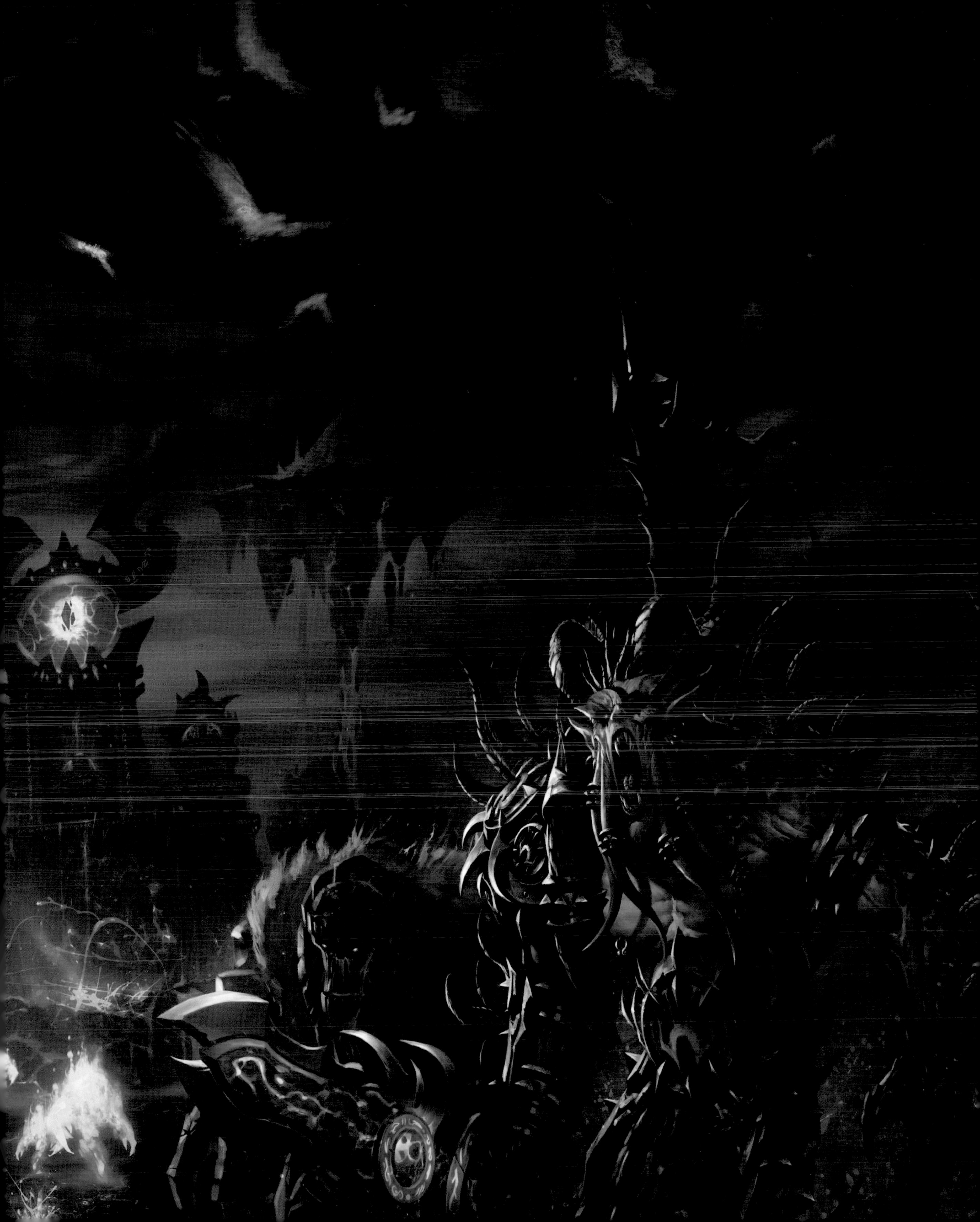

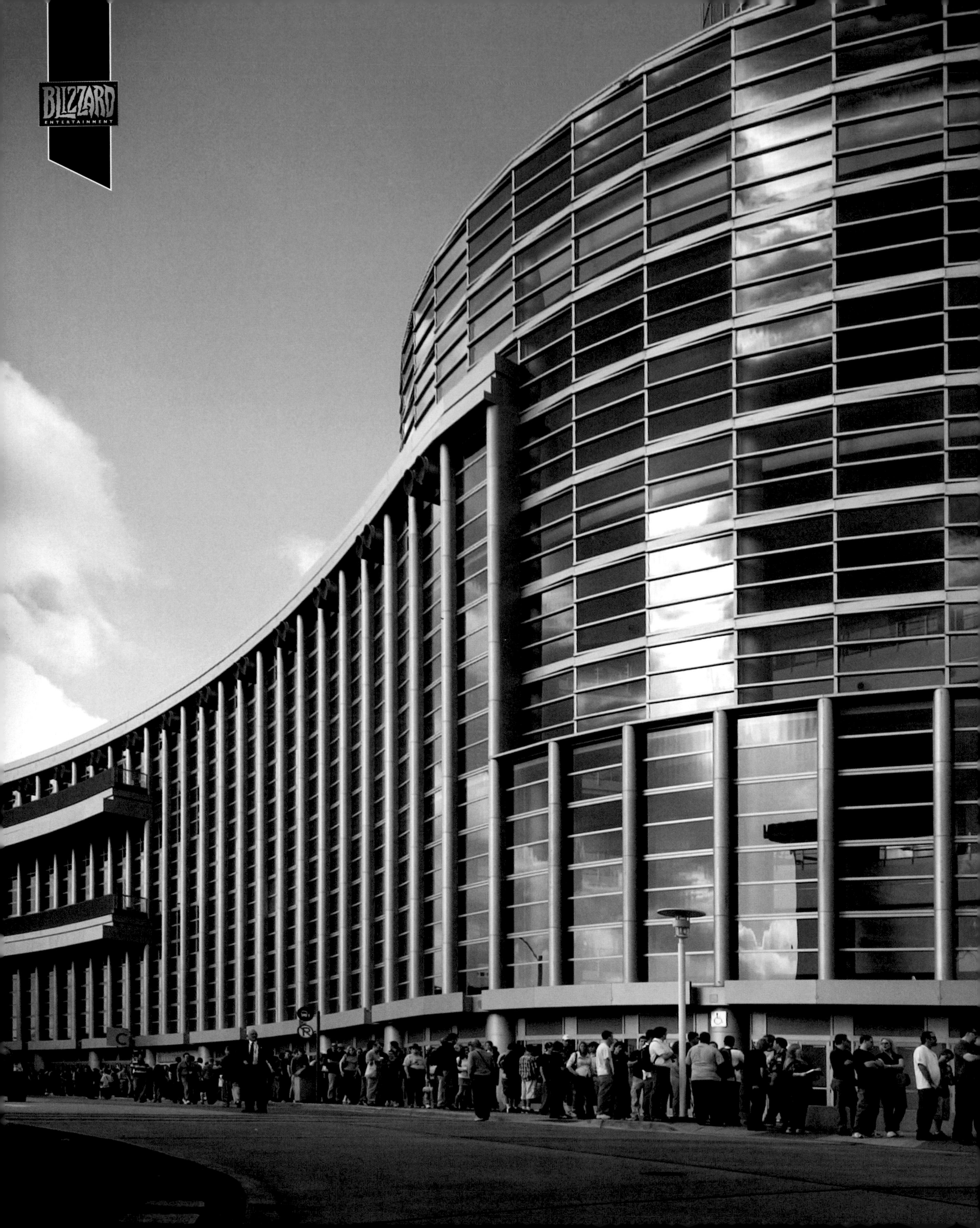

BEHIND THE SCENES

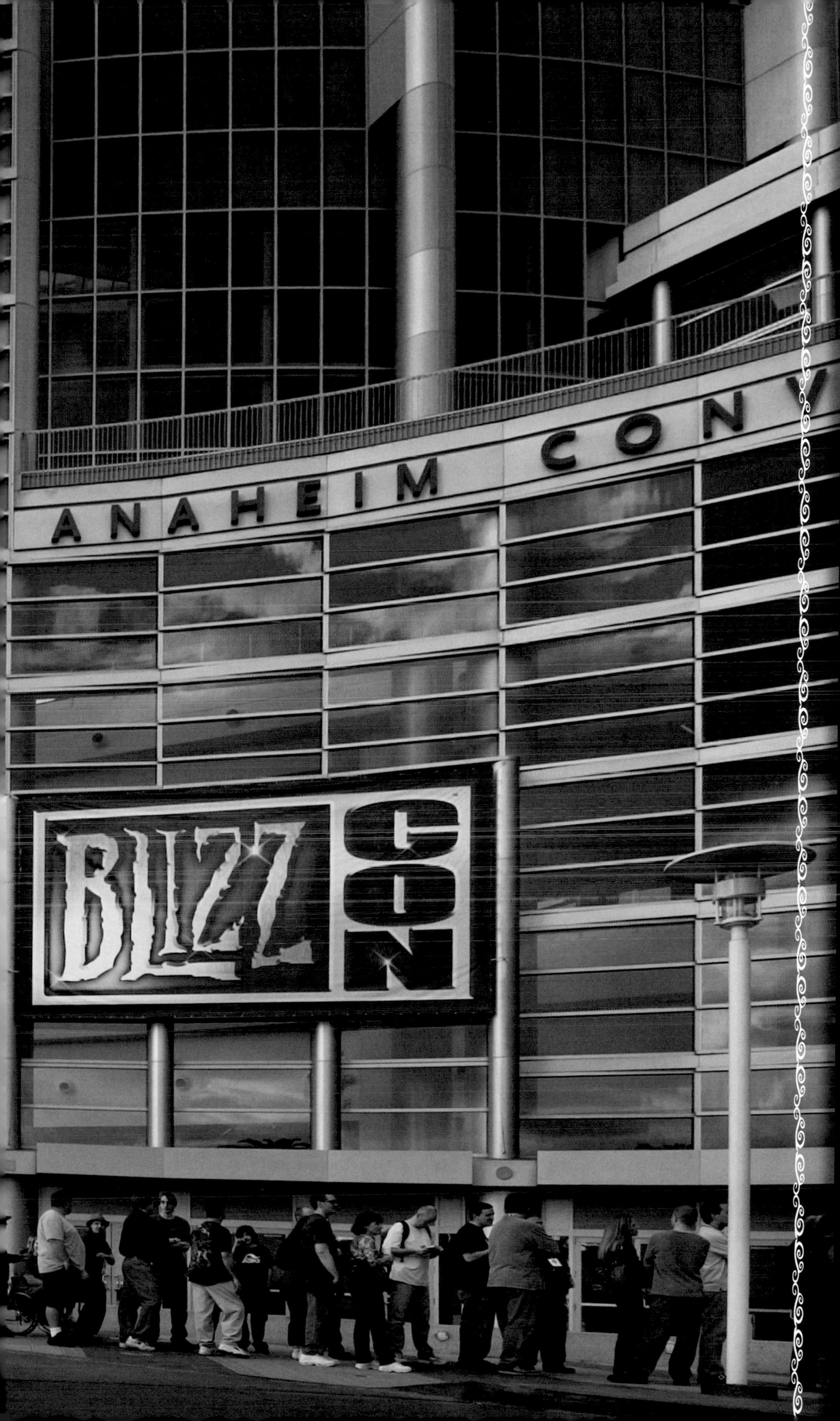
ANAHEIM CONV
BLIZZ CON

BLIZZARD ENTERTAINMENT

EARLY WARCRAFT

The *Warcraft* universe began long before *World of Warcraft* hit the shelves in late 2004. It started with a series of real-time strategy games in which players built structures and commanded armies in order to defeat their opponents. The stories behind the games sparked the imagination of players—and inspired the world's most beloved massively multiplayer online role-playing game (MMORPG).

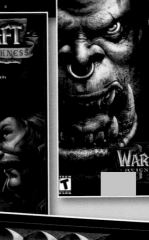

Each entry in the *Warcraft* series featured a clash between two factions: the Alliance and the Horde. This essential story continued to unfold in *World of Warcraft*.

BEFORE WORLD OF WARCRAFT

Three *Warcraft* real-time strategy (RTS) games were released over the span of nearly 10 years. The first, *Warcraft: Orcs & Humans*, was released in 1994. *Warcraft II: Tides of Darkness* arrived in 1995 and was later followed by the *Beyond the Dark Portal* expansion pack in 1996. *Warcraft III: Reign of Chaos* was released in 2002 to tremendous success. This was followed by *The Frozen Throne* one year later.

REIGN OF CHAOS CONCEPT

Reign of Chaos, the third installment in the RTS series, introduced the night elves, an ancient, previously undiscovered, race that proved to be hugely popular with players.

METZEN·96

Originally hired as an artist and animator, Chris Metzen created many of the illustrations for early Blizzard titles, as well as contributing to story development. Today, he is Senior Vice President of Story and Franchise Development at Blizzard. The artist Sam "Samwise" Didier was also responsible for many early character designs, and now works as art director for a variety of Blizzard games. Didier has made many notable contributions to Blizzard's style, and was responsible for the creation of the pandaren race.

> "WARCRAFT WAS SHAPED BY A LOT OF DIFFERENT VISUAL STYLES... ALL THE CLASSIC FANTASY TROPES... IT WAS BORN OF ALL SORTS OF WEIRD THINGS THAT WE WERE INTO BACK IN THE DAY."
>
> CHRIS METZEN

BREAKING RECORDS

As the *Warcraft* RTS series evolved, so did the developers' ability to tell stories through the games. *Warcraft III: Reign of Chaos* shattered all prior records held by the franchise, winning Game of the Year awards from a variety of publications for its engaging gameplay, thrilling story, and beloved cast of characters.

CINEMATICS
The plot of the RTS games was told through the use of cutscenes, cinematics, and additional information found in the manuals. Cinematics were used to frame each act of the story, and highlight moments of particular emotional significance.

MAPS
Included with the manuals were highly detailed maps of each of the regions of Azeroth. Early maps show a slightly altered view of Azeroth, which was refined over the years to the familiar maps and layout of today.

ART
The art for the RTS series illustrated scenes from the world of Azeroth, showcasing the vast potential of a realm rife with conflict and inspiring the imaginations of players.

THE WOW PHENOMENON

On November 23, 2004, Blizzard Entertainment released its highly-anticipated MMORPG *World of Warcraft*. It immediately exceeded expectations, launching to critical acclaim and quickly becoming the most popular subscription-based MMORPG of all time. Since then, millions of players have dived into the world of Azeroth, and the game has spawned expansions, novels, comics, and much more.

AN EVER-EXPANDING UNIVERSE

Following the success of the original game, additional expansions were released to further advance the story and provide new content. Introducing new races, classes, skills, professions, mounts, and continuing to develop Azeroth's vast story, each expansion has been enthusiastically embraced by players. *The Burning Crusade* was released in 2007, followed by *Wrath of the Lich King* in 2008, *Cataclysm* in 2010, and *Mists of Pandaria* in 2012.

PENNY ARCADE
World of Warcraft has shown up in a variety of media, including the long-running digital comic *Penny Arcade*. The strip has featured the world of Azeroth several times in its run, poking fun at some of Azeroth's more ridiculous situations.

MAKE LOVE, NOT WARCRAFT
Popular animated sitcom *South Park* aired an entire episode dedicated to *World of Warcraft*. The episode featured scenes that took place in the game world, created with the direct help of Blizzard Entertainment.

ENRICHING THE EXPERIENCE

Collector's Editions of each expansion include many extras, such as hardcover books that showcase art created during the game's development. In addition, strategy guides have been released with each expansion to assist players with gameplay, as well as atlases, dungeon guides, and other print material designed to complement the gameplay experience.

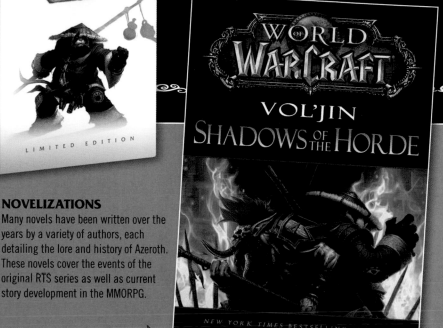

> "HIS SEARCH LEFT HIM STARING AT A VOID. ITS DARKNESS REACHED AND ENGULFED HIM, LEAVING HIM WITH NO ANSWER AND CERTAINLY NO PEACE."
>
> VOL'JIN, SHADOWS OF THE HORDE

MERCHANDISING

World of Warcraft's popularity has led to the launch of a variety of additional products designed to further enhance and expand upon an already massive universe. Trading card games, comics, manga, art books, apparel, strategy guides, novels and more are available to players of the game, offering a variety of ways to delve into *Warcraft*'s multi-layered and complex story, meet up with fellow players in hobby shops and tournaments, or simply wear their enthusiasm with pride. In addition, many passionate members of the *World of Warcraft* community have created a variety of resources to assist players both new and old with gameplay, story, and discussion about the game they love. *World of Warcraft* has created a legacy that unites millions of like-minded adventurers across the world.

NOVELIZATIONS

Many novels have been written over the years by a variety of authors, each detailing the lore and history of Azeroth. These novels cover the events of the original RTS series as well as current story development in the MMORPG.

TRADING CARD GAME

The *World of Warcraft Trading Card Game*, produced in collaboration with Cryptozoic Entertainment, turned the *Warcraft* universe into an incredibly popular collectible card game with its own passionate community. The TCG spawned weekly battleground tournaments hosted at hobby stores, as well as travelling Darkmoon Faires—weekend events featuring demos for newcomers, competition for players of all skill levels, exclusive cards, and epic prizes.

APPAREL

Online retailer J!NX offers a variety of custom clothing inspired by the *Warcraft* universe, including hats, t-shirts, polos, jackets, and a variety of accessories.

DC COMICS

DC Comics produced the *World of Warcraft* comics series from 2007-2009. In addition to the monthly title, manga adaptations of Azeroth's stories and graphic novels were created, featuring engaging art and imaginative storylines highlighting Azeroth's varied cast of characters.

NEWS AND FAN SITES

Player response to the series has been notably enthusiastic, inspiring the creation of fan fiction, art, machinima, songs, podcasts, and many news sites dedicated to *World of Warcraft*. WoW Insider, *Wowhead*, and MMO-Champion are just three of the many highly-regarded online publications for the latest in *Warcraft* news and resource guides.

© J!NX

THE *WOW* COMMUNITY

World of Warcraft has united players from all around the world in their enthusiasm for the game, its characters, and its ongoing story. Players band together in the game itself by forming guilds to combat the perils of Azeroth, making long-lasting friendships along the way that extend out of the game as well. Online forums and websites serve as gathering sites for players, but many choose to meet up in real life as well, all with a common bond: a tremendous passion for *World of Warcraft*.

LARGER-THAN-LIFE
The convention halls themselves are temporary homes to massive sculptural masterpieces. These statues depict many popular characters from Blizzard Entertainment titles, including Tyrael, Kerrigan, Illidan Stormrage (pictured), and more.

BLIZZCON

BlizzCon is a regularly reoccurring convention, first held in 2005 in Anaheim, California. Hosted by Blizzard Entertainment, BlizzCon celebrates players' love of all of Blizzard's games, showcasing the latest titles and providing attendees with a meeting ground to discuss the games with the developers themselves. Because it's an incredibly popular destination, tickets to the convention are notorious for selling out shortly after they are made available for purchase.

GAME PREVIEWS
As a gaming convention, BlizzCon provides access to all of its titles, including sneak peeks of upcoming games. New games, and new expansions, such as *Mists of Pandaria*, are typically made available for play at the convention halls, sometimes before they are even available for beta testing. These sample sessions provide attendees with a unique early glimpse of releases long before the rest of the public.

Opening ceremonies at BlizzCon are packed with players eager to see new cinematics and hear the latest updates about Blizzard Entertainment's variety of titles.

THE FANS
Crowds of enthusiastic Blizzard gamers throng the convention halls, playing games, attending panels, and providing a unique, charged, and engaging atmosphere at the convention.

BlizzCon is a great opportunity for fans to interact with *World of Warcraft* developers. From left to right: Chris Robinson, Greg Street, Tom Chilton, and J. Allen Brack answer questions at one of the convention's many panels.

BE THERE—OR GO ONLINE

Tickets for BlizzCon always sell out fast, but even if fans miss out, they can still watch the entire convention online. Virtual Tickets allow fans live-streaming access to all of BlizzCon's panels, tournaments, and information. Many players unable to attend the convention host parties to watch BlizzCon from the convenience of their own homes. Fan sites often run companion live streams, providing commentary and discussion about the panels. BlizzCon offers both in-person and digital attendees an opportunity to gather, discuss, and share their unbridled enthusiasm for their favorite franchises.

ARTISTS
Artists from Blizzard Entertainment are on hand at BlizzCon for live Q&A sessions, often creating art while fans watch.

COSPLAY!

One of the major highlights of every BlizzCon is the Costume Contest, featuring player-made costumes and recreations of characters from all of Blizzard's games. Cosplayers typically spend months designing, gathering materials, and crafting their creations, painstakingly recreating armor and weapons from World of Warcraft and other games in astonishing, lifelike detail. The Costume Contest is a tremendously popular event, drawing huge crowds eager to see what the exceptionally creative side of Blizzard's community has put together.

"THE TRUEST SPIRIT OF BLIZZCON IS YOU."

CHRIS METZEN ADDRESSING PLAYERS, BLIZZCON 2010

INDEX

E

F

G

H

I

J

K

ACKNOWLEDGMENTS

The publishers would like to thank the following DC comic book artists, whose artwork appears in this book:

Mike Bowden, Jon Buran, Samwise Didier, Gabe Eltaeb, Richard Friend, Derek Frindolfs, Sean "Cheeks" Galloway, Sandra Hope, Mark Irwin, Jim Lee, John Livesay, Ludo Lullabi, Randy Mayor, Pop Mhan, Jerome Moore, Philip Moy, Milen Parvanov,, Allen Passalaqua, Jonny Rench, Chris Robinson, Trevor Scott, Andy Smith, Carrie Strachan, Lee Townsend, Tony Washington, Joe Weems, Jeff Whiting, Walden Wong.

Penny Arcade comic (www.penny-arcade.com) commissioned for *World of Warcraft Official Strategy Guide* by kind permission of BradyGames.
WoW apparel image by kind permission of J!NX, Inc. (www.jinx.com)
South Park image from the episode "Make Love, Not Warcraft" (#1008–Oct. 4, 2006) by kind permission of Comedy Central. © 2006 Comedy Partners. All rights reserved.

The publishers would like to thank the following:
Scarlett O'Hara for proofreading, Zoe Hedges for editorial assistance, Hilary Bird for the index.

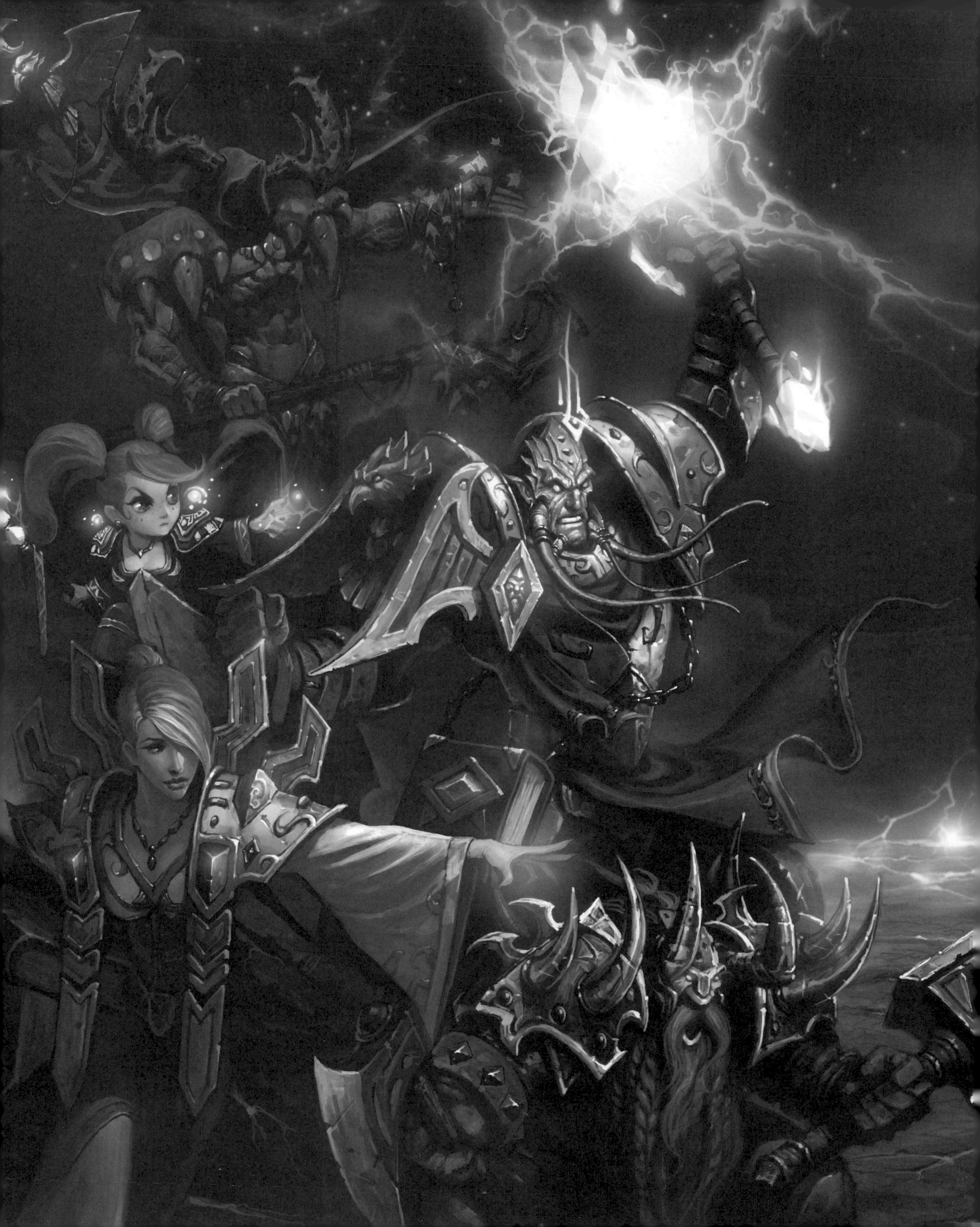